Literary Lives
General Editor: **Richard Dutton**, Professor of English, Lancaster University

This series offers stimulating accounts of the literary careers of the most admired and influential English-language authors. Volumes follow the outline of the writers' working lives, not in the spirit of traditional biography, but aiming to trace the professional, publishing and social contexts which shaped their writing.

Published titles include:

Clinton Machann
MATTHEW ARNOLD

Mary Lago
E. M. FORSTER

Jan Fergus
JANE AUSTEN

Shirley Foster
ELIZABETH GASKELL

Tom Winnifrith and Edward Chitham
CHARLOTTE AND EMILY BRONTË

Neil Sinyard
GRAHAM GREENE

Sarah Wood
ROBERT BROWNING

James Gibson
THOMAS HARDY

Janice Farrar Thaddeus
FRANCES BURNEY

Gerald Roberts
GERARD MANLEY HOPKINS

Caroline Franklin
BYRON

Kenneth Graham
HENRY JAMES

Nancy A. Walker
KATE CHOPIN

W. David Kaye
BEN JONSON

Roger Sales
JOHN CLARE

Phillip Mallett
RUDYARD KIPLING

Cedric Watts
JOSEPH CONRAD

John Worthen
D. H. LAWRENCE

Grahame Smith
CHARLES DICKENS

Angela Smith
KATHERINE MANSFIELD

George Parfitt
JOHN DONNE

Lisa Hopkins
CHRISTOPHER MARLOWE

Paul Hammond
JOHN DRYDEN

Cedric C. Brown
JOHN MILTON

Kerry McSweeney
GEORGE ELIOT

Peter Davison
GEORGE ORWELL

Tony Sharpe
T. S. ELIOT

Linda Wagner-Martin
SYLVIA PLATH

Harold Pagliaro
HENRY FIELDING

Felicity Rosslyn
ALEXANDER POPE

Andrew Hook
F. SCOTT FITZGERALD

Richard Dutton
WILLIAM SHAKESPEARE

Literary Lives
Series Standing Order ISBN 0-333-71486-5 hardcover
Series Standing Order ISBN 0-333-80334-5 paperback
(outside North America only)

You can receive future titles in this series as they are published by placing a standing order. Please contact your bookseller or, in case of difficulty, write to us at the address below with your name and address, the title of the series and one of the ISBNs quoted above.

Customer Services Department, Macmillan Distribution Ltd, Houndmills, Basingstoke, Hampshire RG21 6XS, England

Plath

A Literary Life

Linda Wagner-Martin

Hanes Professor of English
University of North Carolina
Chapel Hill

Second Edition
Revised and Expanded

First published 1999 by Macmillan Press Ltd
Second edition published 2003 by
PALGRAVE MACMILLAN
Houndmills, Basingstoke, Hampshire RG21 6XS and
175 Fifth Avenue, New York, N.Y. 10010
Companies and representatives throughout the world

PALGRAVE MACMILLAN is the global academic imprint of the Palgrave Macmillan division of St. Martin's Press, LLC and of Palgrave Macmillan Ltd. Macmillan® is a registered trademark in the United States, United Kingdom and other countries. Palgrave is a registered trademark in the European Union and other countries.

ISBN 978-1-4039-1653-2

This book is printed on paper suitable for recycling and made from fully managed and sustained forest sources.

A catalogue record for this book is available from the British Library.

Library of Congress Cataloging-in-Publication Data

Wagner-Martin, Linda.
   Sylvia Plath: a literary life / Linda Wagner-Martin. – 2nd ed.
      p. cm. – (Literary lives)
   Includes bibliographical references and index.

   1. Plath, Sylvia. 2. Poets, American–20th century–Biography. I. Title. II. Literary lives (Palgrave Macmillan (Firm))

PS3566.L27Z964 2003
811'.54–dc21
[B]   2003051159

Transferred to Digital Printing 2011

For Andrea

Contents

Chronology of Plath's Literary Life

1932	Sylvia Plath born October 27 in Jamaica Plain, a part of Boston, Massachusetts, to Aurelia Schober and Otto Plath. Family living in Winthrop, Massachusetts.
1936	The Plath family, including son Warren, who was born in the spring of 1935, moves to 892 Johnson Avenue in Winthrop Center, near the grandparents' Schober home.
1938	Hurricane of 21 September (described in Plath's poems).
1940	Otto Plath dies of an embolism following surgery (complications from undiagnosed diabetes caused amputation of leg). Sylvia and Warren do not attend funeral.
1942	The Plath family, now including the Schobers, moves to 23 Elmwood Road in Wellesley ("inland") and Aurelia takes a teaching post at Boston University. Sylvia moves back a grade at Marshall Livingston Perrin Grammar School.
1944	Sylvia enrolls at Alice L. Phillips Junior High School; writes for *The Phillipian*, the school's literary magazine.
1947	Sylvia enters Gamaliel Bradford Senior High School in Wellesley; during her senior year, she co-edits *The Bradford*.
1950–51	Scholarship student at Smith College, Northampton, Massachusetts, as an English major; lives at Haven house. Dates, among others, Dick Norton (the model for Buddy Willard of *The Bell Jar*).
1951	Works as a mother's helper in Swampscott, Massachusetts, during summer.
1952	After sophomore year at Smith, works during the summer at the Belmont Hotel in West Harwich, in Wellesley, and in Chatham, Massachusetts. Lives in Lawrence house beginning with her junior year at Smith.
1953	*Mademoiselle* College Board experience in New York during June. Returns to Wellesley for the remainder of the summer and becomes depressed. Receives bipolar electroconvulsive shock treatments and on August 24 attempts

suicide. Recovery at McLean Hospital, Belmont, Massachusetts.

1954 Returns to Smith for spring semester. Plans honors thesis on Dostoyevski's use of the double. Attends Harvard summer school.

1955 Graduates *summa cum laude* from Smith in June; in the fall, attends Newnham College, Cambridge, England, on a Fulbright.

1956 Meets Ted Hughes February 25 and marries him secretly June 16, with her mother in attendance. Grandmother Schober dies in May. Honeymoon in Benidorm (Spain) and Heptonstall, West Yorkshire. In December Plath and Hughes rent a flat at 55 Eltisley Avenue, Cambridge. Studies with Dorothea Krook.

1957 June, Plath takes her degree and moves with Hughes to America. They summer on Cape Cod and then move to Northampton where Plath teaches freshman English at Smith for the year; Ted teaches part-time at The University of Massachusetts, Amherst.

1958 Moving to Boston in order to write, Sylvia takes part-time jobs and resumes therapy with Ruth Buescher. She attends Robert Lowell's poetry seminar where she becomes friends with Anne Sexton and George Starbuck.

1959 After the summer spent traveling through the US, Sylvia and Ted are residents at Yaddo, the writers' colony in Saratoga Springs, New York, until they sail for England in December. Plath never returns to the United States.

1960 After holidays in West Yorkshire, they rent a flat at 3 Chalcot Square, London. Their first child, Frieda Rebecca Hughes, is born there April 1. *The Colossus* is published in England in October.

1961 February 6, Plath has a miscarriage; February 28, an appendectomy. In late July, she and Hughes buy the manor house, Court Green, in North Tawton, Devon.

1962 Nicholas Farrar Hughes born January 17; Plath writes "Three Women." Marital difficulties intensify in the spring and by October Hughes has moved into London. Plath writes her late ("October") poems, the main part of *Ariel*. In mid-December, she and the children move to 23 Fitzroy Road ("Yeats' house") in London.

1963   *The Bell Jar* is published in England under Plath's pseudonym Victoria Lucas. She dies a suicide on February 11.

1965   Ted Hughes publishes his version of her poem collection *Ariel*, and the cult of Sylvia Plath begins.

1966   *The Bell Jar* is published in England under Plath's name.

1969   Assia Wevill dies a suicide; her child with Ted Hughes, Shura, also dies.

1970   Ted Hughes marries Carol Orchard.

1971   Hughes publishes *Crossing the Water* and *Winter Trees*, additional poem collections drawn from Plath's unpublished work.

1977   Hughes publishes *Johnny Panic and the Bible of Dreams and Other Prose Writing*, Plath's stories, essays, and some journal excerpts.

1981   Hughes edits and publishes *Sylvia Plath: The Collected Poems*.

1982   *The Collected Poems* is awarded the Pulitzer Prize for Poetry, posthumously. *The Journals of Sylvia Plath, 1950–1962* is published only in the United States, with Hughes's admission in the Introduction that he destroyed Plath's last journal, and that her journal dating from late 1959 to the last had been lost.

1983   Ted Hughes is named Poet Laureate of England.

1998   Hughes wins Whitbread Book of the Year Award for *Tales of Ovid*, his reworking of Ovid's *Metamorphosis*. In February, his poems about Plath appear as *Birthday Letters*. In October, just two weeks before his death from cancer, he receives The Order of Merit from Queen Elizabeth II.

Preface

The twenty-first century will furnish the moment of canon revision for the immense literary production that the twentieth century witnessed. Sifting through thousands of poems, plays, short stories, memoirs and novels, today's reader must begin to see what works have the resonance, the imaginative verve, the crucial newness to continue to speak for the modern. Among the works still standing – even cherished – are the poems, fiction and essays of Sylvia Plath.

This statement is as true writing now in 2003 as it was in 1982, when her *Collected Poems* won the Pulitzer Prize for Poetry; during the mid-1980s, when I was privileged to edit two collections of criticism on Plath's work (one for a British house, one for a United States' publisher); in 1987 when my Plath biography appeared in the States, in the UK, in Spain and in Germany; and in 1999, when the original *Sylvia Plath: A Literary Life* was published in the Macmillan Literary Lives series. Over these two decades, readership for Plath's work has never diminished. It is the enthusiasm of these readers that fuels the publishing of critical and biographical work about Plath. These secondary books exist, legitimately, because of these readers' hunger for information.

I am grateful that the editors of the Literary Lives series suggested a need for this revised edition of the 1999 book. Adding the new section which speaks to the existence of Ted Hughes's book of poems about his wife, or related to Plath and her poetry, has been a way of truly completing this project. *Birthday Letters* appeared six months after the first edition of this book started through the publishing process. Hughes's book surprised readers in both Britain and America; there was no way to anticipate its existence. But because *Birthday Letters* garnered an unusual amount of critical attention, the revised edition of this book now includes commentary about it and about the intertextuality that exists between the Hughes' poems in it and the *oeuvre* of Plath's work. Additions have also been made to the Chronology, Notes and Bibliography.

LINDA WAGNER-MARTIN
February 2003, Chapel Hill, North Carolina

Part One

That's where writing comes in. It is as necessary for the survival of my haughty sanity as bread is to my flesh.

Plath, *Journals*, September, 1951

1

The Writing Life

Sylvia Plath trained all her life for her art. She read because, like many word people, she loved words and the arrangements of them. But before she was very old, she read to learn how to make those arrangements for herself. Her first small poem was published when she was eight; from that time on, she worked diligently – almost voraciously – to hone in on what made writers writers.

Her family consistently privileged learning in a steadfast European way. Otto Plath, her father, had emigrated to New York City from Germany in his adolescence, and had such facility with languages that he absorbed his English by sitting in the back of elementary classrooms and promoting himself once he had learned enough to go on to the next level. As a result, he spoke English with a clear American pronunciation. He also spoke German, French, and Polish, and he later taught German and High German at university level. He then made his way from his uncle's home in New York to his grandparents' home in Watertown, Wisconsin, where he had been offered the chance to attend college so long as he studied for the Lutheran ministry. Otto majored in classical languages at Northwestern. Deciding that he could not become a minister, after his study of Darwin and other nineteenth-century scientific thought, he was drummed out of the family – his name erased from the family Bible, support of any kind withheld.

Otto Plath's life – and family, if you will – became his intense study. By the time he taught Aurelia Schober in Middle High German at Boston University, he had won the MS and ScD from Harvard, and had secured a teaching position that was divided between languages and science. He had succeeded in academic fields that were based on languages not his own, and his primary characteristic had become his strong, determined will.

He was attracted to Aurelia Schober in part because of her able and tenacious mind. An accomplished teacher of English and German at secondary school level, Aurelia had also trained for a career in business. An avid reader, she too was the child of a German family whose primary language was German. Her imaginative world was filled

3

with "the novels of Scott, Dickens, Thackeray, Eliot, the Brontës, Jane Austen, Thomas Hardy, Galsworthy, Cooper, Hawthorne, Melville, and Henry James"[1] and, later, with Continental authors. Once married to Otto Plath, however, after a year and a half courtship and a long drive to Las Vegas to obtain the divorce necessary because of his very early marriage, Aurelia came to occupy the center of her own imaginative world.

In a classic European patttern, her "work" became caring for Otto and the children they would soon parent. Sylvia was born not quite ten months after their January, 1932, wedding; Warren, as planned by his father, almost exactly two and a half years after Sylvia's birth. Instead of Aurelia's working at her own teaching, she also became Otto's research assistant. Otto's doctoral dissertation was rewritten into a book, *Bumblebees and Their Ways*, published in 1934 by Macmillan; then he and Aurelia composed a long chapter on "Insect Societies" for an important collection. As Aurelia recalled, "The first year of our married life, all had to be given up for THE BOOK. After Sylvia was born, it was THE CHAPTER."[2] Although she did not continue the analogy, the rest of her married life would be given over to THE ILLNESS. For Otto Plath finally died in 1940 of complications of diabetes mellitus, an illness with which he might well have lived for many years. Because of his own misdiagnosis of the malady as lung cancer, however, the diabetes was so far advanced as to cause the amputation of his leg – and his resulting death from an embolism.

While he lived, however, even during periods of increasing invalidism, the family's emphasis on reading, learning, and language permeated every segment of Sylvia's life. Her father's days were spent reading and studying, preparing for lectures in both his teaching fields. Teaching loads, particularly for a hybrid assignment like his, were heavy; most of the day was spent on campus. In his free time, Professor Plath was expected to write and publish. Aurelia not only prepared her husband's manuscripts; as time went on, she also did much of the writing of them, just as she found new material for his lectures and graded his papers. Eventually, it was as if both the Plath parents were professors, and the atmosphere of the house was a steady quiet. To be "good" children, to earn their parents' love and attention, both Sylvia and Warren needed to spend their time in quiet, language-based pastimes.

Aurelia, with characteristic thoroughness, had read Maria Montessori. She believed that children should create their own interests.

It was lucky for her that both Sylvia and Warren were so attracted to books, letters, speech. Both talked early; both read long before kindergarten. Sylvia showed herself almost from infancy to be a systematizer: she created order out of buttons, small stones, tiles, blocks, any kind of portable object. After Warren's birth, when she was the likely-to-be-jealous age of two and a half, she became more visibly precocious: her quest then was for attention. Hurt by her parents' seeming preference for their infant son, Sylvia became an aggressive toddler, angry that her life of being the center of everyone's attention had changed. Warren was not only male – in an age when even enlightened parents preferred boys; he was also sickly, and so usurped much of Aurelia's attention. Her mother recalled the tactic she used when Sylvia's envy of the baby's nursing was troublesome. Because Sylvia had begun learning the alphabet from packaged foods in the pantry, "each time I nursed Warren, she would get a newspaper, sit on the floor in front of me and pick out all the capital letters to 'read.'"[3]

The Schobers, Sylvia's maternal grandparents, lived nearby, and Sylvia often spent extended periods of time with them. Some of the earliest writing collected in the several Plath archives are Sylvia's "letters" to her mother, written while she stays with her grandparents in the magical ocean-fronting house. In "Ocean 1212-W," her late essay titled for their telephone number, she recalled, "The road I knew curved into the waves with the ocean on one side, the bay on the other; and my grandmother's house, halfway out, faced east, full of red sun and sea lights."[4] Time with the Schobers also reinforced her own family ethic of valuing learning and reading, as well as work. Whether at home or at Grammy's, Sylvia's world was truly shaped by books.

And so it continued. The world of education in the 1930s was also book-governed. Schools were run on the principles of discipline (good behavior was more important than intellectual prowess) and interminable spelling tests. On blackboards and on yellow lined tablets ran the icons of civilization – the neat straight lines of the magic printed letters. These lines could open doors to anywhere a person wanted to go. And for the advanced if still tiny student, the even more magical world of cursive letters awaited on a chalkboard in the corner. Sylvia learned early that writing was as important as reading.

She had always read, it seemed. She could not remember a time when she was not reading, or someone – her mother, both her grandparents – was not reading to her. Favorite books went with Warren and Sylvia on walks to the Schobers or to friends in the neighborhood – or on rare auto trips in the grandparents' car. Favorite stories surrounded them, and piqued their young imaginations. Aurelia created several ongoing tales as bedtime stories for them ("The Adventures of Mixie Blackshort" was based on Warren's favorite bear; and he in turn created a parallel set of adventures, the "other side of the moon" series). From their earliest speaking days, both children made up limericks, poems, stories and fantasies. The process of creating in words was natural to the Plath children, and it became a great source of comfort after the unexpected death of their father.

Immense changes in the Plath household were disturbing for both Sylvia and Warren. In need of income, Aurelia took a teaching job that meant she had to travel long hours in addition to the normal school day. The Schobers moved into the Plath home to care for the children, and later the household moved from the ocean to a modest house in Wellesley. Aurelia had been offered a teaching position at university level, and even though it was poorly paid and non-tenured, she recognized that it was a means to security and stability for her family. Faced with her own health problems, and her father's eye condition, macular degeneration (which cost him a good accounting job and meant that he gratefully worked at the local country club, coming home only a few days a week), Aurelia made good choices. The years at 26 Elmwood Road were generally happy ones.

Sylvia, however, wrote often and consistently about her sudden fall from happiness into despair. At eight years old, she was forced to accept the death of her beloved father – with very little warning or explanation, because neither her mother nor the physicians attending Otto Plath had realized that death was imminent – and then to adjust to the rapid sequence of changes in both living patterns and places. Moving from one school to another was naturally traumatic, and although Aurelia wrote with pride that Sylvia had turned in an extra forty book reports the first year she was in the Wellesley system, one can understand how the tall bright girl's compensatory behavior might have made her less than popular. It was, after all, the early 1940s, and everyone knew that girls rarely went to college. Women were trained to marry well, to be literal helpmates, and to turn whatever ambitions they had for themselves into ways of supporting their husbands. Even primary school education made children aware of gender differences.

Just as Sylvia had been praised for writing poems and stories while her father lived, so she continued that practice. Her writing skills competed with her artistic abilities, and she went through many years of thinking she would become an artist as well as a writer – she could then, after all, illustrate her own books. Decorated napkins, wallet-sized pictures, notecards with pen and ink sketches appeared almost nightly at the Plath-Schober dinner table. Giving people things that she had made or written was a sure way to continue to receive attention. There was nothing wrong with that tactic, except that it became so habitual that years later – when she was ill or experiencing writer's block – she had no alternative ways of feeling that she was worthy of attention, or of love. Sylvia the child's notions of why she was loved were short-circuited with the unexpected death of her father, and because she was so quickly bright and so good at covering up her genuine fears about her life, her future, and her role in her mother's affection, her family did not understand how deeply rooted was her fearfulness. By continuing in their previous family patterns, they thought she was reassured. But Sylvia needed much more comfort, much more explanation about what had happened, much more language about being a valuable part of her family. She never quite believed she was as integral to its existence and healthy life as she, in fact, was.

Assessing what remains of Sylvia Plath's childhood writing (and there is a considerable amount of it in the Lilly Library Plath Archive, the repository of her mother's materials) shows the innate talent of the child, but it also shows her tendency to express those often unreasonable fears. Among her poems, there are the expected paeans to nature, to flowers, to the moon, phrased with the natural exuberance that the language of conventional poetry lends itself to expressing. Perhaps more significant, because it seems stronger – less what we might expect from the usual bright adolescent – is Plath's short fiction. She was fortunate, of course, in being taught at Bradford High School by a number of accomplished and dedicated teachers, and under their tutelage, she wrote a great deal. More than that, she received expert commentary on what she was writing, particularly from the man who was her English teacher for three of her secondary school years, Wilbury Crockett.

Of the fiction that remains, three stories dating from her junior year in school (circa 1948), when she is sixteen, are somber tone pieces. Each focuses on women protagonists who see no promise in their lives. The mood of their collective boredom or, worse,

depression is caught in the description of the summer's heat in the
story of that title ("Heat"): "There was no escape. The heat was
everywhere. It penetrated the apartments and the air-conditioned
offices. It penetrated steel, brick and stone. It rested like a palpable
blanket over the city..."[5] Living in this oppressive atmosphere,
stifled by work she finds hateful, the character Judith is still better
off than the unnamed protagonist of "The Attic View," a woman so
presenceless that the other boarders in the ocean-side rooming
house do not notice that she has died. Frustration about her life as
an adult, fear about her choices, and consistent personal doubt
underlay each woman's personality. The bleakest of these stories is
"The Brink," a fragmented mood piece in which the female
protagonist rides a bus and muses about the lives of the people
riding with her, and those on the street she observes from inside
the vehicle. She does not claim to understand herself or her
emotions, but she presents them clearly. Contempt for the "pup-
pets" she observes, all with "no identity," and for their "frenzied"
and "absurd" lives modulates into outright hatred: "Janet could
have seen all the people lying dead in the gutters and not felt one
twinge of emotion."[6] The plot of the story, however, shows that this
is more than a typical pretentiously adolescent "I-hate-the-world"
statement. As Janet sees that the bus is unexpectedly headed toward
a dark tunnel, she rouses herself to leave it, expressing her sense that
her own life may be worth saving. Her irrational fear of the tunnel
prompts her to act (though, in keeping with her superiority, she
does not alert anyone else on the bus as to what might be danger),
and the story ends with that movement away from the bus. A story
in such suspension seems an advance over the definite, and limiting,
endings of the other two narratives.

The dark tunnel in "The Brink" becomes a mysterious ebony river
in a longer piece written the following year, 1949. "The Dark River"
adopts the flimsy narrative of an older protagonist telling her life
story to an eager young female listener. Plath presents the older
woman as appealing, with "a fluid youthfulness in her features
and a strange, radiant light in her eyes." The narrator tells of her
peaceful fantasies as a child, and of the threat to her existence when
she falls in love with Colin, a boy as mysterious as he is lovable.
Destined to be different, to be separate from even those she loves,
the older woman has traded her love of this man for that of "the
dark, singing waters." As she tells the young listener: "with awful
clarity I realized that the mysterious black river of my youth would

be with me forever, always withholding me from a complete communication with those I wished to love." Her escape from Colin and his love is described as blissful: "It was good to run. As her feet thudded over the gravel path, the blood pounded in her ears and drowned out the sound of the river, which still echoed in her brain. Something pent up inside her broke, free and wild."[7] What is perhaps most touching about the story is the fact that the woman – lonely and self-sufficient, as are most of Plath's female characters – sees in her young listener a sister of the spirit. Some sense of communion between women is introduced here, and grows intermittently through many of Plath's fictions – especially those in which a male antagonist is less fully visible.

A paired story from 1949 is another river piece ("East Wind") which introduces Miss Minton, a woman character who is to recur in Plath's prize-winning 1952 story, "Sunday at the Mintons'." Here a lonely professional woman leaves her drab apartment at twilight to walk to the bakery. As night falls, she follows an "elfin child" through the city streets, and almost succumbs to the suicide the strange child points her toward.

> She reached out over the railing, and there was the water down below. Way, way down the dark surface of the river leered up at her. If she leaned just a little farther, just a little, . . . there would be no more apartment, no more ugly brown cloak, no more . . . The wind would bear her up. She would be floating on the wind . . . For one breathless exultant moment she leaned out, her eyes shining. She laughed giddily. She was going to . . .[8]

With the shift in the wind, Miss Minton leaves her fantasy and goes sanely home to bed, forgetting the episode and the child (and forgetting, Plath suggests, that moment of clarity as well).

Admittedly, these are the fictions of a high school student. Yet it is interesting that the pervasive themes of Plath's fictional *oeuvre* appear here in miniature. The struggle to shape her mature life becomes the plot of Esther Greenwood's narrative in *The Bell Jar*, a novel filled with the woman protagonist's fears of never finding a suitable career, a worthy husband, or her own mental health. Plath's interest in defining health and madness seems, too, to stem from these earlier fragments of stories, for all of the women characters here are at least unusual rather than predictable and normal.

Retrospectively, in 1983, in one of the last things she published about her daughter, Aurelia Plath concluded that Sylvia was, at all stages in her life, a writer; and that she "achieved release when troubled by writing things out, thereby dissipating her frustration, even her fury, by the act."[9] It is a contradictory conclusion, I think, to equate the therapeutic benefits of being a writer with Sylvia Plath's steady progress toward her achievement – great skills employed in expressions that show her unusually mature comprehension of the human condition. But at least her mother had come to terms with the force that did drive Plath far from the tranquil 1950s, far from the passive roles that so many well-educated women at mid-century were willing to accept. But in that brief essay, her mother continued, suggesting that most of Sylvia's best writing stemmed from "the toll of the death bell... the obsessive return to the period of emotional confusion and the horror of that first shock treatment."[10] As we have sampled here, the undercurrent of unease, the attraction of the dark mystery of the inexplicable, is evident long before Plath's own breakdown. Unless we accept the plausible notion that the toll of the death bell is that ringing for her dramatically absent father, the parent whose death left her vulnerable to a world she was not ready to meet on her own. It was, after all, Otto Plath who was the published author.

2
Creating Lives

As decades have passed, it has been difficult to return in time to assess Sylvia Plath's relationships with either of her parents, though it is the persona of the father who exists more tangibly in her writing. Otto Plath as readers know him from her fiction and poetry was from the start a highly fictionalized character. According to Plath's mother, the warm and loving father figure created in her early fiction was "90% her adoring grandfather," Aurelia's father, "Grampy" Schober. In an unpublished 1988 letter, Mrs. Plath expanded on the description of her husband's invalidism, expressing for perhaps the first time how dismal the family's life was during the four years of his misdiagnosed illness – and how separate the children's lives were from their father's existence. She described the "four years of horrible illness, reactions I kept the children from witnessing" by making their upstairs playroom the center of their lives, the place "where their meals were served and eaten while I either read to them or made up wild and humorous stories to fill them with imagination and *fun*. It was a world apart from the huge 'bedroom-study' on the first floor on the other end of the house which was silent." Because of the specter of Otto Plath's illness, Aurelia concluded, "My husband never hugged, never kissed his children, fearing he had something communicable that closeness would transfer...[he] never took a walk with them, played [with] or touched them. [There were] no 'talks' – [only] a pat on the head at bedtime."[1]

Rather than villify Otto Plath, his wife chose the tactic throughout the children's lives of deifying him (see her introduction to her collection of Sylvia's letters, *Letters Home*). Only late in life, fearing that her deteriorating eyesight would soon prevent her from communicating, did Mrs. Plath write this remarkable description.

Sylvia Plath's younger cousin, Anita Helle, supplies another kind of information as she reads the hundreds of letters her mother and Aurelia Plath exchanged once she, Anita, had been born on Sylvia's birthday. The distance that Otto Plath felt from most human beings, Helle speculates, began in his own boyhood, when his mother was forced to leave her children to follow their father. The children, left "with various relatives," heard nothing from their mother during the last thirty years of her life. Otto's personal history, Helle suggests, created his own "hard-bitten anguish" and led to his, and Aurelia's, investment "in the future of their children" even as they may have denied "their own histories of injury."[2]

Perhaps only in her wry 1959 poem, "The Colossus," does Plath catch this sense of the father as an unattainble sphinx- like statue, an entity more foreboding than real. In most of her early writing, the father persona is either the lovingly affectionate grandfather or the absent man she yearns to bring back into her existence. Plath's writing often focuses on the guilt the daughter feels for her bereavement – she has somehow been responsible for his death, if not the direct agent of it. "The Colossus," too, for all its remoteness of place, poses a burden – the poet is charged with cleaning, repairing, resurrecting him. As the poem opens, "I shall never get you put together entirely,/ Pieced, glued, and properly jointed."[3] Even amid the unpleasant noises of the barnyard (she likens his ephemera to "mule-bray, pig-grunt and bawdy cackles" as she punctures his tendency to think of himself as godlike, "an oracle"), she continues her labor; but even after a virtual lifetime of this effort, she concludes, "I am none the wiser."

The diminution of the poet's self appears here – she is "an ant in mourning" – or such a small being that she is able to squat "in the cornucopia/ Of your left ear." She has relinquished hope of rescue or of reprieve as she says simply, "My hours are married to shadow." The poem asks, What is the child's role in the aftermath of a brilliant scientist's and father's death? To reconstruct his *oeuvre*, and perhaps through that, his persona. Characteristic of the temper of the 1940s and 1950s, when men held most of the prestigious teaching posts as well as the same kinds of positions in industry, women saw themselves as assistants rather than as primary actors. Plath saw that pattern in her own household, as her grandfather worked outside the home while her grandmother stayed within, and her mother resumed her teaching career only after Otto had died. Men's work was the significant effort.

As Steven Gould Axelrod points out in his 1990 work, Sylvia was impressed with the fact that her father had written a book. She also saw that Otto's treatise was dedicated not to his wife but to his "'teacher and friend,' William Morton Wheeler and [that he] had merely acknowledged the 'service' of his wife 'in editing the manuscript and in proofreading'...he had generated language, whereas her mother only transcribed it."[4] Again, men held privileged positions in the literary world; no wonder her mother's later suggestion that Sylvia learn shorthand, so that she could be an efficient secretary, enraged her. As she wrote angrily in her journal, "I will not submit to having my life fingered by my husband... nourished by tales of his actual exploits. I must have a legitimate field of my own."[5] Entering college, she admitted, "My greatest trouble is jealousy. I am jealous of men...It is an envy born of the desire to be active and doing, not passive and listening."[6] Looking to books for women models, she asked, "Why did Virginia Woolf commit suicide? Or Sara Teasdale or the other brilliant women? Neurotic? Was their writing sublimation (oh, horrible word)...If only I knew how high I could set my goals, my requirements for my life!...Whom can I talk to? Get advice from? No one."[7]

What Plath the young writer did in much of her adolescent fiction was to create the father she had never had – and in so doing, to elaborate on the father that Aurelia had constructed for her. Yet there was always something wrong with that construction, as she later realized: she and Warren had not gone to his funeral, had never mourned for him (neither had Aurelia mourned Otto's death because she did not want the children to see her crying). Instead of admitting that Otto's misdiagnosis of his illness (coupled with his refusal to see any doctor) had led to his death, the family colluded to shape a distant noble figure – a colossus – and accepted as their burden a permanent state of bereavement. Only much later does Plath begin to question the paternal image she has been given.

"Among the Bumblebees," a 1952 story written for an English class assignment at Smith, is her most direct recounting of the wide gap between the presence of her father while she is young and the long progression of his dying. Transferring the role played by Grandfather Schober to the father persona, she opens the story with the Biblical echo, "In the beginning there was Alice Denway's father, tossing her up in the air until the breath caught in her throat, and catching her and holding her in a huge bear hug."[8] From that comforting image of the father in charge, protecting the child whether swimming or walking, the story becomes a detailed narrative of his illness. The texture of the young daughter's memory is caught in her complete confidence: with him, "she could face the doomsday of the world."

Yet as he declines, grows remote, and spends his energy waiting to die, she realizes the essential separateness of all human beings. Despite the allure of thinking that her father could and would always protect her, Alice knew in her heart that she was alone. Plath's closing scene intensifies what might have remained somewhat sentimental; she focuses on Alice standing separate at his bedside, monitoring his weaker and weaker pulse. What is most devastating about her father's condition, however, is not that he is dying but rather that he has withdrawn completely from her. His whole being is centered in the "core of himself."

Plath attempts to probe the experience of a father's death again in her 1955 story, "The Day Mr. Prescott Died." In this narrative she is Lydia, the crude-talking grown daughter who is coerced into joining her mother in a visit to the bereaved household. Rather than dying young, Mr. Prescott is old – and in the quasi-tough idiom of the narrator, "old Mr. Prescott had it coming. Just because nobody's sorry...you know Mr. Prescott was twenty years older than Mrs. Prescott and she was just waiting for him to die so she could have some fun. Just waiting. He was a grumpy old man even as far back as I remember. A cross word for everybody..."[9]

It is a boldly angry move – to describe "Mr. Prescott" as a bystander might have described her father, the aloof – and most of the time, grumpy – Otto Plath, twenty-one years older than his eager-to-please wife. This is Plath writing after her therapy with Ruth Buescher, trying to see her family in a more honest light than the rosy tint her mother consistently gave it.

And yet even at this time Plath could not write in her own voice. Instead, she adopts the tough observer stance, aiming to create humor through the unsympathetic description of Mr Prescott's heart attack and death as he returned from swimming. She adds to the humor by creating grotesque family members who are gathered to mourn – the fat sister, the callous and bored children, the young and well-powdered wife. Relegated by her mother to doing the kitchen work for the mourners, Lydia washes dirty dishes in the sink before setting out supper. Thirsty and impatient, she drinks from one of the still unwashed glasses, only to be told that Mr. Prescott had drunk from that very glass as he lay dying in the yard. Ben, the son, reassures her that someone would have had to drink from it sometime. As she talks with Ben, he admits that, while he is not exactly sorry that his father has died, "I could have been nicer. Could have been nicer, that's all." His honesty triggers her own view of what her life might be like without her often irritating mother; then her anger at having to come along changes to understanding: "I thought of Mama, and suddenly all the sad part I hadn't been able to find during the day came up in my throat. 'We'll go on better than before,' I said. And then I quoted Mama like I never thought I would: 'It's all the best of us can do.' "[10] Here Plath is able to express antipathy at the mother's controlling behavior even as she treats the theme of bereavement and family reaction to the death of a man who might be said to resemble Otto Plath.

Some of Plath's dwelling on the deaths of beloved people was a probable result of her grandmother's being ill with incurable cancer. In 1955, frustrated that she was not in the States to tell Grammy Schober goodbye, or to help Aurelia care for her mother and soon to face her death, Plath was naturally recalling the only other death experience her family had endured, that of her father. As she wrote in her journal, "I love that woman [Grandmother Schober], I can't believe she could go out of the world and me not there; I can't believe home could be without her. It sickens me; afar off, I think of her, and cry. Those presences, those people loved and gone into the dark; I rail and rage against the taking of my father, whom I have never known."[11] Her fear of death, coupled with her understanding of the allure of it, leads her to write, "I feel somehow much too old, with all the older ones dead before I have known them, and only the young ones, the babies, under me. I am so close to the dark. My villanelle was to my father; and the best one."[12]

While in her first year at Smith, she had assumed a brusque tone in reminding herself that she was part of Otto's lineage ("There is your dead father who is somewhere in you").[13] Later journal entries, however, like the one above and this, express her loss more directly: "it hurts, Father, it hurts, oh, Father I have never known; a father, even, they took from me."[14] And there can be little question that part of the reason Plath had difficulty expressing any criticism of her mother, no matter how stifling and unsuitable she sometimes found Aurelia's behavior, was the very natural fear that she would lose her as well – what she calls "the terror of having no parents."[15]

The latter is the controlling image of the persona's vacillation between fear and self-loathing expressed in her story, "Tongues of Stone," where she engages in meaningless sex as a way to find physical closeness, all the while repressing her fears of abandonment by her family. It is clear in the story that her father has already died, but she worries now about the wellbeing of both her grandparents and her mother. Narratively, the story works in ways similar to "Superman and Paula Brown's New Snowsuit," a story in which the father's death is foregrounded so that the young daughter has nowhere to turn. In the neighbor's accusation that she has shoved Paula and ruined her snowsuit, the persona is found guilty even though she is entirely innocent. Plath implies that the character's isolation, her inability to communicate – in this story, even with her beloved young Uncle Frank – stems from the loss of her father.

In many of Plath's poems after 1957, during the years when she was consciously choosing rich subjects to evoke the deepest of her poetic skills, the subject of Otto Plath's death surfaces – either as primary theme or as a subtle embroidery on the ostensible content of the work. Of her earlier poems, however, it is only her "best" villanelle, as she calls it in the 1955 journal entry, that treats of his absence. In "Lament," published in *New Orleans Poetry Journal*, she chooses as the refrain line one that links the subject persona with bees: "The sting of bees took away my father."[16] Economically, with the swift impact that a well-constructed villanelle can achieve, 'Lament' cries out in every tercet for the absent parent. The second refrain – "and scorned the tick of the falling weather" – indicates both the late autumn time of Otto's death and his cavalier defiance of his health problems. The end of harvest, November recurs frequently in Plath's later poems – signaling both Otto's death and her period of living alone after her husband had moved out of their Devon house. November is also the month that follows four days after her late-October birthday. In themes of absence, aging, and bereavement, it names a time of sorrow.

"Lament" captures the imperiousness of Otto Plath even as it joins his persona with that of Grandfather Schober: "Trouncing the sea like a raging bather,/ he rode the flood in a pride of prongs." For all his strength and bravado, however, and despite the fact that he "can mangle the grin of kings," the father persona is dead. Strangely, so is the mother. Her death, however, stems from a different cause: "A scowl of sun struck down my mother." That death occurs in only one stanza, and appears not to be the reason for the speaker's lament.

Many of Plath's earlier poems that appear to be about Otto Plath, or about his death, might also be read as investigations of power – particularly gendered power. During 1957 and 1958, "On the Decline of Oracles" begins with the death of the persona's father but goes on to question the ways she, as daughter and poet, has come into his voice/authority. "Ouija" and "Snakecharmer" also work from the theme of authority, and "Full Fathom Five" sets up the first half of a dialogue which "Lorelei' completes. The women's voices in the latter poem supply the soundings that the poet only awaits in 'Full Fathom Five." By 1959, the time of "Electra on the Azalea Path," "The Beekeeper's Daughter," "The Manor Garden," and "The Colossus," Plath is dealing much more directly with her personal loss of her father – and with the deep and almost crippling effects her therapy has shown that death to have had. The pattern is like that of Plath's early "East Wind" and "Heat." Writing that seems to be about death also serves to characterize the two sexes. It is the male who is mourned at the time of his death, presumably because of the loss of his ability; the woman – even if tempted by death – usually continues her life.

As the reader might expect, no matter how bright Sylvia Plath was, her early writing remains the product of a very young person. Much of her first fiction was written for the three years of high school English classes that she took with Wilbury Crockett. As with many of her college English classes, the fact that she had a male instructor – and that she read literature almost exclusively by male authors – was to set patterns, and to encourage critical approaches to texts, that became the norm. Crockett encouraged Plath to write about what she knew best, and she did write several stories about women trying to become writers; but what he taught most – and loved best – were works by men.

The pattern had been set even earlier. When Plath graduated from junior high school as the outstanding student for the year, and was given as a prize *Understanding Poetry*, Robert Penn Warren's and Cleanth Brooks' New Critical textbook, she found herself already caught in mandates for reading – and, implicitly, for writing – that had traditionally inspired (male) writers. Literature was "about" the quest, the search for the best of human and spiritual values, the adventurous achievement through which a person could find identity. No wonder that when the young Plath thought about writing fiction, she decided she would not try to be "great." She would instead choose to write "pot boilers" for women's magazines. Being a girl, she had had very few adventurous trips to mountain tops, nor had she spent years in Swiss sanatoria. While she could read Thomas Mann and T. S. Eliot accurately, she did not much identify with their traditional themes.

One of Plath's best early short stories grows from her observing this inherent gender difference between the established, great male authors whose works comprised the reading lists for English courses and the fact that she was herself a female writer – one as interested, during some summers, in improving her tennis game as her poetry. Her consciousness of the privileging of male writers was heightened during her first years at college because she was then the steady girlfriend of Dick Norton, a Yale medical student whose parents were close friends of her mother's. When she began dating Dick, she had written to Aurelia that he knew "everything."[17] Her sense of inferiority increased when Norton was found to be tubercular and sent to a sanatorium; there he decided to become a writer himself (whereas he had previously criticized the fact that Sylvia had such an impractical ambition). Seeing Dick write and publish, or rather, seeing that he now had the leisure to read and write and publish, while she spent her time doing homework for required courses, increased her antipathy to his know-it-all attitude, and in frustration she wrote what became her prize-winning story, "Sunday at the Mintons'."

The contrast between the fragile retired librarian, Elizabeth Minton, and her authoritative, successful brother Henry is the fulcrum of the story. Plath's metaphors establish lines of sympathy for Elizabeth, who now keeps house for her critical brother; the story, in fact, opens with her wishing that Henry were not so "supremely fastidious."[18] Her brother's neatness, however, is not Elizabeth's real worry: she is afraid the differences between her personality and his will spoil their life together. Elizabeth, after years of being self-supporting, is now faced with the need to please Henry who owns the house, and has rigid ideas about how things – all things – are to be done.

As the early scenes show clearly – and with humor, Elizabeth is a dreamer whereas Henry fixates on order. Plath shows this difference in several remarkable scenes, filled with intentionally comic dialogue. The long story turns into fantasy – but fantasy with a bite. As the two siblings take their Sunday walk to the ocean, Elizabeth loses her mother's brooch and when she asks Henry to retrieve it for her, he falls and is scooped away by waves. Freed literally as well as figuratively, she in turn sails away into space, no longer submissive, "enjoying herself thoroughly, blowing upward, now to this side, now to that, her lavender dress blending with the purple of the distant clouds."[19] Framing "Sunday at the Mintons'" so that the personae eventually awake, Plath balances imagination with logic, finally reuniting the characters.

It becomes, then, a palatable story, its more frightening elements that speak of gender power covered over by the peaceful – if fantastic – ending. That it won for Plath a $500 prize, in a year when she anguished over Smith College having increased its annual tuition by $150, marked her strategies as brilliant. To write about the inequity of being female in such a way as to pacify readers – to keep them from seeing how deep her anger was about the topic – was to learn to succeed in the commercial marketplace.

Plath writes different kinds of stories about her romance with Dick Norton (the model for Henry Minton) in both "The Christmas Heart," an unpublished fiction, and the 1954 Hemingway-like "In the Mountains." In the former the protagonist Sheila goes to visit Michael, her former boyfriend, as he recovers from tuberculosis. As in the Mintons' relationship, Michael has been dominant, learned, scientific, and less than sympathetic to her. Sheila remembers, early in the narrative, that Michael had "always treated her frequent sinus infections like a rather unnecessary feminine indulgence."[20] That insightful memory leads her to think over more of their past and to, finally, conclude, "He had wanted only to master her, to cut out her tender softness like a cancer spot, until she saw life as he did: a stimulating scientific experiment where people are guinea pigs."

For all its didacticism, the story is full of apt, comic images: "She no longer felt the old desperate passion to identify with Michael, to leap through the flaming hoops he set up for her until she reached the summit where he sat, calling the stars by name and clocking her heartbeats with his watch." The crux of the separation in "The Christmas Heart" is that dichotomy between intuition and rationality that ocurs in "Sunday at the Mintons'" but here Plath has stayed close to the literal truth.

"In the Mountains," written the next year, is a softer story, with responsibility for the break up more evenly divided. Austin, the tubercular medical student, wants to keep the romance going: the normality of having a girlfriend helps keep his fears of death at bay. The story begins with Austin and Isobel on the bus, traveling back to the sanatorium after his holidays at home. It is a physical story, his thigh resting against hers, his fingers twisting her hair: sexuality surges through the distanced description. But the sexuality is past. It has been six months since they have been together, and, Isobel thinks, whatever Austin did "did not make her want to go to him." What suffuses her memory is "the old hurting fear."[21]

Once they are together in the house, he confesses to her his fear of both his illness and of losing her. She, however, remains remote, even cynical. This time, Isobel is the stunted persona: Austin has changed, improved, become more human. Allusions to Hemingway's *A Farewell to Arms*, and its ending scene with Frederic leaving the dead Catherine and walking into the rainy night, draw the inferences into a close: their love is over. Austin's illness – which prevents his kissing or being intimate with Isobel – is as good as a death.

This is the more mature picture Plath creates of the Dick Norton character, and of the love she shared with him. The reader's impression from "In the Mountains" is quite different from that created by the Buddy Willard character in *The Bell Jar*. In comparison with Austin in this story, Buddy is more caricature than character.

In seeing how Plath learned to *draw from* the real events of her life – rather than to write *about* those events, the reader can appreciate her skill as a writer. Never a simple one-to-one equation, creating scene and character is an imaginative coalescence of knowledge – intimate or distant – mixed with more shadowy impressions, all fused at the right catalytic moment. Learning to watch for the exactly right set of circumstances was part of Plath's education in writing. By 1954, she was making good, steady, progress.

3

Creating the Persona of the Self

More important than stories that deal with Plath's first serious romance are those that investigate her developing sexuality. Several of her early stories that try to approach that controversial theme take as heroine Marcia (or Mary or Dody) Ventura. One of Plath's high school friends, Mary Ventura, was the prototype for this character, a woman of a lower social class than Plath. Daring and candid, Mary/Marcia readily admitted to being sexually experienced. Plath's stories "The Island" and "Den of Lions" are based on this character, and there are suggestions of the same sexual defiance in "The Estonian," re-titled "The Latvian." In the story "Mary Ventura," the title character, the daughter of a poor Italian family, has not been able to think of going to college. When she mets the Plath persona on the street and they talk, Mary's sense of defeat is tangible. As she tells her friend about her life experiences, all defined sexually and beginning with an affair with her piano teacher, her cool objectivity is puzzling, disturbing. The mystery of her attitude is intensified by the unexplained presence of a train in the background, a train moving steadily to some unknown destination.[1]

The inexplicable train becomes the center of Plath's 1952 story "Mary Ventura and the Ninth Kingdom," and here the woman character is passively awaiting the train's arrival. Warned by a fellow passenger that she will "pay" at the end of the journey, Ventura is complacent, unafraid. The enigmatic story does not work, but it seems to have been an experiment in using religious imagery in an apparently non-religious story. As Plath explained in a note that preceded the text, the story is meant to be "a symbolic allegory,"[2] with the train trip representing "the journey of many young people through life, bored, won over by the pleasures of creature comforts." Narratively, Plath writes, "The Christian symbols which appear in the story are intended to be subtle suggestions of the ever-presence of Bible figures in modern life." She then directs her reader to the scene in which brothers quarrel as "present-day prototypes of Cain and

Abel," and to her use of mother and child, "A lady in a blue jacket, carrying a baby wrapped in a soiled white blanket..."

Hardly subtle, each of these events in the story fits so poorly into the narrative that it calls a great deal of attention to itself; for example, Plath incorporates a Wise Man scene, complete with ironic modern disregard for a crying infant, and the three men, drunk from cocktails, can say only "Darn brat."[3]

While Plath may have been too inexperienced to use religious allegory well, she later employs that approach in *The Bell Jar*, changing the twenty actual *Mademoiselle* college editors to the symbolic twelve of Jesus's disciples[4] and heightening each narrative scene so that it has some parallel with the last years of Christ's life.

What "Mary Ventura and the Ninth Kingdom" shows about Plath's early fiction is her fascination with the theme of women's sexuality. The contrast between this 1952 story and the 1957 Dody Ventura fiction is striking. Keeping the same family name, with its sound of "adventure," she here speaks much more bluntly about the persona's sexuality. As an American woman studying in England, Dody sleeps with a number of men, justifying her behavior with the notion that "as long as it was someone who didn't matter, it didn't matter."[5] But her longing for real fulfillment – for someone who did matter – finally breaks into the quasi-objectivity of the narrating voice: "let something happen. Let something happen. Something terrible, something bloody. Something to end this endless flaking snowdrift of airmail letters, of blank pages turning in library books. How we go waste..."[6]

This intense plea comes as a surprise to the reader. It appears amid descriptions of tasteless food in the dining hall and the snow-covered statue which Dody brushes off each evening (the "stone boy with dolphin" of the title, who becomes her winged fantasy lover). Meanwhile she goes to parties with assorted men, this time with Hamish – "safe, slow. Like travling by mule, minus mule kicks." But it is Leonard, the "statue-breaker" whom she meets at the party, with whom she experiences that violence she has been hungering for. In response to his violent kiss, she bites him on his unshaven cheek, and her decisive act brings all the imagery of icy waste to a heated conclusion: "wasted, wasting, her blood gone to redden the circle of teeth marks on Leonard's cheek, and she, a bloodless husk, left drifting in limbo. Here with Hamish."[7]

Because so many of Plath's early stories sound as if she were trying to win American Legion essay contests, this much more explicit narrative shows her growth into a fiction writer with a distinctive voice. The cynical Dody, for all her privileging of the mind, knows that she hungers for the physical, the sexual. And the reader shares with her the impatience of having to mark her time by fulfilling the social rituals demanded of "nice" American women during the 1950s. While the story is clearly autobiographical, it is more importantly a step forward into the effective use of scenes that strike the reader as plausible. The desperate hunger to be satisfied, to find a man worthy of being a mate for the unusual woman persona, is believable.

Identifying the woman protagonist with herself is another step forward for Plath the fiction writer. We have seen the manner in which she wrote stories during high school about protagonists who were older women, career women, often unfulfilled. There were, too, the charming adolescent narratives about first dates ("And Summer Will Not Come Again," "First Date," "The New Girl"), but more of the stories were then focused outward. Toward the end of her college years, she began trying to work with stories of women's friendships. The slight fictions "Platinum Summer" and "The Smoky Blue Piano" are less "romance" narratives than they are women's friendship stories. While the protagonist is trying to trap the perfect mate, she does her romancing under the tutelage of a woman friend. In "Platinum Summer," Happy is the sensible roommate who keeps Lynn Hunter from succumbing to a wealthy playboy's attentions. As a newly blonded vamp, Lynn has little experience fighting off the kind of men who are attracted by her platinum hair. In "The Smoky Blue Piano," Lynn is the brilliant apartment-mate, but it is the plain girlfriend who has spent the summer studying German who ends up with Lou, the older man next-door. Much of the intrigue of watching Lou occurs during the women's daily lives together. In fact, it is the protagonist's concern for Lynn's crush on Lou that leads to the intimate conversation that brings him to confess that he has liked her, not Lynn, all along. In a move toward what will become her more satiric voice in very late fiction, Plath creates her upfront protagonist:

> "Look, Lou," I said in a big sister tone of voice, "so you don't know how to treat Ava Gardner when she also has the brains of Marie Curie. So I am here to tell you. I am your fairy godmother, in person, complete with chocolate cake."

Lou looked as if he really believed the fairy godmother part, so I forged on.

"You see, Lou," I began reasonably, as if I were selling an expensive insurance policy I sincerely believed in...[8]

The theme in both stories is the affection between women, a new figuration for Plath's narratives.

While in both stories the women are away from home – working as waitresses on the Cape, or in summer school at Harvard – and therefore the absence of parents or families is reasonable, in most of her fiction Plath avoids mentioning the character of a mother, even when the presence of that persona would be logical. There is this kind of absence, just as there is (in her archives) a lack of the fiction she did write about her mother, or a mother, or the fusion between daughter and mother. For even as the father figure is a dominant presence in Plath's early writing, the mother figure is comparatively neglected.

There are, literally, very few of her poems or stories that even mention a mother. The disdainful tone of her early poem "housewife" suggests her consistent lack of admiration for such a figure, a woman who might "slam the kitchen cupboards/ of her mind/ and walk down to the beach/ to be alone and free."[9] But from this positive move to free herself from mundane chores, in Plath's poem the natural world disdains her. One of her earlier poems, "Song of the Wild Geese," uses the mother persona to answer the balladeer's interrogation: "Why do you sigh, mother?" and "Why do you cry, mother?"[10] In this lament, the mother is only a stock character required by the poetic form.

Psychologist Alice Miller explains that there were many reasons for Plath's avoiding the representation of her mother in her art. In *For Your Own Good, Hidden Cruelty in Child-Rearing and the Roots of Violence*, Miller uses the symbiotic relationship between Plath and her mother as an example of the way parental power coerces a child into belief in, and representations of, a false self. Miller sees the falsity of Plath's *Letters Home* as significant – not because she is disguising her pain from Aurelia, but because she has no other choices but to present herself as accomplished, successful, happy.

Sylvia Plath's life was no more difficult than that of millions of others...the reason for her despair was not her suffering but the impossibility of communicating her suffering to another person.

In all her letters she assures her mother how well she is doing. The suspicion that her mother did not release negative letters for publication overlooks the deep tragedy of Plath's life. This tragedy (and the explanation for her suicide as well) lies in the very fact that she could not have written any other kind of letters, because her mother needed reassurance, or because Sylvia at any rate believed that her mother would not have been able to live without this reassurance. Had Sylvia been able to write aggressive and unhappy letters to her mother, she would not have had to commit suicide. Had her mother been able to experience grief at her inability to comprehend the abyss that was her daughter's life, she never would have published the letters, because the assurances they contained of how well things were going for her daughter would have been too painful to bear. Aurelia Plath is unable to mourn over this because she has guilt feelings, and the letters serve her as proof of her innocence.[11]

The crux of the problem, according to Miller, is that no one cared for Sylvia for herself, but rather as the product of all the success her mother had had in rearing her. In that process, Plath never had the permission to be anyone other than her mother's daughter, and her true self was repressed at every turn. In Miller's analysis, "The letters are testimony of the false self she constructed (whereas her true self is speaking in *The Bell Jar*)."[12] Miller concludes, "suicide really is... the only possible way to express the true self – at the expense of life itself."[13]

Keeping in mind the duality of Plath-as-self and Plath-as-daughter, then, the fact that it is a decade later before Plath incorporates her mother's character into a poem is less surprising. Otto Plath was a static and comparatively known quantity. Because he was dead, the writer had no fear of either losing his love or hearing his reactions. But in the case of Aurelia, Plath feared both. Unfortunately, because she often shared her writing with her mother, she faced the double and triple bind of knowing that she would hear what her mother thought about her portraiture. In "The Disquieting Muses," she fuses the history of the poet, the poet's mother, and that same figure as the daughter of the Schobers to shape a rich, if ambivalent and perhaps intentionally confusing tapestry of women's experiences.

As the poem opens, the history is recognizable. There is Aurelia telling stories of Mixie Blackshort, baking bad witches into ginger-bread, teaching Warren and Sylvia cheerful songs when storms threaten to blow in all twelve porch windows of Otto's study. Although Plath does not mention her father, she gives the reader Mother as "denying figure," one who puts the best face on everything – and asks her children to do the same, just as she had at the time of Otto's illness. (Most children find thunderstorms frightening; in this narrative Aurelia turns them into an occasion for play-acting and performance.) The tone in this opening section of the poem can be read as objective; the poet's reliance on "fact" sends one sort of message.

But then the narrative recalls the child's ballet experience and becomes obviously unpleasant; suddenly the mother figure fuses with that of the poet in a non-factual way. Heavy-footed, this daughter cannot dance, and her disappointed mother accordingly "cried and cried."[14] Rather than find some meaning in Sylvia's need to draw a daughter who cannot perform well, who disappoints her mother, Aurelia Plath instead read the narrative very literally. In a late essay which was supposed to be her contribution to a collection of essays about Sylvia Plath's art, Aurelia took it upon herself to correct her daughter, to explain what she saw as the erroneous circumstances of the image: "The fact is Sylvia never took ballet lessons. I did – and told her about my delight, especially during the ballet recital, when, at nine, I was a member of the chorus of about thirty other 'fireflies.' On the dimly lit stage as, in our winged costumes, we danced, tiny 'blinking flashlights' in each hand, I felt myself exalted, for I knew that in the front row my parents were sitting with eyes for me alone – I was for *them* the prima ballerina!"[15]

Aurelia continues, with definite sorrow that her daughter had changed the tone of a thoroughly happy experience, and had then coupled the dance scene with a subsequent one of a daughter failing to play the piano well. In her essay, Aurelia corrects that impression as well: clearly, she notes, poetic license was being used to make these childhood experiences – regardless of whose they rightfully were – more dramatic. It is interesting that Aurelia seems not to notice the real import of the poem, in which the persona's being surrounded by disquieting muses, uninvited spirits, is more palatable for her than living the cosy suburban life her mother has provided: "I woke one day to see you, mother/ Floating above me in bluest air/ On a green balloon bright with a million/ Flowers and bluebirds that never were/ Never, never, found anywhere..."[16]

Plath's anger toward Aurelia, expressed in notes about her therapy with Dr. Beuscher, was focused on the faulty information her mother provided her. Whatever Aurelia said, or whatever Aurelia believed, life was not the way she represented it as being. For Sylvia – who looked and even sounded so much like her mother,[17] the wide discrepancy in their beliefs and expectations was continuously disappointing.

In her 1991 study, critic Pat Macpherson sees this poem as "an accusation in which the mother's denial creates the daughter's disturbed reality...The daughter has learned to use her mother's denials against her, announcing their cost to her and then bravely swallowing the martyr's pill." She also quotes Aurelia Plath's comment on the *Voices and Visions* program, " 'I think it was a remarkable poem but I was hurt by it [because] she manipulated what I said.' Unwitting still, the mother's literal-mindedness in the court of mother-blame blinds her to the daughter's 'reality' of the symbolic, the uncanny, where speaks all that hurts, manipulates and – worst crime – is ungrateful."[18] What Plath had learned, according to Macpherson, was that her mother's attitudes were supposed to become hers, no matter how objectionable she personally found them.

In the only two of Aurelia's letters that remain in the Plath archives, what is most remarkable about them – especially in her letter of December 4, 1962, after she had received page after page of angry lament and rage, always countered with letters of seemingly unreasonable optimism from her daughter – is the sense of competition. Sylvia has written Aurelia about a book review she did for pay, so her mother writes her daughter a lengthy book review of something she has just read. Commenting on a poetry reading Sylvia has been asked to give, Aurelia instructed her about choosing 'simple poems' for her audience. She should be like Robert Frost, her mother says, and then she will be "immortal."[19] Worse, she chides Sylvia about her carelessness, wonders at her inability to manage the move from Court Green to London, and seems not to respond in any way to the serious problems Sylvia has admitted to having. It is as if Aurelia Plath, as the writer of this letter, is not the same person who has been receiving Sylvia's anguished missives. It is also as if Aurelia Plath is only an acquaintance, not her daughter's mother.

Perhaps Plath was not surprised by such ineffective parenting (though the fact that this letter survived among her papers suggests that she, too, was appalled by it). As her college poems from this earlier period show, what she was endeavoring to learn was how to survive alone, how to keep her balance without the sugary lies she thought her family, particularly her mother, was likely to feed her. Poem after early poem – from "Aerialist" to "Morning in the Hospital Solarium" to "April 18" – traces her struggle to write honestly, and yet without admitting the terrors of the defeats she experiences. External or internal, visible or hidden, Plath's defeats provided the fabric of much of her writing.

The three poems contrast but each has the theme of bare survival: "Aerialist" is a well-shaped narrative of eight sexains, its theme that "this adroit young lady" has been so well trained that she survives all physical threats (which include whipcracks, "black weight, black ball, black truck") as she leads a cartoon-like life of escaping people and things out to get her. It is only when she awakens and faces the real challenge that she feels despair: if she cannot maintain her performance of being the bright and capable woman, then "the whole/ Elaborate scaffold of sky overhead [will]/ Fall racketing finale on her luck."[20]

"April 18" is the terse, intentionally shocking free form lyric that opens "the slime of all my yesterdays/ rots in the hollow of my skull."[21] It concludes that "a future was lost yesterday," and in between the short lines scan a series of bleak and pungent images. Private to the point of ellipsis, poems like these add to the tonal impact of a series or collection but they remain too enigmatic to reach most readers on their own.

The best of this group of poems, and the one that offers more possibility of later poetic development, is the clearly titled "Morning in the Hospital Solarium." Perhaps Plath did not try to publish this writing, since it so obviously relates to her institutionalization. As readers know, it is not until 1960 when she begins to write *The Bell Jar* that she resurrects those painful (and socially objectionable) memories. (One can imagine Aurelia Plath's horror at her daughter's drawing art from that period of her life.)

The three stanzas of nine lines each impress the reader with an easy colloquial voice; here, attention to form works for the naturalness of the language, not for the need to fit into a structure. Describing the sun room where women gather in this private, and therefore upscale institution, the poem begins, "Sunlight strikes a glass of grapefruit juice,/ flaring green through philodendron leaves/ in this surrealistic house/ of pink and beige...patronized by convalescent wives." Isolated as a female place and beautified in expected decorative ways (even the medications are "a flock of pastel pills,/ turquoise, rose, sierra mauve"), the mental hospital is the setting for "Morning: another day." The poem hints that it is also a place "where ills/ slowly concede to sun and serum." But Plath lets it remain a feminine location, and fills it with women who turn "pages of magazines in elegant ennui," waiting for "some incredible dark man/ to assault the scene." Victims of mid-century ideas about heterosexual love, these women are dreamers rather than actors. Plath's concluding line punctures their fantasies: "at noon, anemic husbands visit them."[22]

Embedded in the physical descriptions of place is the women's reason for being there; the persona mentions "Needles/ that sting no more than love." Romantic love, complete with its imagery of sexual penetration, is the gloss that fits best with the context of the poem; but for Plath's own circumstances, the love of her mother validates the image. For hardest of all the personal elements in keeping her balance was the continuing necessity of living with a woman who had seldom admitted defeat. Aurelia Plath had not been handed an easy life, but she rose above discouragement time after time. Seeing her keep on was in itself a kind of warring note in Sylvia's life: what could she accomplish, given her comparatively pleasant existence, that could equal her mother's courage? Typically, Aurelia spoke in platitudes: she was, after all, a woman of the war years, a woman whose friends had lost husbands, as she had; a woman of confident parentage who knew she could survive. And she was also a woman descended from the hardy Schobers of Austria, not from the depressive Plaths. Genetically, Aurelia had few tendencies toward mental instability.

It goes without saying that Plath knew she should not dislike her mother, and that knowledge meant that her feelings of irritation and active impatience caused her great guilt. When she wrote in her journal about the story (now lost) "Trouble-Making Mother," she referred to it as "close to my experience, slice out of a big pothering deep-dish pie."[23] She summarized the plot of the narrative:

mother dominates daughter, only nineteen years old, or twenty: girl 17, mother 37: mother flirts with girl's dates. Girl fights for freedom & integrity...Get tension of scenes with mother during Ira and Gordon crisis.[This is the Harvard summer]. Rebellion. Car keys. Psychiatrist. Details: Dr. B.: baby. Girl comes back to self, can be good daughter. Sees vision of mother's hardships. Yes yes. This is a good one. A subject. Dramatic. Serious...Dynamite under high tension. Mother's character. At first menacing, later pathetic, moving."[24]

Excited as Plath was about this complex narrative, she wrote a few days later, "I'm surprised at the story: it's more gripping, I think, than anything I've ever done. No more burble about Platinum Summers manipulated from behind my eye with a ten-foot pole. Real, dramatic crises. A growth in the main character. Things and emblems of importance."[25]

Ironically, Sylvia wrote this story during July 1957, when she and Hughes honeymooned at the "Hidden Acres" cottage at Eastham where they had uninterrupted time to write – a vacation paid for entirely by Aurelia. Plath's only other journal comment about "Trouble-Making Mother" is that *The Saturday Evening Post*, the magazine to which she sent it first, rejected it without a comment of any kind.[26]

Reading Sylvia's July, 1957, letters back to her mother in Wellesley, however, is finding an entirely different narrative. Exuberant that she and Ted are both writing well (though she does not tell Aurelia anything about the story she has just written), she graciously thanks her mother, "You could have done nothing more wonderful than giving us these seven weeks..."[27] To follow Sylvia's "letters home," from her earliest days at Smith College, through her travel to England and her return to the States, to Northampton for her teaching job at Smith, to Boston, and then back to England for the rest of her life, is to read a narrative of sheer success. According to these letters, nothing ever stops Sylvia, and although she does not publish as much as she would like – ever – she tells Aurelia that she remains confident about her writing prowess. These letters never mention her seemingly endless days of writing block, the endless depressions, the heartbreaks that pepper her journal entries.

The *Letters Home* narrative is, obviously, a fantasy. It might be explained – all the years of it – by saying that whenever Sylvia tried to write honestly to her mother, days and months of that parent's cajoling and lecturing came into play. She would do nothing to hurt her wonderful mother, her mother with ulcers, with other physical problems, with her heavy workload. She also would not take on the puritanical, morally upright woman who had known only one sex partner in her life, and who believed that monogamy was the only way to experience sexuality. Whenever Sylvia broke any of the family laws – whether written or unwritten, spoken or silent – she added to her mother's burden of crushing weight.

The guilt had begun with the death of Otto. There was no way Sylvia and Warren, good as they were, could be silently good throughout the four or five years of their father's illness. There were days – and nights – when they simply misbehaved, intentionally, purposefully, meanly. Small as they were, they had no idea that their bad behavior would "cause" their father to die. Once Otto did fail to return from the hospital, and was said to have been buried (even if the children never saw his grave), both Sylvia and Warren were filled with guilt.

It continued throughout their lives, though Warren might have been able to deflect it at times (because he went to prep schools, he was away from the Wellesley house much earlier than Sylvia, who attended the local high school). Soon after they were both in college, Sylvia wrote her brother and chastised him for worrying Aurelia. After a long paragraph about their taking care of their own college expenses (whatever they would need besides their scholarships), she came to the more personal item on her agenda: "One thing I hope is that you will make your own breakfasts ... so mother won't have to lift a finger. That is the main thing that seems to bother her. You know, as I do, ... that mother would actually kill herself for us if we calmly accepted all she wanted to do for us ... I have realized lately that we have to fight against her selflessness as we would fight against a deadly disease."[28] With foreshadowing that was eerily accurate, Sylvia here expressed her need to separate from Aurelia, to become the person she saw herself as being. Yet she remained torn with all the ambitious hopes her mother had fostered within her – who was Sylvia? The Sylvia her mother had shaped or the Sylvia who knew her own desires and abilities? Ted Hughes later wrote that "her [Plath's] real creation was her own image ... all her writings appear like notes and jottings directing attention towards that central problem – herself."[29] The question of Plath's identity, then, was crucial to her continued development as a writer.

By this time in both Warren's and Sylvia's lives, they were legally past their mother's control; but Aurelia's influence ran deep, at least partly because they had only one parent. Offending the remaining parent was risking outright abandonment. The dilemma for the reader of both Plath's poetry and fiction and the letters to her mother that comprise *Letters Home* is being able to sort through the

various kinds of fantasies that these writings represent. As critic
Jacqueline Rose writes about the possibility of our understanding
the Plath–Hughes relationship, similarly, it is the difficulty of reading fact from fictions that proves insurmountable. She writes, "But
we cannot assume ... that because this is what Hughes writes about,
this is also what he *does*. In fact beyond – or for in excuse of – the
unanswerable question of what really happened, the drama
between Plath and Hughes, in the form in which they write it, can
be read as one of the most stunning illustrations of the brute reality,
the lived effectivity, of fantasy life."[30] While Rose focuses her reading of Plath's late poems on the marital relationship, there are
numerous poems that continue to speak for the difficulty of Sylvia's
deciding who and what she is or might become, themes that stem
from her continuing imbroglio over her emotional bondage to Aurelia. So convoluted is this bondage that Plath the writer needs a
large canvas to explore it. Impossible to handle in a single poem or
story, the heartily symbiotic relationship between Sylvia and her
mother provides the governing metaphor for Plath's only extant
novel, *The Bell Jar*.

4

Recalling the Bell Jar

Ironically, in Aurelia Plath's own assessment, the crucial event of Sylvia's life was her breakdown and recovery.[1] That her mother never admitted any complicity in that psychological malaise was, as we have seen, endemic to her psychology – and, of course, to her daughter's. Mrs. Plath tended to focus on what most readers would think were the externals of the situation: whose car they drove to the out-patient facility, or how Aurelia managed her work schedule to be home most of the time with her daughter. One element of that continuum of details which Mrs. Plath seldom mentions was the existence of what Sylvia saw as frightening electroconvulsive shock treatments – those given during the summer by a psychologist she did not respect, and those given during her rehabilitation at McLean Hospital, this time under the care of Dr. Ruth Buescher, a psychiatrist she did admire and respect – and love.

The entire year that was occupied by her decline into the depression that caused her suicide attempt, and her recovery from that depression, was a time she tried in several ways to erase. There are no journal entries from that year; there are few letters; and there is almost no poetry or fiction. If Plath saw herself as living the life of a writer, existing through the life of the mind and its language, then the period of her breakdown was, in truth, not only a lost year but a death. She subsequently faced the terrifying loss of memory that was bound to accompany shock treatments, but that loss was more easily disguised.

What could never be disguised was the event – breakdown, suicide attempt, treatment, incarceration in an institution. Society would not forget, nor could society forgive her that indignity. The brilliant and beautiful Sylvia Plath, the Smith scholarship coed whose photograph ran in newspapers across the United States while she was missing during her suicide attempt, was irretrievably moored in the cultural memory of the American 1950s. The question of what would become of that brilliant woman had become a larger cultural question: what man would marry a mad woman? Or as Plath wrote the moving line for Esther Greenwood's boyfriend in

The Bell Jar, " 'I wonder who you'll marry now, Esther . . . I wonder who you'll marry now, Esther. Now you've been,' and Buddy's gesture encompassed the hill, the pines and the severe, snow-gabled buildings breaking up the rolling landscape, 'here.' "[2]

Given all the separable themes that intertwine in Plath's novel, the pervasive one is the autobiography of her breakdown. It is that illness that brings the bell jar down on her, that weakens her grasp on accomplishment and life, and that makes her question the family power that had been so coercive a force in her life choices. *The Bell Jar* shows the ways in which Esther Greenwood is the unquestionable product of her ambitious mother and family,[3] and the ways in which she must deny the influence of those elements before she can come into her own fully defined birth. Esther must reconcile what she wants out of life with the pain she will have to cause her family during her process of attaining her needs. She must stop being the good daughter and become the woman who wants.

An unpleasant book to write, freighted with pain for people she knew loved her deeply, this novel became yet another way to crash through the emotional obstacles that were hedging her in, keeping her from realizing her characteristically wry and often hurtful voice. It is only after Plath finishes writing *The Bell Jar* (she turns the manuscript over to its English publishers in November 1961 although the book does not appear until late January 1963) that she comes into the powerful, relentless voice of her last poems.[4]

From its opening scenes, with the recovered Esther Greenwood giving her baby the plastic starfish off the College Board sunglass case, the novel charts what it means to be wife, mother, daughter. Every detail in the novel speaks to some ritualized feminine behavior – whether it be keeping lipsticks in the case they belong in, winning prizes in the New York writing market, dating the eligible Yalie, or finding out with relief that one is not pregnant. From the smallest scenes to the largest, *The Bell Jar* is a tapestry of women's experiences, women's comedy, and all too often, women's tragedy.

It is also a narrative that pays strict attention to what the reader will need to know. Part I sets the novel in the summer of 1953, with the electrocution of the Rosenbergs,[5] an event caught in historical time that foreshadows Esther's own electroconvulsive shock treatments later that same summer. Part II lets the reader know that Esther has survived, that she has married and had a child (effectively answering Buddy Willard's interrogation above), and that she has tried to resume a normal existence. As Plath wrote candidly,

"I realized we kept piling up these presents because it was as good as free advertising for the firms involved, but I couldn't be cynical. I got such a kick out of all those free gifts showering on to us. For a long time afterward I hid them away, but later, when I was all right again, I brought them out, and I still have them around the house."[6]

In her description of the "Amazon" hotel (the Barbizon), Plath draws an economic dividing line between the protected and rich young women (going to Katy Gibbs or being secretaries for executives after having gone to Katy Gibbs) who comprise most of the Amazon's residents and the intellectual elite, the College Board women who do not have such clear ambitions to marry well. Esther begins her quasi-nasty monologue, "Girls like that make me sick. I'm so jealous I can't speak." Yet she backtracks to point to the obvious problems with the wealthy playgirl story: "These girls looked awfully bored to me...I talked with one of them, and she was bored with yachts and bored with flying around in airplanes and bored with skiing in Switzerland at Christmas and bored with the men in Brazil."[7] The dichotomy between women who have a chance to marry well – and thereby solve all their career problems for the rest of their lives – and those who must make it on their own is forcefully drawn.

The key narrative in *The Bell Jar*, however, is less economic than it is sexual. If there were ever a point of contention between the generations of Aurelia Plath and her daughter, it was the problem of unmarried women having sex. Nice girls didn't. Pages of women's magazines, basic sex education classes, veiled movies and novels were all devoted to the mandate that women experienced sex only after they married.

Plath's introduction of the other eleven College Board women had to do with their sexuality. Doreen, the Southern woman who was recognizable by her "slightly sweaty smell" in her "dressing gowns the color of skin,"[8] was after fun; Betsy, or 'Pollyanna Cowgirl" as Doreen called her, was after staying in straight and narrow paths; and invited Esther to do things with her "as if she were trying to save me in some way."[9] The assortment of various episodes that take place in New York are arranged around either pole of sexuality. With Doreen, Esther feels morally superior; with Betsy, she feels corrupt and worldly. Finally, neither woman can serve as a pattern for appropriate behavior, though Esther borrows Betsy's skirt and blouse to wear on the trip back home. The most decisive act she takes toward Doreen is leaving her friend, drunk and sick, to sleep in the hallway after Doreen collapsed at her door.

The way Esther behaves in regard to these friends, and the other college women – as well as toward Jay Cee, the fiction editor, and other magazine personnel – is to become her mother. That disapproving attitude that finds reasons for disliking nearly everyone becomes her trademark; and yet her cynicism leads her into sexual situations she knows would appall her mother. Pretending she must work harder to please Jay Cee, she creates further isolation, when in reality she cannot find a moral balance to use when she interacts with the other college women.

Being unsure is one dilemma, but being angry is another, and different, situation. In *The Bell Jar*, Esther's anger is aimed toward the experienced, successful magazine staff; these women become the objects of her hatred: "Jay Cee wanted to teach me something, all the old ladies I ever knew wanted to teach me something, but I suddenly didn't think they had anything to teach me."[10] For a novel about young women in New York, the fiction spends much of its time dwelling on a bevy of "old ladies." Here is the crux of what Plath defines as a generational mandate: she must listen to older women with money, power, and knowledge because she is dependent on them – for money and knowledge. They pay for her education, they pay for her therapy, they pay for her beauty aides. They instruct her on how to catch a man, how to do well in college, how to write. All these clones of her successful mother, Mrs. Greenwood, who is the epitome of self-satisfied careerism, seem to share an ability to lead non-sexual lives, throwing themselves into their work and their volunteerism (which includes Esther and her mental health) as if they were nuns.

Much of the narrative of *The Bell Jar*, in fact, describes the kind of interaction Esther has with these "old ladies." The initial scene with Jay Cee, when the fiction editor berates Esther for not working hard enough, not knowing enough languages, not trying to learn all there is to know about the fashion magazine world, leads to Esther's memory of the way she has outsmarted her college dean so that she is allowed to take whatever classes she wants, instead of following the schedule for majors. The connection between her memory of getting her way about requirements and her present-time chastizing from Jay Cee is that she knows full well, in retrospect, that she has only hurt herself by changing classes. Pretending to be smarter than authorities, pretending that she knows her own needs, has cost her. The scene with Jay Cee winds down into Esther's hard realization that part of her angst in New York is fueled by her anger at her mother.

The next scene in the novel concerns the writer-mentor who not only funds Esther's college scholarship, but provides advice about the literary world as well. Another memory piece, this episode recounts the way the inexperienced Esther drank the water out of Philomena Guinea's elegant fingerbowl when she had gone to her benefactress's home for lunch. About the voiceless, and victimized, Philomena the reader knows only that she doesn't say a word about Esther's gaffe, but instead tells her only that "she had been very stupid at college."[11]

When Alice Miller says that Plath's *The Bell Jar* was her honest if partially subconscious assessment of the way her psyche had developed, and was developing, in contrast to *Letters Home* which continued the fantasy that she and Aurelia together created, she calls attention to the way art stems from the subconscious as well as the conscious. What does happen in the fusion between conscious and subconscious that writing the novel evoked for Plath is that many of the "old ladies" took on characteristics of her mother. Whereas one might suppose that Philomena Guinea would be more understanding of Esther's writerly talents, in *The Bell Jar* she seems as obtuse – and as set on diminishing her fame and money-making ability – as a Mrs. Greenwood might have been.

Through Mrs. Willard, the mother of her beau Buddy, Esther meets and goes out with Constantin, an interpreter for the UN. In this narrative, Plath can assess notions of romantic love and marriage, but her focus falls more directly on the life of Mrs. Willard, mother of three children, wife of a college teacher, and maker of kitchen rugs. In her choice of the anecdote about Mrs. Willard's devoting hours to weaving a kitchen mat out of strips of her family's clothing, Plath signals her anger about the way society values work. She would have hung the mat on the wall, she says, and viewed it as a piece of art. Instead, Mrs. Willard (only once in the book called "Nelly" and that time by her husband) used it on her floor so that "in a few days it was soiled and dull and indistinguishable from any mat you could buy for under a dollar in the five and ten."[12] In *The Bell Jar*, Mrs. Willard becomes the voice of society's wisdom about women. It is she who describes a woman's being the place that a man, imaged as an arrow, shoots off from; and it is her son Buddy who explains to Esther that once she has children, she won't want to write poems any longer – that she will understand that poems are dust.

Plath reserves the major part of the novel for the characterization of Mrs. Greenwood, developing it from the perspective of the

by-now thoroughly depressed Esther when she arrives home from
New York. Even the "motherly" breath of the suburb horrified her,
as she noticed that "A summer calm laid its soothing hand over
everything, like death."[13] And the first person Esther sees from her
bedroom window is the ever-pregnant Dodo Conway, one of the
successful debs who had trapped a worthy husband so that she
could immediately begin her life work of having children. The plot
of matrophobia[14] kicks in earnestly, for Esther must sort through
the tangible ramifications of being sexually active, succeeding in the
female quest to capture a man, and still being something other than
one's mother.

Everything reprehensible about older and asexual women –
minor as well as major – comes into play in this section of *The Bell
Jar*. Snoring, wearing pincurls "like a row of little bayonets,"[15] being
dictatorial yet knowing nothing, Mrs. Greenwood is a paragon of
generational difference. In some ways, she is also a paragon of
parental *in*difference because she clearly does not hear what Esther
tells her, nor does she respond to Esther's needs in any meaningful
way. What comes from Mrs. Greenwood is a set of platitudes, so
commonplace that Esther need not listen to them: "My mother said
the cure for thinking too much about yourself was helping some-
body who was worse off than you,"[16] she noted at the start of her
daughter's depression; "We'll act as if all this were a bad dream,"[17]
she states with some emphasis after Esther's suicide attempt. And
the acts that Mrs. Greenwood performs – like getting out an old
blackboard and using it to show Esther shorthand symbols – parallel her useless maxims. The most useless, of course, is her dramatic
and stubborn reply after Esther has declared that she will have no
more shock treatments: her mother then confidently says, "I knew
my baby wasn't like that...I knew you'd decide to be all right
again."[18]

Claiming ownership of Esther (referring to her as "my baby,"
which, at 19, Esther no longer is) and claiming all knowledge that
pertains to her daughter's illness (that her improving is only a
matter of will) shows Mrs. Greenwood's true personality. Nothing
can jar her complacent belief that she knows all about everything,
that she is the perfect mother to a perfect set of children, children
whose only responsibility is to present themselves to the world so
as to validate their mother's goodness. It is because Esther
knows this about her mother that she has decided early in the
book, "I would spend the summer writing a novel. That would
fix a lot of people."[19]

Coming to terms with some of her more intense motives, Esther sees that anger at her mother is at the root of her illness. She does not need her therapist to explain her anger to her; the first night she spent at home, seeing her mother sleeping in the adjoining twin bed in her room, Esther realized: "My mother turned from a foggy log into a slumbering, middle-aged woman, her mouth slightly open and a snore raveling from her throat. The piggish noise irritated me, and for a while it seemed to me that the only way to stop it would be to take the column of skin and sinew from which it rose and twist it to silence between my hands."[20] No wonder Plath wrote to her brother that this novel was to be published secretly, under a pseudonym, and – as a "pot-boiler." Death wishes about one's mother were not the stuff to satisfy parental dreams.

Whatever comic effect Esther's recognition might have had for the cursory reader, she knew that, if her mother read the book, there was no way of disguising the hatred that motivated such a paragraph. There was no way of explaining away the fact that Esther tried to hang herself with the silk cord of her mother's bathrobe, and that she stole fifty sleeping pills from her mother's supposedly locked cabinet. Mother and daughter are thereby shown to be complicit in this suicide effort, however innocent of Esther's aims her mother pretends to be.

It may be that another of Plath's lost stories about her mother, "A ten-page diatribe against the Dark Mother. The Mummy. Mother of Shadows," also dealt with this symbiosis. As she noted in her journal, she needed to "get some horror into this mother story" so that it did not become "the monologue of a madwoman."[21] A few days later she had finished the story but "then was electrified ... to read in Jung case history confirmations of certain images in my story," and she draws comparisons between her story and the Jung account: "The word 'chessboard' used in an identical situation: of a supposedly loving but ambitious mother who manipulated the child on the 'chessboard of her egotism'; I had used 'chessboard of her desire.' Then the image of the eating mother, or grandmother: all mouth, as in Red Riding Hood." Plath concludes this later journal entry, "However, I am the victim, rather than the analyst. My 'fiction' is only a naked recreation of what I felt, as a child and later, must be true."[22]

As a victim who could never wrest enough power from her mother's grasp, Plath chose the alternative route to adulthood. Pat Macpherson points out that Plath "turns from the dead-end with the mother (who can never be completely mummified and killed in the daughter), to 'rescue' by the Right Man from the Mother: the classic escape-attempt from female adolescence into one's 'own woman'hood. The illusion is that the mother blocks the exit. The illusion is that only the Man, like God Himself, can create woman. The culturally enforced illusion is that the daughter needs to be purged of the devouring mother, by being 'born again' from the Prince's kiss."[23]

The baleful hatred that Plath's novel evinces has other maternal targets as well. Whenever Dodo Conway as earth mother appears, it is to either censure or ridicule. Plath weaves a few other child–adult woman scenarios into the text, as if to make clear that her antipathy may have been with the role of mother as much as with the way her own mother played that role. Reminiscent of her story "Sweetie-Pie and the Gutter Man," in which the college friend finds that she has more in common with the bad small child than with the svelt, controlled mother, Esther's scene of trying to bribe the small boy on the beach with candy also sets up that anti-mother plot. Thinking he will stay with her for candy money, rather than answer his mother, Esther then realizes, "I could sense the boy's interest dwindle as the pulls of his mother increased. He began to pretend he didn't know me."[24]

Part of Plath's task in writing *The Bell Jar* may have been to explore that complicity between child and mother, the fact that the child/daughter would in fact do exactly what the parent asked – i.e., would respond to "the pulls" of the mother here. This dilemma is what Marilyn Yalom investigates in her study of contemporary women writers, including Plath, and their attitudes toward maternity. She finds that writers and readers alike must deal with what she calls "woman's ambivalence to her own flesh," and she asks, "Where is the subjectivity of the mother in our investigation of the crazy-making potential of motherhood?"[25] Pointing out that *The Bell Jar* is filled by what she calls "The narrator's obsessive maternal fears – her 'infantophobia,'" Yalom notes that "Esther is haunted by visions of babies in various stages of existence: 'bald babies, chocolate-colored babies, Eisenhower-faced babies...big glass bottles full of babies that had died before they were born.'" She says directly, "If I had to wait on a baby all day, I would go mad."[26]

This obsessive fear brings Buddy's taking Esther to view the birth to the center of the narrative. Her mental image of the drugged mother, so torn with pain that she does not realize her child has been born, surfaces repeatedly, always accompanied by the background voice of the young would-be doctor Willard as he reassures Esther that the woman will not remember, that she will soon return to birth still another child. Between this vivid scene and Esther's oblique vision of the row of laboratory jars holding fetuses at different stages of development, Plath manages to comment on the patriarchal control that not only makes pregnancy possible, but delivers babies with all the mechanical finesse of a factory assembly line. In comparison to the malevolence associated with childbirth, Plath's depiction of Buddy's sex play with Esther, as he shows her his penis and asks to see her vagina, is comic. From the couple's first kiss to his farewell visit to the institution, the romance has been a travesty, filled with anything except real emotion. Yet this is a pairing that society would find suitable, and Buddy Willard would be the best possible mate for the Esther Greenwood her family has constructed.

The masterful change in the last quarter of *The Bell Jar*, a narrative move that takes the novel out of the realm of autobiography – even if comparatively honest autobiography, is that Plath transfers the parental role from Mrs Greenwood to Dr Nolan. By ending Esther's torture in the mental institution by providing her with both an apt physician and a refuge from her mother's frightening control, the novel takes on the aura of promise that Plath was trying to create. Finally, *The Bell Jar* convinces the reader that its author understands the subtleties and the full ranges of mental and physical health.

5

Lifting the Bell Jar

During the 1950s, most women didn't pay much attention to being healthy. Being thin, model-like, with cinched waists and long legs, was the ideal, and to attain that thinness, women chose diet rather than exercise. Because of her height of five feet, nine inches, Plath usually had no worries about gaining too much weight. But in McLean, like other patients on insulin treatment, she became heavy.

Disdain for her own health was part of the feminine self-sacrificing ethos that dominated many women's lives at mid-century. People were beginning to worry about men's health, in the context of stressful corporate jobs and unadmitted alcoholism; conversations about Type A and Type B personalities were common. But so seldom was the concept of women's health discussed that most women would not have known how to participate in such a discourse; their experience with health was limited to which kind of painful diet they were choosing to be on (one popular one was the orange and celery week, during which time the dieter ate only those two items and drank gallons of water). From this abyss of ignorance about general health, it follows that information about mental health would have been correspondingly scant – and correspondingly inaccurate.

The reason Dr Nolan becomes the hero of *The Bell Jar* is that she has a quantity of what seems to be expert and relevant information about women's health; she knows things Esther has suspected (only to have her mother contradict those suspicions). Nolan knows, for instance, that Esther needs to be protected from well-meaning visitors. Her decision keeps away Philomena Guinea; Esther's Christian Science employer; her teacher Mr Crockett who plays Scrabble with her; and, of course, her mother. Nolan makes her decision after Mrs. Greenwood has brought Esther a dozen red roses on her birthday, and Esther has thrown them in the wastebasket. Though the novel does not comment on her mother's choice of flowers, the fact that the red rose symbolizes enduring romantic love – and the institutionalized, and mad, Esther can hardly be thinking of marriage – makes Mrs. Greenwood's gift highly inappropriate. Mother–daughter symbiosis is not heterosexual love.

Dr Nolan knows that Esther does not need to re-visit the close relationship she has been forced to have with her mother; separating from that strong woman is one of the paths to Esther's regaining her health. So isolating her from the outside world, making her focus on the asylum world, which is a means of making her focus on herself, is good strategy. In psychological terms, as she removes her attention from her mother, Esther transfers it to Dr Nolan – and for a time to Miss Norris, the patient next door who never speaks. Hoping to be the first to encourage her, Esther has given up the pleasures of the institution – movies, badminton, and walks – to sit by Miss Norris's bedside, eagerly watching "the pale, speechless circlet of her lips."[1] Perhaps she is enacting her mother's earlier prescription of doing good things for the less fortunate; in this case, it is *Esther's* ability to speak and to recognize letters and words that her doctors have worried about.

Ironically, as a presence in the novel, the reader knows very little about Dr Nolan. Her appearance is somewhere between that of movie actress Myrna Loy and Esther's mother. This description surprises the reader, who has come to envision Mrs. Greenwood as old and ogre-like; this image, instead, is of a thin, dark, attractive woman in her early forties. But Dr Nolan is not just any middle-aged woman; she does that highly unsuitable thing: she smokes, and uses tiny wooden matches to light her cigarettes. Because of her smoking, Nolan has immediately moved into Esther's category of intellectual, independent, perhaps defiant woman. And while she has degrees and information that will be useful to Esther, she does not constantly talk about what she knows. She is a very quiet persona on the institutional scene.

What the reader does know about Dr Nolan is that she listens. Without interfering with Esther's own thought processes, Nolan gives her time – and context – to make her own decisions. Her listening is non-judgmental. Even though Esther is institutionalized, for one of the first periods of her life, she feels independent, in control. She manages to tell the doctor that she hates her mother (even as she waits for "the blow to fall" in reaction to her admission). No blows fall. With her usual serenity, Dr Nolan smiles and replies, "I suppose you do."[2]

When Esther is critical of Joan's lesbianism, Nolan reminds her that women who love women find tenderness. When she complains angrily about men being able to have sex without the worry of pregnancy, Nolan gives her an appointment for a diaphragm fitting. When Esther is to have electroconvulsive shock, Nolan comes early to tell her, and stays with her during the treatments. And it is Dr Nolan who leads Esther into the physicians' board room, and stays with her there, during her release hearing. As *The Bell Jar* charts their relationship, Dr Nolan is with Esther for the major events of her rehabilitation: her treatment brings Esther privacy, calm, the possibility of sexual experience, and freedom.

Yet eventually, Nolan must turn Esther back over to her cloying mother, whose solution after months of being kept away from Esther is to pretend that the half year has been a bad dream. Plath gives the key, painful scene short shrift in the tapestry of the novel as a whole:

> "We'll take up where we left off, Esther," she had said, with her sweet, martyr's smile. "We'll act as if all this were a bad dream."
> A bad dream.
> To the person in the bell jar, blank and stopped as a dead baby, the world itself is the bad dream.
> A bad dream.
> I remembered everything.
> I remembered the cadavers and Doreen and the story of the fig tree and Marco's diamond and the sailor on the Common and Doctor Gordon's wall-eyed nurse and the broken thermometers ... and the twenty pounds I gained on insulin ...
> Maybe forgetfulness, like a kind of snow, should numb and cover them.
> But they were part of me. They were my landscape.[3]

Esther's poignant statement of who she is, what she has become, does not reach her mother's ears because she says it only to herself. While the book has shown that Dr Nolan will "hear" that response, because she already knows the way Esther must react to her mother's nonsense, the novel also shows the reader that Esther will at some time return to the impasse that had brought her to suicide in the first place: Mrs. Greenwood has not changed. She understands as little about her daughter as she did in the beginning of the narrative.

As a result of her treatment, and Dr Nolan's understanding, Esther has chosen not to have a lobotomy: she has refused "forgetfulness."

She has, instead, chosen memory, and she cherishes the recollection of even the twenty pounds she gained, the frightening cadavers Buddy Willard used to show off his superiority, Marco's brutal rape-attempt, her dilemma over the fig tree choices . . . whether significant or insignificant, the events of Esther's life are precious to her.

Much of the text of *The Bell Jar* works on the juxtaposition of images. Here, if she is forced to hide her responses, Esther knows she will become, once more, a "blank, stopped – and dead – baby." In an earlier scene when she has the positive reaction to insulin treatment, and feels herself to be coming out of her depression, Esther drinks hot milk provided by the understanding nurse, metaphorically becoming a nursing child: "tasting it luxuriously, the way a baby tastes its mother."[4] In this step toward health, Esther is able to return to her infancy and re-create a relationship with her mother that has long troubled her – she is willing to start over, beginning with mother's milk. Yet the scene quickly sours as Mrs. Greenwood puts her own repressive gloss on the notion of her daughter's rebirth. For Mrs. Greenwood, Esther does not need to be reborn; she has, rather, developed according to plan. That she is unhappy to the point of attempting suicide is of less consequence than that she has been successful, so successful that the townspeople all congratulate her mother on "her" brilliant child. As Esther's impatient tone in this excerpt suggests, her mother has no understanding of what Esther has experienced – nor will she try to come to any kind of understanding. Mrs. Greenwood is, simply, going to erase this year.

The most effective characterization of Dr Nolan is her great difference from Esther's mother. Smoking the cigarettes she enjoys, Nolan is the soul of sanity. Never afraid to laugh, she can also be firm. She is herself. She is confident in her profession, and she does not need any external accolades for the fact that she has helped Esther regain her health.

The reader feels that this portrait of Dr Nolan is the one Plath the writer intends. Midway through the book, she creates a scene in which Esther admits to herself, "I liked Doctor Nolan, I loved her, I had given her my trust on a platter and told her everything . . ."[5] Yet for the 1990s reader, Nolan seems almost too reticent about what real health might mean for Esther. Is her strategy as a psychiatrist only to get Esther over her depression rather than to lead her to find new modes of accepting a healthy mind and body?

What happens to Esther Greenwood in *The Bell Jar* is hardly a healthy scenario, whether one reads the book in the 1950s or the

1990s. In New York she drinks a great deal, becomes virulently sick
with food poisoning, overworks, and is emotionally abused,
attacked and almost raped. That she arrives in Wellesley with the
blood from Marco's wounding still on her face is meant to provoke
questions from Mrs. Greenwood. It does not. There, "at home,"
with all the irony Plath can build into the word, Esther loses her
power to write or read, or even to decipher letters. She cannot sleep.
Again, her family does not notice her disorientation. It takes her
telling her mother about attempting suicide by cutting her legs to
gain any kind of treatment. She undergoes a quantity of electroconvulsive shock treatments, usually without correlated therapy.
After several days of self-burial, while the fifty sleeping pills she
has taken deaden her system, she bruises and scrapes her cheek and
eye on the wall of her hiding place, and carries a permanent scar.

During her six months in mental institutions, Esther gains weight
from insulin treatments, receives another series of electroconvulsive
shock treatments, and undergoes a serious vaginal tear during her
first sexual intercourse. The graphic description of blood loss suggests its parallel injury, here understated, Esther's emotional loss as
she tries to work through Joan Gilling's mimicry of her illness and
that woman's subsequent suicide. In a world of so few supporters,
Joan was at least someone who wanted to be friends with Esther.
Misguided in the way she showed her admiration, Joan was a
casualty of women's lives during the 1950s, but she was still someone to be mourned.

As *The Bell Jar* expresses the concept of women's health, the best a
woman at mid-century could hope for would be an absence of fear
and trauma. The novel does not show any positive means of
Esther's learning to sustain her own mental and physical health.
It, rather, shows the reader that returning home is dangerous, that
continuing to be in therapy will be necessary, and that Esther in her
post-institutionalized state has lost most of her friends, male and
female. There are many reasons why today's readers have difficulty
reading the novel as a positive statement about women's lives and
prospects.

Women's health, for readers at the end of the twentieth century,
might be more readily determined by the woman's obtaining – and
fulfilling – the subject position. Yet Esther Greenwood remains
anything but a subject; she cannot even act at the end of *The Bell
Jar* without the physical support of Dr Nolan, who leads her into the
examiners' interrogation. The haunting metaphor of the bell jar in

its last mention in the book suggests that it is poised to be lowered again, somewhere, perhaps in Paris or England or Italy. Running from her circumstances at home, then, may not keep Esther from another depression. Esther's willingness to consider these possibilities brings the reader back into the more realistic state of mind that *The Bell Jar* encourages – anything other than Mrs. Greenwood's saccharine, and inaccurate, assessment that forgetting is possible.

If Plath were to have given Esther the subject position, particularly in the sex scenes, Esther would have not only been the aggressor, she would have reveled in her naked body and its sensual reactions. Instead, in *The Bell Jar*, Esther is never naked. She sleeps in a room with her mother; she seems to be fully clothed when Buddy Willard shows her his penis; she is carried by Irwin into bed (we see no undressing, we have no information about the process of making love with that macabre man, though we hear him taking a shower afterward). So far as we can tell from the novel, Esther never sees anyone's body naked, including her own.

Most of the courtship scenes are mere rhetorical exercises. Even in the swimming passages, characters' bodies in swim suits are uninteresting to the writer, and the later key scenes between Buddy Willard and Esther play out amid snow drifts and in skiing garb. Location conspires to keep even a touch of skin on skin from occurring. Interestingly, even in the attempted rape scene, the sense of real skin showing through Esther's formal dress is disguised by the speaker's attention to Marco's cruelty to Esther. In this scene, the gruesome – if purposefully detached – account of Marco's malevolence is extended: he initially bruises her arm with his thumb and all four fingers, he slams her drink to the floor, he drags her around the dancefloor, he throws her to the muddy ground and lands on top of her, spitting on to her lips, not kissing her. Then, as Plath writes, he "set his teeth to the strap at my shoulder and tore my sheath to the waist. I saw the glimmer of bare skin, like a pale veil separating two bloody-minded adversaries."[6] Marco tears her clothes not out of passion, however, but only to insult her further – " 'Slut!' " and then after Esther hits him in the nose and causes it to bleed, "Sluts, all sluts … Yes or no, it is all the same."[7] Ironically, Plath had introduced this scene with Esther's weary lack of response to another blind date: " 'I am an observer,' I told myself, as I watched Doreen being handed into the room by the blond boy to another man."[8] Yet Esther's expectation of control, of maintaining distance, crumbles under the force of the woman hater

Marco. He ends their battle on the lawn of the prestigious country club by threatening to kill her if she does not return the diamond to him, and she realizes that he would, indeed, "break her neck."

As Esther covers her now "bare breasts" with her shawl in order to find a ride back to the hotel, she is sickened by the pretense of clothing and by the hypocrisy of Marco and his well- dressed friends who want only to maim women. Her immediate reaction is to rid herself of the means of being a part of this sham, so she throws her fashionable New York clothes off the hotel rooftop. "Piece by piece, I fed my wardrobe to the night wind, and flutter-ingly, like a loved one's ashes, the gray scraps were ferried off..."[9] Rather than flaunting her control, or her nakedness, however, Esther is still expressing the fear of being in control that her experience with Marco has only intensified.

Even in this long scene, it seems clear to the reader that what Esther holds throughout the novel is the object position. Looked at and evaluated by her mother, looked at and evaluated by the New York magazine photographer, looked at and evaluated by Buddy Willard, by Irwin, and by Marco, Esther has no chance to become a real person. The stereotype of the 1950s woman – tall, thin, long-haired, smiling, appealing, she has made herself into the commodity that women's magazines, cultural attitudes, and gender roles had trained people to expect.

Even in the midst of the sex act, Esther is the proper good girl; that she takes herself out of Irwin's apartment when the messy bleeding continues is expected behavior for the nice (and guilty) mid-century woman. Better to inconvenience one of her girlfriends than the man responsible for her injury. Better to inconvenience no one and to possibly bleed to death than to make the sexual partner pay for his pleasure.

When does Esther get to be the subject? When does she get to do the observing? Only twice, in the scene at Irwin's as she maneuvers herself into his bathroom to see from the window who his woman caller is; and as she awakens in bed with Constantin, who is "lying in his shirt and trousers and stocking feet"[10] beside her, is she in any position of power. When she looks at Buddy's penis, she does so at his instructing and not from any curiosity or sense of adventure of her own. Similarly, during her visit to him at the hospital where he interns, she observes but she does so without adequate information, so that what she "learns" is only frightening. Dressed in hospital whites and pretending to be interested, she admits to her insecurity,

"I was quite proud of the calm way I stared at all these gruesome things."[11]

Not that Plath omits the possibility of nakedness; after all, *The Bell Jar* was to be a "pot-boiler" and Plath was a woman who had once shared a writers' conference stage with the sensational detective (pot-boiler) writer Mickey Spillane. Rather, she builds into the novel the sense of nakedness as objectionable in itself, at least under the coercion of someone else. When Buddy suggests that Esther take off her clothes, for example, using the adolescent directive "Now let me see you," the text replies for Esther, in its best comic tone,

> But undressing in front of Buddy suddenly appealed to me about as much as having my Posture Picture taken at college, where you have to stand naked in front of a camera, knowing all the time that a picture of you stark naked, both full view and side view, is going into the college gym files to be marked A B C or D depending on how straight you are.[12]

The phrase "stark naked" and the distinction of "full view and side view" accurately reflects 1950s attitudes about revealing one's body. The cultural message was, a woman does not reveal her body, at least not without loss of social position; a woman does not enjoy revealing her body, because such enjoyment would suggest that she knew the ranges of physical pleasure that body could provide.

The information about sexuality which Plath embeds in *The Bell Jar* is scant, and comes only from Mrs. Greenwood about the early days of her marriage: "Hadn't my own mother told me that as soon as she and my father left Reno on their honeymoon – my father had been married before, so he needed a divorce – my father said to her, 'Whew, that's a relief, now we can stop pretending and be ourselves'? – and from that day on my mother never had a minute's peace."[13] Mrs. Greenwood's euphemism for avoiding the male sexual chase – having "a minute's peace" – echoes ironically the slang locution, *piece*. Again, Plath achieves the tone of the upright, uptight mother, in a scene that is intentionally misleading. As the novel proceeds, the reader must come to see that the omission of nakedness in *The Bell Jar* parallels the omission of knowledge of any physical, bodily pleasure. As a trope for Esther's paralyzing ignorance about the sensual, as well as the sexual, her fully clothed state in nearly all segments of the novel sends a pathetically accurate message.

In this stilted context of a woman writer's withholding information about the physical and sexual side of the protagonist's life,
Plath would have erred tremendously if she had given readers
information about lesbianism. If heterosexuality, and its pleasures,
were forbidden topics for a novel to be published in the early 1960s
to discuss, then any mention of the lesbian, woman-to-woman
sexual experience would have been scandalous. Critics in the
1990s who wonder at Plath's introduction of the subject, and the
quick and seemingly punitive demise of Joan as a possible lesbian
character, seldom relate the topic of Plath's treatment of what in the
1950s would still have been labeled "deviant" behavior to her
general prudishness about the body.

It seems more than ironic that the only sensual experience Esther
has, at least as described by Plath in the novel, is drinking hot milk
after her insulin reaction. Throughout the book, there is an extended
image of food, or the possibility of food, as when Esther stands in
the hospital kitchen and stares at the breakfast trays: "I looked with
love at the lineup of waiting trays – the white paper napkins, folded
in their crisp, isosceles triangles, each under the anchor of its silver
fork, the pale domes of soft-boiled eggs in the blue egg cups, the
scalloped glass shells of orange marmalade."[14] In contrast to these
comforting images, Plath has earlier established Esther's frustrating
vision of her necessary choice among "fat purple" figs on the tree of
life, one "a husband and a happy home and children;" another, "a
famous poet;" a third, "a brilliant professor," etc. Her positioning of
Esther in this vision is the closest Plath comes to sexualizing her
protagonist's frustration: "I saw myself sitting in the crotch of this
fig tree, starving to death, just because I couldn't make up my mind
which of the figs I would choose. I wanted each and every one of
them, but choosing one meant losing all the rest, and, as I sat there,
unable to decide, the figs began to wrinkle and go black, and, one by
one, they plopped to the ground at my feet."[15] Visible decay sets in
as years of indecision move on, and Plath envisions the kind of
female protagonists she had drawn in her earliest fiction, the Miss
Mintons, the Judiths, the women who live relentlessly sterile and
asexual lives because of their careers. Even in the crotch of experience, even with the phallic imagery replicating vaginal forms
instead of penile, Esther Greenwood cannot make good choices,
possibly because she cannot explore each of the fig-like construc-
tions. Knowing the figs becomes a metaphor for knowing the female
body.

Accordingly, in *The Bell Jar*, the best Esther can do regarding lesbianism is to accept Dr Nolan's single-word explanation of what women saw in other women – "tenderness" – and cease her questioning. Yet there is a more explicit subtext to the lesbian narrative, in that Esther turns to Joan after her sex with Irwin. To have Irwin, the partner of this intercourse, drop Esther at Joan's house – complete with a kiss of Esther's hand, the only mention of any kiss in their love-making – so that Joan can repair the injured woman is a strange development in the running subtext about sexual preference. Yet Plath seems not to load the event with any particular meaning. Joan is, in fact, almost obtuse when she telephones the doctors, explaining something about Esther's period when she needs – as Esther finally makes clear – to make the situation into an urgent emergency. It is Joan, however, who strips Esther's clothes off to get to the "original royal red towel."[16] It is Joan who applies fresh bandages. And after getting Esther to the hospital and paying the cab driver, Joan joins her in the examining room: "Joan stood, rigid as a soldier, at my side, holding my hand, for my sake or hers I couldn't tell."[17]

After the abrupt ending to this scene, with the emergency room doctor assuring Esther that he can "fix" the injury, the text moves to someone's knocking on Esther's door back at the asylum. Purposely misleading, this arrangement suggests that Esther is waking from her gynecological repair – but what has in fact occurred is that Joan is missing. Plath gives the reader only a loose indication of how much time has elapsed, leaving one to picture the unwritten hours of Joan's story, her going home to find the blood-soaked beige carpet and the remains of Esther's ordeal throughout her house. By conjoining Esther's hemorrhaging with Joan's later hanging herself, Plath links the two women in a way which seems relevant to this discussion of their subject–object roles. Clearly, even if Joan had the power to act, to become a subject, she needed to have learned appropriate uses for that independence. Misleading in her pretense of capability and of wellness, and in her plans to become a psychiatrist when she returned to college, Joan has turned away from her own progress. Her assumption of control equips her only to leave the world of therapy and psychiatric medicine entirely.

Regardless of sexual preference, then, *The Bell Jar* keeps returning to the question of women's identities. Plath gives the reader a signal of Esther's discomfort with her "old" image in the scene in the woman's lounge, as Joan points out Esther in her "strapless evening dress of fuzzy white stuff"[18] as part of the College Board summer issue of the fashion magazine. Esther's outright denial that the photograph is of her, coupled with the women's willingness to accept Esther's denial (ostensibly because she is now twenty pounds heavier and therefore has become a different woman), adds another metaphor to the definition of self-acceptance. If Esther refuses to "be" the person she clearly was only a few months before, if viewers cannot accept the physical accuracy of a photograph – a photo the reader has seen being shot in the fashion magazine scenes, then all definition of reality is up for question.

It is following this scene that Esther realizes that Joan is somehow connected with her sense of her own reality, and she meditates "Sometimes I wondered if I had made Joan up. Other times I wondered if she would continue to pop in at every crisis of my life to remind me of what I had been, and what I had been through, and carry on her own separate but similar crisis under my nose."[19] Just as in her senior thesis Plath had studied literature that focused on characters and their doubles, she here tried to give the character of Joan Gilling some correspondence to Esther, an erstwhile double with a difference. Esther says of Joan that she liked her, and continues, "Her thoughts were not my thoughts, nor her feelings my feelings, but we were close enough so that her thoughts and feelings seemed a wry, black image of my own."[20]

As criticism has shown, the intentionally positive ending of *The Bell Jar* that Plath tried to craft conveys neither rescue nor recovery for some readers.[21] The book ends with three juxtaposed scenes, each one bringing to closure several narrative lines. In the third from the end, Esther phones Irwin and tells him to pay the overdue emergency room bill. Though he asks to see her, she refuses. At the close of that scene, Plath writes, somewhat ironically, "I was perfectly free."[22]

The second episode from the end is the scene of Joan's funeral, to which Esther goes even though Dr Nolan said she need not do so. At the close of the burial, Plath writes a longer paean to Esther's health: "I took a deep breath and listened to the old brag of my heart. I am, I am, I am."[23] Starkly presented, the scene portends irony, but it is not here achieved.

The last episode is the much-discussed interview which Esther is to have with the examining board of the mental institution. Somewhat strangely, the book ends before she has the interview. The last scene is of Esther's preparing for the meeting, waiting in the library

as she looks at a "tatty" *National Geographic*. At this time she speculates that there should be some ritual for "being born twice –
patched, retreaded and approved for the road."[24] As Dr Nolan
comes to lead her into the board room, the reader pauses with
Esther on the threshold while she looks into the faces of the powerful doctors. What happens next may reflect Plath's clear-headed
ambivalence about the procedures of caring for the unstable, and
the unresolved issues of recovery and cure. In this closing scene,
Esther is still in the object position. She is still going to be acted
upon by the authorities; she, in fact, does not even have the volition
to walk into the room on her own. The closing sentence of the novel
reads: "The eyes and the faces all turned themselves toward me,
and guiding myself by them, as by a magical thread, I stepped into
the room."[25]

The volitionless Esther, even accompanied by her doctor, does
not inspire the reader to believe she has yet become her own person.

6

Plath's Hospital Writing

It was not that Sylvia Plath went from having the experience of breakdown and recovery in 1953 to immediately begin writing probingly about it. Rather, as soon as she came under the control of her mother once more, she began writing about the various disguised personas that she was comfortable with. Of course, she did not write seriously for many months: all her energies went into staying up with her coursework, trying to come to terms with her memory loss, and proving to friends and acquaintances at Smith and on other campuses that she was herself again – whoever that self might be. One of the reasons during her writing of *The Bell Jar* in 1961 that she chose to end the book with Esther still in the hospital is that such a conclusion obviated her re-living the following years, times of discontent and anger, times of even more outright conflict with her mother.

In addition to the months of therapy and rehabilitation at McLean Hospital after her suicide attempt, preceeded by the earlier weeks at Massachusetts General, Plath worked at the latter hospital as a secretary during the Boston year, a time when she and Ted were both, supposedly, spending all their time writing. After their move to England in late 1959, Sylvia gave birth to Frieda at home, attended by a midwife; in the spring of 1961, however, she spent a week in a London hospital for an appendectomy. In early 1962, Nicholas also was born at home, so Plath had no other hospital experiences – perhaps some of her fear about going to the hospital in February of 1963, as her doctor urged, was the fact that she had very little direct experience with being hospitalized. Whenever she wrote about hospitalization or hospital life, then, she was drawing on her earlier experiences – as both patient and as employee – in American institutions during 1953 and 1959.

One of the ways Plath used her hospital experiences in her writing was as a source of interesting knowledge, a means of getting out of her myopic college-girl voice and life. By focusing attention on the hospital *per se*, she was able to treat groups of people who worked for their living, who daily observed the sick and ill and mentally unstable, and who seldom did much philosophical reflecting about the people they saw. From the 1955 poem about the hospital solarium, Plath moved easily to one of her best stories, one originally titled "This Earth Our Hospital" and published in 1960 as "The Daughters of Blossom Street." Intriguing in its reference to "Blossom Street" as a euphemism for death, this fiction works with several rather intricate narrative lines to create hospital employees whose pragmatism balances their sensitivities.

The authorial persona in this story, similar to that in Plath's better known narrative, "Johnny Panic and the Bible of Dreams," is a somewhat impatient secretary who keeps patients' records in Adult Psychiatry, in the Clinics' Building of the hospital complex. On a humid day filled with hurricane warnings, she goes to a staff meeting where her friends Dotty (from Alcoholic Clinic), Cora (in Psychiatric Social Service), Minnie Dapkins (from Skin), and other women discuss hospital news. Among the items is that Emily Russo, a long-time employee in Admissions, is dying of cancer; and that the young Billy Monihan from the Record Room is a patient in Adult Psychiatry.

By the end of the story, Emily and Billy have died, both under strange circumstances. When the protagonist and Dotty take a large bouquet of flowers to Emily lying semi-conscious in her hospital room, and assure her that the girls on the hospital staff are thinking of her, they find Billy waiting outside her room, intent on visiting. Although he tells the nurse he is her nephew, they know that Emily has no family. When Emily dies during his visit, the nurse reports that Billy is much affected by her death. What Plath's story does is make all these factual details insignificant: as the women huddle in the darkened room to play cards together that evening, unable to leave the hospital because of the hurricane, news comes that Billy too has died. In deft characterization, Plath draws a believable scene:

Everybody is very quiet all of a sudden.

"He was running up and down these *stairs*," Cora says, her voice so teary you'd think she was talking about her kid brother or something. "Up and down, up and down with these records, and no lights, and he's in such a hurry he's skipping two, three steps. And he *fell*. He fell a whole flight ..."

"Where is he?" Dotty asks, slowly putting down her hand of cards. "Where is he now?"

"Where *is* he?" Cora's voice rises an octave. "Where is he, he's dead."

It's a funny thing. The minute those words are out of Cora's mouth, everybody forgets how little Billy was, and how really ridiculous looking, with that stammer and that awful complexion...memory throws a kind of halo around him. You'd think he'd laid down and died for the whole bunch of us sitting there..."[1]

In this story, Plath does not mock the altruistic impulse – as the story concludes, Billy has indeed become a hero and the possible connection between his presence and Emily Russo's death evaporates. For the reader, a narrative no longer has to do anything except present realistic people, and most people in this world – whether or not the world of the hospital – are predictable and mundane. The good impulses, as the women pool their money to buy flowers for Emily and make Billy into a hero, more than balance the bad.

With the Johnny Panic story, Plath is not content to do realistic presentation; this time her interest is in the incipient madness of the secretary – and perhaps the staff of the psychiatric ward – who devotes herself to the fanciful transcription of mad patients' dreams, fictions, and tales. As Ted Hughes commented in his introduction to Plath's story collection, which he titled for the Johnny Panic story, "She escaped from this into a job in the records office for mental patients in the Massachusetts General Hospital in Boston, and a few months later, after writing the story 'Johnny Panic and the Bible of Dreams,' where she turned that experience into a private literary breakthrough which ran on underground through the rest of that year, she wrote: 'It is the hate, the paralysing fear, that gets in my way and stops me. Once that is worked clear of I will flow. My life may at least get into my writing: as it did in the Johnny Panic story.' What that story had actually done was tap the molten source of her poetry as none of her poems up to then had."[2]

In "Johnny Panic and the Bible of Dreams," Plath assumes the persona of a secretary of the psychiatric ward, who is also – secretly and on her own time – the secretary to none-other-than Johnny Panic. The name emblemizes the fear that usurps people's personalities; as this Plath persona says, "I figure the world is run by one thing and this one thing only. Panic with a dog-face, devil-face, hag-face, whore-face, panic in capital letters with no face at all – it's the same Johnny Panic, awake or asleep."[3] Her days are spent typing up the patients' dreams, as well as their daytime complaints: "trouble with mother, trouble with father, trouble with the bottle, the bed, the headache that bangs home and blacks out the sweet world for no known reason."[4]

As these quotations show, whether because she had found an interesting idiomatic voice or because her prose style had become more inflected, free of the essay tone that was customary for her, it is the rhythmic texture of "Johnny Panic" that makes it such good writing. It is, in fact, more poem-like than many of Plath's 1959 and 1960 poems. An analysis of the structure of the entire story is not possible, but her effective movement from long run-on paragraphing to single lines which underscore emotion shows her developing skill. In this paragraph, she uses the sentence fragment for that same underscoring:

> Some nights I take the elevator up to the roof of my apartment building. Some nights, about three a.m. Over the trees at the far side of the park the United Fund torch flare flattens and recovers under some witchy invisible push and here and there in the hunks of stone and brick I see a light. Most of all, though, I feel the city sleeping. Sleeping from the river on the west to the ocean on the east, like some rootless island rockabying itself on nothing at all.[5]

As Plath lulls the reader with this highly rhythmic prose, the persona's fascination with Johnny Panic gives him life. She has learned that he leaves a signature on each dream transcript, that he excels at his calling – the creation of macabre, but usually appropriate, dreams. Her admiration shows in her economiums of praise – "He's sly, he's subtle, he's sudden as thunder"[6] – but above all he is interesting. (Plath contrasts her mentally ill dreamers with the recovered patient Harry Bilbo, who was "doomed to the crass fate"[7] of what his doctors call "health and happiness.")

So much for normalcy, the story implies; and, no matter what the reader's persuasion about the controlling power of fear, he or she comes to share the protagonist's opinion. When she hides out all night amid the darkened file cabinets, in order to transcribe the older dream records for herself, the reader wants her to succeed in fooling the administrative staff. When she is caught by the Clinic Director, and taken to be punished with electroconvulsive shock, the reader's sympathy is genuine – despite the surreality of the narrative.

The story is, however, more complicated than this synopsis suggests. Playing a secondary role in the protagonist's life has been
Miss Milleravage (the last part of the name is intended to suggest
"Ravage," Plath wrote). As the Secretary of the Psychiatric Observation Ward, this woman is a muscled, uniformed control freak
("Her face, hefty as a bullock's, is covered with a remarkable number of tiny maculae, as if she'd been lying under water for some
time and little algae had latched on to her skin, smutching it over
with tobacco-browns and greens").[8] Evidently lesbian, Miss Milleravage mourned the disappearance of her nurse friend in London
during the bombings by joking about her loss; she puts the protagonist off for many reasons. But it is into her clutches, literally, that
the Clinic Director gives the protagonist, and it is out of her hard
and muscled body that the bed for the shock treatments appears.
Calling the protagonist "sweetie," Milleravage makes a kind of love
to her as she subdues her under the wires of the electroconvulsive
shock bed: "Against her great bulk I beat my fists, and against her
whopping milkless breasts, until her hands on my wrists are iron
hoops... 'My baby, my own baby's come back to me...' "[9]

As part of the readying for her punishment, Miss Milleravage
undresses her: "With a terrible gentleness [she] takes the watch
from my wrist, the rings from my fingers, the hairpins from my
hair... When I am bare, I am anointed on the temples and robed in
sheets virginal as the first snow."[10] The ritual of bedding complete,
the protagonist knows she is doomed – either as the bride of this
demon disguised as a female (with milkless breasts) or as the
sacrificial victim.

But even as the current is turned on, the protagonist finds escape,
of a kind. There on the ceiling "the face of Johnny Panic appears in a
nimbus of arc lights... I am shaken like a leaf in the teeth of glory.
His beard is lightning. Lightning is in his eye. His Word charges
and illumines the universe."[11] At the all-too-significant age of
thirty-three, the mundane secretary has come into her own, and is
now sheltered by the god of fear she has devoted her life to serving:
"His love is the twenty-storey leap, the rope at the throat, the knife
at the heart."[12] Whether this is an ironic parody of religious belief,
or a pathetic voicing of the protagonist's madness, it serves
Plath well in creating a supposedly fanciful ending for one of
her strongest stories, a fiction that as Sandra Gilbert points out,
rewrites the famous – and misogynistic – D. H. Lawrence story,
"The Woman Who Rode Away." Gilbert rehearses the similarities

of a thirty-three-year-old misbehaving woman, according to the patriarchy, the five robed priests, the sacrifice and the ritual that accompanies it, and concludes that Plath had created a true intertextual answer – to Lawrence and whatever misogynists existed in her writing life.[13]

"Johnny Panic and the Bible of Dreams" as title also emphasizes the frailty of the formal belief systems of both psychiatry and religion. These "bibles" that the protagonist reads are old record books, and they chronicle lives and dreams only back thirty-three years. While the protagonist thinks that is a long time, it is of course almost meaningless in the annals of human knowledge.

Various methods of dying appear here, set in the positive context of the protagonist's "going to" whatever god in whatever realm he lives. Completely controlled by his power, she willingly succumbs to his direction – a plot line that bears a great deal of similarity to Plath's relationship with her husband. In a 1957 story drawn directly from life with the Hughes family, "All the Dead Dears," Plath had similarly used belief in an other-worldly spirit connection to explore the supernatural. Her interest in this subject came from visiting the Hugheses on the Yorkshire moors (Edith Hughes was said to have second sight although in a journal entry Plath commented wryly that her mother-in-law "almost"[14] had it) and being literally surrounded with the miasma of acceptance of the occult. Paul Alexander states it directly, "Edith, it was rumored, studied magic... Finally this explained Ted's avid interest in horoscopes, hypnosis, and mind control."[15]

Not only is Plath practising with her creation of atypical characters, people so firmly grounded in their beliefs that they are not self-conscious about them; she is also continuing her exploration of the effects of her permanently unsettling shock and insulin treatments in 1953. Once the mind and spirit have been so devastated by the impact of shock treatments, the acceptance of conventional boundaries is difficult. Pat Macpherson notes that in her writing Plath often uses the symbolism of shock treatments, "male instrumentality seeming to have the last word over the woman's mute body."[16] In the Johnny Panic story, Miss Milleravage takes on a male persona – being inordinately strong, fast, brutal, and lusty – as she overpowers the small protagonist. But as this critic recognizes, in both this story and *The Bell Jar*, the woman as protagonist is waiting for rescue by a man. In the story, Johnny Panic himself appears; in the novel, the supposedly positive ending that sends Esther out into the world as a whole, healthy person fails to convince readers of her wholeness. She is a character still in need of rescue.

There is no shock treatment *per se* in "All the Dead Dears." As written, it is an observed narrative, with the protagonist's interest focused on Nellie Meehan and her gift of second sight, a gift that also occasions interest from her friends and neighbors. Aside from the contrived ending, a mark of Plath's need to bring her early stories to some kind of "magazine sale" conclusion, this narrative explores a number of themes new to Plath as writer. The most obvious is the calmly accepted violence of the Northcountry culture. Within the first page the reader is apprised of Dora's brother-in-law's suicide by drowning; Nellie's brother's, Lucas's, suicide by hanging; the fates of Clifford Meehan's friends who served with him in World War I; and the fact that the Meehan's lodger Herbert had forced his wife to leave him years before. The seemingly peaceful voices of the four friends drinking tea and gossiping about past events weave a misleadingly tranquil fabric over the violence of factual biographies. As Plath noted in her journal, the family regularly told "tales of hanging, pneumonia death (implied murder), mad cousins..."[17]

An experiment in creating different voices, this story divides responsibility for the narrating of these horrific events by having Nellie Meehan tell part of a tale and Clifford, other parts. For instance, when Clifford tells the story of Lucas's suicide, his pace is almost soporific: as the protagonist-observer says,

> he, too, had told his part of the story so many times, and each time it seemed to him as though he were pausing here, expectant, waiting for some clear light to spring out of his own words, to illumine and explain the bleak, threadbare facts of the going of Lucas. "Lucas went upstairs after dinner, and when Daphne [his daughter] called him to drive out, it was a couple of minutes before he came – his face was puffed funny, Daphne said afterwards, and his lips kind of purple. Well, they stopped for a few bitters at the Black Bull, as was Lucas' habit of a Thursday night, and when he came back home, after sitting about downstairs with Daphne and Agnes a bit, he put his hands down on the arms of his chair and heaved himself up – I remember him getting up like that a hundred times – and said 'I guess I'll go get ready.'"[18]

Interrupted as he had been in his first suicide attempt – hence, the disfigurement and purple lips, Lucas calmly resumed his effort; he had indeed gotten ready. What Plath emphasizes in the subsequent conversation, and in that which accompanies Dora's account of her brother-in-law's more recent suicide, is the interrogation the family puts itself through. Why do such things happen? Why do people commit suicide? The factual explanations they offer satisfy no one, and as if in contrast, Nellie tells the story of her brother Jake, a man married to an invalid, a woman whose health seems to be the reason their child is retarded. If anyone should be depressed, it should be Jake, the friends imply, because his only healthy child died of pneumonia when young.

Attributing reason to suicide is one strand of the narrative, but the key story concerns Nellie's being visited by angels. On the night of Lucas's suicide, she has seen the angel Minnie, her older sister who died when she was just seven. Minnie was dressed in "A white Empire smock...All gathered about the waist, it was, with hundreds and hundreds of little pleats. I remember just as clear. And wings, great feathery white wings coming down over the bare tips of her toes..."[19] Seemingly a sensible woman, Nellie recounts her experiences as seer with great calmness. She describes knowing that "presences" are with her, and that she finds comfort in those manifestations. With Clifford, she continues "the fugue of family phantoms," and with the observer narrator, agrees that they have lived their lives by "reliving each past event as if it had no beginning and no end, but existed, vivid and irrevocable, from the beginning of time, and would continue to exist long after their own voices were stilled."[20]

The beauty of this narrative, phrased as it is and reflective of a genuine belief in the possible existence of the presences of loved ones who are dead, is cut short by the death of Nellie as she waits, alone in her house, for Clifford to return from walking Dora home. As she sees the glittery pillar-like appearance of a long-dead friend, Nellie realizes too late that it is her own demise that has called forth the presence.

Plath's poem of the same title ("All the Dead Dears," 1957) has little of the charm and believability of the story, though it continues to probe the space that would divide the living from the dead. Focused on a stone coffin containing the remains of a woman, a mouse, and a shrew from the fourth century AD in the Cambridge Archaeological Museum, the six stanza poem works through regular form and cryptic voice to point out the irony of the woman's gnawn ankle. At its heart is the persona's connection of herself – and her imagination – to the ancient story, and it is in stanza four that the couplet so evocative of the writer's trying to both link and erase her own story occurs:

> Mother, grandmother, greatgrandmother
> Reach hag hands to haul me in . . . [21]

As an integral part of what she envisions as a line of matriarchal power, the persona can only accept her role – and perhaps her guilt for her father's death. As in the story of the same title, the inexplicable deaths are enacted by men. The implied question becomes, at whose direction did those men's suicides occur?

The rest of that stanza evokes the image of a drowned father, and the next few lines sound a little like a Nellie-Meehan voice: "All the long gone darlings: they/ Get back, though, soon,/ Soon: be it by wakes, weddings,/ Childbirths or a family barbecue:/ Any touch, taste, tang's/ Fit for those outlaws to ride home on."[22] Presences, as Nellie would say, create our living lives as well as our dead ones.

Just as Nellie appears in this poem, Esther and Mr Greenwood (also from the "Dead Dears" story) will become key names in *The Bell Jar*, and in that later work, the protagonist falls into unconsciousness as "in panic I bit down"[23] during the preparation for shock treatment, it seems clear that Plath was viewing her creative work from 1957 on – when she had given up her teaching job at Smith in order to become a writer – as a single continuing text. That may be the explanation for her including as a finished work one of her shortest poems, "The Hanging Man," written in June of 1960. If the threat of future shock treatments accompanied her concern about recurring depression, if the experience of shock treatment had scarred her so badly, then her probing the meaning of consciousness, as well as of knowledge and even life itself, takes on more than intellectual interest.

Fear is certainly apparent in this short poem. Again, "some god" has the aura of a Johnny Panic as well as a formalized deity, a figure whose grasp is anything but positive: "I sizzled in his blue volts like a desert prophet." Most moving is Plath's description of the effects of the treatment, "A world of bald white days in a shadeless socket," and the apathy, which she calls "a vulturous boredom." Christ-like, the speaker too is "pinned . . . in this tree." To close, and to end the speculation about suicide that dominates "All the Dead Dears," she announces in an assured voice, "If he were I, he would do what I did."[24]

"The Hanging Man" is a kind of crystallization of a number of themes that Plath had attempted to write about in her impressive seven-part "Poem for a Birthday." Electroconvulsive shock occurs in many of the segments ("Now they light me up like an electric bulb./ For weeks I can remember nothing at all"[25] in part 1; "all things sink/ Into a soft caul of forgetfulness"[26] in part 5; a range of burning and electrical imagery in part 6; and a more complete description of the process in part 7). That the actual treatment becomes a metaphor for the loveless behavior of what seem to be both parent and spouse figures as well as animals allows the poet to thread its presence into and through much of this work.

Later in 1960 Plath returns to the image of the woman in recovery, a woman who has "suffered a sort of private blitzkrieg" in an admonitory poem titled "A Life." Here her urging the persona to "Touch it" refers to experiencing life, but she quickly moves from the early abstract stanzas to a "more frank" look at the woman's life. She depicts her "dragging her shadow in a circle/ About a bald, hospital saucer./ It resembles the moon, or a sheet of blank paper." Damaged perhaps beyond repair, the woman has chosen to live "quietly// With no attachments, like a foetus in a bottle."[27] Even as her grief and anger have been exorcised by the blitzkrieg of the shock, so that she can lead her passive, unattached life, she knows that, for her, "The future is a grey seagull/ Tattling in its cat-voice of departure, departure." What is most horrifying about this poem is the last three lines, which follow the repetition of "departure":

> Age and terror, like nurses, attend her,
> And a drowned man, complaining of the great cold,
> Crawls up out of the sea.[28]

Few critics except Marilyn Yalom have given adequate attention to what might well have been the existence of post-partum depression after the births of both Plath's children. For a woman who has waited to have children to create an image which links the woman whose child is not yet a year old with the figure of the drowned man – the paternal curse, the literal body of her father, of all fathers – rather than with the child is ominous. What is this fear, this terror, if not that of the depressed life and its regularly accruing treatment-punishment, electric shock.

In Yalom's analysis, maternity often "serves as a catalyst for mental breakdown. A corollary of this question concerns the distinction between *maternity* and *motherhood*: to what extent is maternity (conception, pregnancy, parturition, lactation, and the nurturing of infants) a fixed biological, existentially loaded reality, and to what extent is motherhood (the daily care of children and the ensuing lifelong lien on the mother) a mutable social construct?"[29] When Yalom connects this general problem of defining and accepting the immense burden of mothering with Plath's loss of a parent when she was a child, an event which probably set in motion her own "death anxiety," she sees the writer as ripe for breakdown. "In the case of individuals who have not developed appropriate psychological mechanisms for containing death anxiety, certain life passages, such as the choice of a career or the experience of childbirth, may have the paradoxical effect of reactivating and intensifying the fear of death, 'freezing' that person in psychotic time."[30]

In accordance with this set of hypotheses, Yalom reads the fig tree scene in *The Bell Jar* as a way for Esther to freeze time. She has not had to choose. It is also a way to sacrilize the predicament Esther finds herself in; fig trees are sacred to Bantu beliefs, and Plath was much involved in reading Paul Radin's African folktales. Similarly, her choice of the image of the dead baby in the poignant if unspoken answer to her mother, that "To the person in the bell jar, blank and stopped as a dead baby, the world itself is a bad dream,"[31] also shows regression: here Esther has become an infant. Once Plath was a mother, then, according to Yalom, her anger toward Aurelia fed into her self-image, and threatened to destroy the happiness she had originally felt in giving birth to a daughter. In becoming a mother, perhaps *her* mother, through the birth of children, Plath was faced with choosing which of those sometimes contradictory mother characteristics she would adopt.

The realization of this complex of developing unhappiness in conflict with joy colors her magnificent 1961 poem "Tulips." Originally titled "Sick Room Tulips" and then "Tulips in Hospital," the work literally explores the persona's anger and guilt when her husband brings flowers into her peaceful, quiet, stark white hospital room. The invasion of the red breathing tulips into her intimate privacy seems more than the recovering woman can bear. These "frightening" flowers "bleed and eat my oxygen," some early lines in the poem complain, as does this couplet which sounds as if the persona is arguing with the man who has brought the tulips:

> Bouquets are for arrivals, departures or sweet connections
> And I have gone and come, but I'm not back yet...[32]

Clearly, beset by the responsibilities of being both mother and wife, the persona wants to be alone, she wants only to drift, to learn peacefulness, "just lying by myself quietly/ As the light lies on these white walls, this bed, these hands."

Repetition is the mode for the lament: "I didn't want any flowers, I only wanted to lie here/ Empty as a cup, well-tended and mending." In a later version the lines read "I didn't ask for flowers, I only wanted/ to lie with my hands turned up and be utterly empty." The cup has disappeared; the empty woman, or her hands, distracts the reader less from the pervasive imagery – of peace, non-active living, and in this case, *empty* is a cogently descriptive word. Later in that stanza, after the line "How free it is, you have no idea how free –" Plath writes two lines which she later deletes,

> I can see the dead come to it, finally
> The dead would talk like this, if they came back

Joining some of her impressions in "Tulips" with the theme of 'All the Dead Dears," she moves through the long stanzas in which she describes the tulips as dangerous (one crossed-out phrase in that section is "the tulips are egotistical").

An interesting change occurs two lines from the end, when Plath originally writes "The water I *weep* comes from another country" before dividing that line into two, and making the conclusion less autobiographical:

> The water I taste is warm and salt, like the sea
> And comes from a country far away as health.

As has frequently been said, this more positive addition hardly saves the reader from experiencing the barrage of the hospitalized woman's impatience with the tulips – and through them, with her husband. Perhaps this ending works like the rebirth image at the close of *The Bell Jar*, to give the reader a more conventional conclusion than the unhappy writer could honestly manage throughout the work.

Often considered a pair poem to "Tulips," "In Plaster" was written the same day. Different in that it describes the poet's experiences when her broken leg was in the heavy plaster cast and she tried to maneuver it around the Smith campus during the winter of 1953, and in response to a woman in a full body cast who shared her hospital room, the poem is similar in tone and effect. Its ostensible theme is the divided self, the woman in plaster and the woman without, one white and one "old yellow." Accepting their symbiosis, the two women need each other, though the older and less attractive one – the speaker of the poem – is planning to break away from the partnership. A double of the recovered self also, Plath describes the white and pure self, saying "In the beginning I hated her, she had no personality – / She lay in bed with me like a dead body/ And I was scared, because she was shaped just the way I was// Only much whiter and unbreakable and with no complaints."[33] The white woman is scarcely human – "She doesn't need food, she is one of the real saints." She also is tidy, calm, and patient, all useful traits for the American doll-wife that Plath consistently criticized. (In the poem "On Deck" she had described "A perfectly faceted wife to wait/ On him hand and foot, quiet as a diamond.") In contrast, the speaker is honestly objectionable, "ugly and hairy."

More descriptive than "Tulips," "In Plaster" might have been intended to be a very different sort of poem. With its emphasis on the "new absolutely white person," who neither answers accusations or responds to physical punishments, this poem could be read as a meditation on sainthood on the order of the 1956 "Dialogue Between Ghost and Priest." Later in the work, Plath notes wryly that the self in question thought she was immortal, or certainly superior. What happens next is drawn from the African ritual of stealing, absorbing, the spirit from its body: "secretly she began to hope I'd die./ Then she could cover my mouth and eyes, cover me entirely/ And wear my painted face the way a mummy-case/ Wears the face of a pharaoh..." Given this ritualized tone, "In Plaster" as title leads the reader into that shadowy realm of replicas of saints and martyrs, and other artifacts of worship.

While this poem creates an ingenious metaphor, it does not evince the tautness and surprise inherent in Plath's best writing. There is a calculation about "In Plaster" that suggests that the poet may be censoring her impressions, rather than letting her imagination respond to life's necessary ambiguities.

7

Defining Health

The strangely unsettled longing in the ending lines of "Tulips" foreshadows the tone for much of Plath's later writing. The reader is left with the unasked question, why does "health" appear to be so far away? What is it that weighs down the persona's body, and – accordingly – her spirit?

Thinking back to the early draft of "Tulips" brings other inquiries. Why does the persona weep after this almost exuberant expression of her need for separateness, for peace? She might rather be relieved to have made such a vehement statement, to have brought to consciousness anger and angst that had been buried under her accepting wife-and-mother facade. In that original line, the water the speaker weeps comes from "another country," a phrase indelibly marked with Hemingwayesque associations. (It is a given in the romantic scenes the much-revered American writer created that the more idealistic of a couple would insist that love can be found, if not on this earth and in this life, then "in another country" – and of course the phrase resonates back to Marlowe as well.) As she changes the ending image, Plath disregards the romantic overtones and cuts from the faintly nostalgic mood of "another country" to a comparison with her touchstone, her source of tranquility from childhood, the sea.

To pair the sea with health is to reveal much about Plath's psyche. She has done this kind of revealing elsewhere in the early draft of "Tulips," in the lines previously quoted – that bouquets are for "arrivals, departures or sweet connections." This set of lines does not appear at all in the finished poem, but the resonance of "sweet connections" helps to gloss possible problems within the marriage. What can have happened to that passionate bonding Plath had been so eloquent about, to have caused the persona to describe "My husband and child smiling out of the family photo"[1] with the line, "Their smiles catch onto my skin, little smiling hooks"? Mentioned only once, the family serves as the omitted term of the wife's unhappiness; and the reader can easily gauge the importance of those now-lost "sweet connections."

Despite hospital care, despite her husband's having brought her flowers, the hospitalized persona cannot find her health (i.e., her tranquility, her rest) under what appear to be inescapable circumstances. Thoughts of responsibilities waiting – of her child and her spouse eager to hook onto her body, her time, her soul – twist through her recovery and wring any joy from her chance of regaining health. To become well, the persona wants only to lie by herself, and to do so "quietly." The suggestion of the biblical "lie with" in the sexual sense is introduced early: this persona, however, wants aloneness, not sex. She wants whiteness, not color. She wants to lose her name (which she has given to the nurses) and all those occasions of reclaiming it – Plath? Hughes? Plath-Hughes? – that might cause anger within the family. Other lines in the early draft of the poem give more detail about the persona's loss of self during her hospital experience: "I watched my identity recede," she writes. Tying up her long hair in a gauze bandage, the nurses make her look like all other mummified patients. "With white adhesive," however, they attach her wedding ring to her finger; even if indistinguishable as herself, she will be known as someone's wife. It is the affixed ring as symbol of her marriage that adds to her sense of entrapment.

There is some sense of contradiction about the province of the persona's name. In stanza four, she notes that she is "Stubbornly hanging on to my name and address," even as she envies a nun-like celibacy. In draft, this line is different, reading, "Hanging onto my name and address stubbornly as money." One of the wife's housekeeping duties is to manage the family's money; her strength of will shows itself as she limits spending, conserves, and tries not to waste their resources on herself, her hair, or her clothing. As a woman without her own name, the poem implies, she also has no need for her own things, for fashion, for beauty operators. These are the themes of Plath's short story, "Day of Success," in which the "country wife" wears her hair long and unfashionably, eschews make up, and lives to help her husband write – without spending his and her hard-earned money. Against the advice of her sophisticated women friends, she does not make herself over. Instead she trusts to her husband's deep love of her in her natural state; she believes that he will ward off the chic and predatory Londoners who much admire the handsome young poet.

The center of "Tulips" springs out of the comparison between the persona and the pure state of nuns. It is stanza five, in which the persona speaks with blunt yet haunting directness: "I didn't want any flowers," a line changed with good effect from "I didn't ask for flowers." The poignancy of the verb *want* reaches into that sense of unsatisfied longing that the whole poem evokes, and the phrase is repeated in the second part of that line: "I only wanted/ To lie with my hands turned up and be utterly empty." The verb *lie* is repeated here, in this case with the intensification of the inanimate – the physical appearance of the body at rest, hands turned up and, most effective, "utterly empty." *Want* and *utterly* form a rhythmic bridge over the stasis of the body at peace.

Lines three and four emphasize, again through repetition and that voiced rhythm, both peacefulness and being free. The summation of what the persona has been trying to express as valuable occurs in the closing lines of the stanza, repeating the idea of peacefulness without repeating the word,

> And it asks nothing, a name tag, a few trinkets.
> It is what the dead close on, finally...

The viability of the name, here conveyed past the persona's ability to speak it in this tag form, overshadows the "few trinkets" which remain of the accumulated treasures of earth. Linking this core image of paucity, of sorting through value, with all the relinquishment images of the early stanzas, the persona reminds the reader that she has earlier said, "I am sick of baggage." With some discomfort, the reader might remember that it is in that list of "baggage" that we see the family photo of husband and child. Then the simile of the red tulips being visible through gift paper, breathing "Lightly, through their white swaddlings, like an awful baby" creates even greater dismay.

Finally, the faceless speaker (brought to the reader's consciousness in the tautly rhyming two-part line, "I have no face, I have wanted to efface myself") seems to become in fact the metaphor she had earlier used to express her lack of volition: "a cut-paper shadow." Ostensibly a poem about recovery and a yearning for health, "Tulips" is filled with contradictory, and disturbing, images. (One recalls Plath's matter-of-fact journal line, "Writing is my health.")[2]

Ted Hughes states in a 1995 essay that the spring of 1961 brought Plath to her real voice ("Tulips" and "In Plaster" were each written March 18, 1961, and were followed ten days later by "I Am Vertical"). His theory is that she had found that voice in 1959, with her writing of the Johnny Panic story, but that the complexities of

her life – "change of country, home-building, birth and infancy of
her first child"[3] – interfered so that it was not until 1961 that she was
able to resume that voice in her work. Hughes's focus in this essay is
on Plath's very rapid writing of *The Bell Jar*, which he claims she
wrote much of in the spring of 1961. He comments on what he sees
as her recurring theme: "That mythic scheme of violent initiation, in
which the old self dies and the new self is born, or the false dies and
the true is born, or the child dies and the adult is born, or the base
animal dies and the spiritual self is born..."[4] While he connects this
theme with its use in the writing of D. H. Lawrence and Dostoevsky,
he also links it with Christianity.

A reader might fit "In Plaster" into this paradigm, but the ambivalence of "Tulips" seems to go beyond any simple theme. The woman
in the hospital is not trading her death for a life, nor is she consciously adopting behaviors that would lead to improvement in
either her physical or her spiritual health. The poem is more of a
sounding board for her current state of disarray than it is a finished
or polished philosophical prolegomenon. Perhaps it needs to be
read in the context of Plath's other writing during the months just
before, and just after, the Hughes' return to England to live. This is
the period of Plath's pregnancy with Frieda, and then of her daughter's birth and infancy; and perhaps for that reason, her writing
deals more pointedly with what it means to be healthy, what it
means to be a healthy woman – now a woman engaged in child-
bearing and rearing.

These issues are raised in one of her last short stories, "Mothers"
(published as "The Mothers' Union"), a North Tawton story that
describes an afternoon meeting of church women. Beneath an
apparently realistic surface, the story works with cruel irony to
expose hypocritical Christianity. Here Plath's focus is on the vindic-
tiveness of the poor parish as it excludes one of its members because
she has been divorced.

The narrative opens as the American Esther wonders why the
English are so nosy; her older friend Rose – like the postman, the
baker, and the grocer's boy – usually walked into Esther's house
without so much as a knock. Rose, who lives with her husband
down the lane, is taking the eight-months-pregnant Esther to a
Mothers' Union meeting. With her comes Mrs. Nolan, the blonde
wife of the pub keeper. Esther has a baby whom her husband Tom
is caring for; Mrs. Nolan has a seven-year-old son. In fact, it is the
scene of Esther's going out to tell Tom that she is leaving, seeing the

infant in the dirt and saying nothing about it, that introduces questions of good or poor mothering. "The baby sat in the path on a pile
of red earth, ladling dirt into her lap with a battered spoon...[she]
turned in the direction of Esther's voice, her mouth black, as if she
had been eating dirt. But Esther slipped away, before the baby
could heave up and toddle after her..."[5]

Escaping her child, feeling petty because she objects to Tom's
unshaven appearance, Esther joins arms with the other two as
they walk to the chill old church, gossiping about their neighbors.
Mrs. Nolan, who has lived in the village for six years, knows very
few people; Esther cannot decide whether or not she wants to know
the townspeople. Past the cemetery and the butcher's to the church,
where seeing the rector leads to Esther's reminiscence of his calling
on them, several times, so that she now sometimes attended Even-
song.

The narrative action occurs after the service as the women climb
to the gathering room where tea – "a startling number of cakes" – is
arranged. Plath catches the tone of the two visiting women, neither
comfortable with either the group of women or the service, in their
conversation: When Mrs. Nolan asks Esther if she is staying for tea,
the American replies,

> "That's what I came for," Esther said. "I think we deserve it."
> "When's your next baby?"
> Esther laughed. "Any minute."[6]

As the eating continues – with the oozing fat sausages carried in on
large trays, Mrs. Nolan's discomfort is clear. She wants to smoke but
is told she cannot; she tries to clarify her married situation for the
rector, but he replies that he knew she was a divorcee. Esther wants
to leave, yet after Mrs. Nolan leaves Rose and Esther to walk home,
the latter forgets her camaraderie with Mrs. Nolan and responds
genuinely to Rose's offer of friendship. Rose has told her that
Mrs. Nolan will not be allowed to join The Mothers' Union (even
though she is a mother), because she was once divorced. Unfair as
the rule is in Esther's eyes, she seems to commit herself to joining
the group, and to behaving toward divorced women just as the
Mothers' Union members do.

"Mothers" catches the reader off guard because its ending is less
critical than Plath has suggested it will be. Esther's own uneasiness
about going to the meeting is quieted as she feels her baby kick and

placidly thinks, "I am a mother; I belong here."[7] Yet the circumstances of Mrs. Nolan's treatment – for the six years of her living in
town as well as at the afternoon meeting – show Esther that belong-
ing, like being a mother, is no simple matter of definition. When the
rector's wife greets them at tea by "bending maternally over them,
one hand on Mrs. Nolan's shoulder, one on Esther's," the reader
assumes she welcomes them. Yet even though she has verbally
asked the two women to join, social forms and religious codes let
everyone know that Mrs. Nolan cannot join. What Esther has
experienced, in addition to the sheer gluttony of the women at tea,
is their flagrant hypocrisy.

Yet there is nothing objectionable in the story. "Mothers" is not a
violent narrative; nothing unpleasant happens, except that
Mrs. Nolan is left to lead her life alone. In writing this story, it is
as if Plath is trying out her skill of suffusing prose with emotional
color rather than relying on action that comes from plot development. Her technique in the story "The Fifteen-Dollar Eagle" is quite
different. In some ways this narrative of the tattooist and his tiny
shop, published in 1960 in *The Sewanee Review*, is much more
obvious than what she achieves in "Mothers."

A character sketch of Carmey, "a real poet with the needle and
dye, an artist with a heart," the story works through the artist's
rough yet warmly untutored voice: "You got a dream, Carmey says,
without saying a word, you got a rose on the heart, an eagle in the
muscle, you got the sweet Jesus himself, so come in to me. Wear
your heart on your skin in this life, I'm the man can give you a
deal."[8] The unfolding of the carnival barker's spiel traps the reader
– and the observers, who themselves have voices and characters.
The ostensible plot of the story is Carmey's tattooing the extra-large
eagle on the sailor's arm; the subtext is Carmey's extravagant use of
his wife Laura as the illustration for many of his stories, only to
have that wife appear, in either compromising or sinister circumstances, at the story's end. While Carmey is the protagonist of the
tale, the observing young girlfriend of Ned Bean, an inexperienced
woman who becomes faint at the sight – and smell – of all the blood,
plays the straight man to Carmey's storying.

Early in the story, Carmey locates her strategically: " 'You come
right in here,' Carmey says to me in a low, promising voice, 'where
you can get a good look. You've never seen a tattooing before.' I
squinch up and settle on the crate of papers in the corner at the left
of Carmey's chair, careful as a hen on eggs."[9] Surrounded soon by

the "powerful sweet perfume" of the blood dropping off the sailor's arm, the woman sees that Carmey tosses blood-drenched tissues that the tattooing produces into the wastebasket at her feet. Cramped into her corner, she cannot avoid the sensation of being surrounded by blood.

Smelling salts revive her. " 'She's never got like that before,' Ned says. 'She's seen all sorts of blood. Babies born. Bull fights. Things like that,' "[10] and so the boyfriend's rescue of her – both from her fainting spell and from the other men's derogation of her as a weak woman – completes that part of the story. Strength is here equated, at least in Ned's eyes, with being able to stand the sight of blood, with being, presumably, one of the guys. An unanticipated emphasis, this negative characterization of the boyfriend, determined by his dialect, who seems to be even less cultured than Carmey.

In its last pages, "The Fifteen-Dollar Eagle" becomes the story of Carmey's marriage, juxtaposed indirectly with the observer's relationship with Ned. What startles the group of people who have been watching him at work tattooing is Carmey's personality change from a confident professional to an abject, cringing man when his beloved "death-lily-white" wife enters the shop. Plath leaves the mystery of his wife's relationship to Carmey and his art, and the identity of the watchdog-like man who accompanies her, unresolved: what matters in the story is that the province of any accomplished artist can be destroyed by hostility, particularly hostility from the beloved.

The irony of the story is that despite his priestly lore, his wide knowledge of his arcane skill, Carmey succumbs to the base emotion of fear when he faces his inimical life partner. Even as a bloodletter, a kind of physician of the heart, Carmey fares badly in the greatest of all such affairs, love. The scene of the adolescents who enter the shop to watch their buddy be tattooed with the name of his girlfriend "Ruth" – a scene that becomes a catalyst for the four adults' comments about love – is integral to the development of Plath's narrative.

The interrogation of the meaning of such designations as *mother, wife, beloved,* and *husband,* depicted in these complex stories, form part of the thematic base for Plath's poems during this period. Difficult to translate into shorter forms, the expression of these issues is sometimes mixed, somehow unresolved, as in her 1960 poem "Love Letter." The voice is that of the girlfriend in the previous story, as the poem opens, "Not easy to state the change you made./ If I'm alive now, then I was dead,/ Though, like a stone, unbothered by it..."[11] The transformation of the speaker through the beloved's passion is, however, described mechanically, with the quality of some of Plath's exercise poems, and seems to take place largely in the last stanza. There, once the persona "started to bud like a March twig," she Kafka-like completes her metamorphosis and becomes "a sort of god/ Floating through the air in my soul-shift/ Pure as a pane of ice."

Apparently positive in intent – after all, the female persona has become "a sort of god," which is a change from all the male-connected deities that sprinkle her poems, "Love Letter" yet catches the reader with that same whisk of recognition: while "soul-shift" may be a happy choice for a fashion writer, the attaching of that attire to a "pane of ice" can only be chilling. The woman's metamorphosis has become ironic: just as she began to bud she has, instead, died or been killed. Circling back to the opening of the poem, the writer has clearly attributed her changes in circumstance – whatever they may be – to the unidentified "you."

Plath's poem "Parliament Hill Fields" makes similar use of the intentionally misleading "you" or "yours." Given the traditional indirection of poetry in the early 1960s, for her to write about miscarriage, directing her meditation to the fetus she had just lost was a daring move. Tonally, the poem aligns itself with other of these winter and spring writings, as it tries to capture the resilience of the bereft woman who yet must go on with her daily life.

One of the most noticeable points about this fairly long poem is that the father of the child, her husband, is not referred to at all (once the reader gets beyond thinking he is the referent for 'your' in line four, a line ironically about absence – "Your absence is inconspicuous").[12] With double meanings implicit in the poet's assumption of metaphor, the line could both record the spontaneous abortion of the fetus and the uncaring, calloused behavior of the husband, who does not even accompany his fatigued wife on her nighttime walk. Separated by the physicality of her loss of the child, aware that it is only the mother's body that feels the loss, the poem's persona is so suffused with grief over the infant's death that she chooses childlike images to express her grief: "the city melts like sugar," a little girl drops "a barrette of pink plastic," ashes "swaddle" roof and tree, she misses "your doll grip" as the developing infant's fantasized cry "fades like the cry of a gnat." All images are diminutive, even to the scene of "your sister's birthday picture" of the little pale blue hill, complete with its blue night plants. All is unreal, as unreal as her now-terminated pregnancy, and of, perhaps, her husband's role in the life of their family.

In the midst of this purposefully artificial description comes one of those stunningly direct lines, as Plath writes, "The old dregs, the old difficulties take me to wife." Matter-of-factly said, the persona moves ahead, and the last line of the poem is "I enter the lit house."[13]

As if Plath were charting the reasons for her unease, her depression and illness, she writes about a brief trip she and Ted, with Frieda, took with Ted's cousin Vicky to the beach. "Whitsun" recounts the disappointment of the holiday in Whitby; the poem opens, "This is not what I meant." Picnicking "in the death-stench of a hawthorn," she notes that her spouse is "no happier than I about it." The poem concludes with the image of the two vacationers lying together "seasick and fever-dry."[14] Plath's description in a letter to her mother reinforces the mood of the poem: "There is something depressingly mucky about English sea resorts. Of course, the weather is hardly ever sheer fair, so most people are in woolen suits and coats and tinted plastic raincoats. The sand is muddy and dirty. The working class is also dirty, strewing candy papers, gum and cigarette wrappers."[15] In contrast to her assessment of their holiday, she lamented in the following paragraph, "My favorite beach in the world is Nauset, and my heart aches for it. I don't know, but there is something *clean* about New England sand, no matter how crowded."[16]

A few weeks later, she admits to Aurelia, "I feel immensely homesick when you talk of white snow! All we've had here since October is grey rain."[17] The nostalgia Plath feels for her American winters, her American beaches, may reflect a deeper malaise as she finds herself less comfortable than she had expected to be living in England. The lack of acceptance drawn in the story "Mothers" both foreshadows and clarifies part of the problem of Plath's trying to live as a productive writer in England – she was American. Most were considered to be at least ugly, if not materialistic, haughty, and meretricious. She was also, for all her pretense of being able to hold her own with Ted, increasingly in his shadow both as writer and as wife. Perhaps her tenacious hold on such household duties as keeping accounts and cooking was a means of claiming equality in their stormy partnership. The constant search for a balance of power, if not for an even more important consideration – unqualified acceptance and love – wore the young mother down.

It is during this winter, in early 1961, that Plath wrote to her mother about her failing health. In her most efficient voice, she tells Aurelia that she has embarked, "with Ted's help, on a drastic program to pull my health up from the low midwinter slump of cold after cold, and am eating big breakfasts (oatmeal, griddles, bacon, etc., with lots of citrus juices), tender steaks, salads, and drinking the cream from the tops of our bottles, along with iron and vitamin pills."[18] Sleepless stretches while Frieda nursed and teethed, the need to accommodate her schedule to keep up with her own work and Ted's, the normal exhaustion of their being first-time parents, and her increasing doubts about Ted's affection for her added to Plath's usual tenuous hold on keeping well. Some of this worry about matters of health seeps into a poem that is ostensibly about something very different. "Zoo Keeper's Wife" cries out in a macabre, even carnivalesque, fashion that this wife – who is willing to let her spouse take up a completely different career, to train to be a zoo keeper (as she writes to Aurelia, Hughes was seriously considering this training) – has just about reached the end of her tether.

The poem begins and ends with references to sleeplessness. "I can stay awake all night, if need be – / Cold as an eel, without eyelids."[19] Not so much super-human as a different kind of member of the animal kingdom, the speaker comes directly to the point in the second stanza, noting that "Old grievances jostling each other" create continued disharmony. In a mock epic address to her beloved, even one so changed as to think of giving up his art for the care of animals, the persona asks, rudely,

> But what do you know about that
> My fat pork, my marrowy sweetheart, face-to-the-wall?
> Some things of this world are indigestible.[20]

Her eating imagery here, with her naming the husband "fat pork" and then commenting on his evident indigestibility, recalls the primitive namings she had used in part 4 ("The Beast") of "Poem for a Birthday," where the bullman is called "Mumblepaws" and "Fido Littlesoul' and insulted by the poet's saying, 'Call him any name, he'll come to it." The heart of her invective occurs when she calls him

> Mud-sump, happy sty-face.
> I've married a cupboard of rubbish.
> I bed in a fish puddle ... Hogwallow's at the window

The poem concludes with the persona's description of herself as "Duchess of Nothing,/ Hairtusk's bride."[21]

Perhaps it was easy to dismiss any personal agenda in the kaleidoscope of fantastic imagery the seven parts of "Poem for a Birthday" evince; but a perceptive reader must have been aware of the deep unease that prompted such descriptions of the Hairtusk figure. Issues of physical habits, sexual contact, literal and figurative appetites are bared here, and if there is self-loathing, there is also clear criticism of the uncouth husband figure.

Having left the States to live in England with Hughes, a man who had found little he could stand in America, Sylvia was now forced to cope with his boredom and disillusion in England. Even though he was making a noticeable career and supporting his family at least meagerly from his writing, Hughes was unsatisfied. Envious all through their marriage of his publishing and prize winning, but more so of his ability to write well and to be interested in his various projects, Plath could not imagine why her successful husband (the man she had given a great deal of her time and energy to making successful) could not be content.

In her letter to her mother which discusses Ted's plan to go back to school,[22] she comments on the fact that they have enough savings to pay the tuition. Her calmness, in fact, seems unreal. The comic energy that suffuses the last three stanzas of "Zoo Keeper's Wife" is the counter balance to that apparently tranquil acceptance of his plan. The poem is starred with lines like "You wooed me with the wolf-headed fruit bats" and "our courtship lit the tindery cages – / Your two-horned rhinoceros opened a mouth/ Dirty as a bootsole and big as a hospital sink/ For my cube of sugar." Yet the speaker admits that although she was wooed, she was also complicit: "I entered your bible, I boarded your ark." He played the zoo keeper; she pretended to be the Tree of Knowledge. Finally, it all came down to sex: "Tangled in the sweat-wet sheets/ I remember the bloodied chicks and the quartered rabbits." Her memory of some mutual violence is part of the cause of her insomnia, and it is that insomnia that has her counting, and flogging, "apes owls bears sheep ... And still don't sleep."[23]

Plath's darkly comic effect here prefigures what she will learn to do even better in her writing during the last year of her life. Taken in the context of the rest of what she wrote in early spring of 1961, however, "Zoo Keeper's Wife" is an anomaly. It will be many more months before she has connected that dramatically intense poem,

"The Rabbit Catcher," the poem that was at one time to replace "Ariel" as the title poem for her planned last collection, to some of these same images, particularly to the central image of the husband as killer of defenseless animals.

As it is, here in the spring of 1961, the poem she wrote just ten days after "In Plaster" and "Tulips" comes the closest to effecting some sense of rest for the persona. Still an inordinately dark poem, "I Am Vertical" takes its first line as title, pairing it with "But I would rather be horizontal." In draft, the first line of this poem was the flat-footed "This upright position is unnatural/ I am not a tree with my root in the soil/ sucking up minerals and motherly love";[24] whereas Plath keeps lines two and three, her new beginning makes them metaphoric rather than literal.

It is in the second stanza of the moving poem that Plath seems to locate a sense of peace, a calm that – even if it is not exactly health – bodes well for harmony. Almost mystically, the persona identifies with the trees and flowers, and the stanza opens with a languid meditation: "Tonight, in the infinitesimal light of the stars,/ The trees and flowers have been strewing their cool odors./ I walk among them..."

An early title for the poem was the descriptive "In a Midnight Garden." Associations with the Garden of Eden, with the power of the myth of creation to form man and woman, and with the healing images of darkness might have created a very different tone for this work. Plath, however, abandons this title and with it more acceptable poetic associations, in order to give the reader this colder, more realistic insight. The reader thinks of Mrs. Plath's late comment, "she [Sylvia] was so exhausted. She carried so much... Ted expected so much of her. She took care of the bills, she made out the tax report, she did all the correspondence because he never would attend to it."[25]

Still located in a sympathetic natural surrounding, the persona moves into a confessional moment, remarking that she is happiest when she sleeps, with "thoughts gone dim." Such an image sounds like the reaction of the fatigued "Tulips" persona. Yet here the final quatrain of the poem expresses what might be a healthful, peaceful stasis for her: "It is more natural to me, lying down./ Then the sky and I are in open conversation,/ And I shall be useful when I lie down finally:/ Then the trees may touch me for once, and the flowers have time for me."

The poet works through metaphor, challenging the reader not to correct that last set of images. We want Plath to say that *she* will touch the trees; *she* will have time for the flowers. But, being a poet and being intrinsically aware of the power of language to express without always revealing, she says something quite different. She says, in effect, that health is beyond her power to achieve, and that consummation will reclaim her for the only world that matters, the natural one.

Part Two

"I must be lean & write & make worlds beside this to live in..."

Plath, *Journals*, p. 157

8

The Journey Toward *Ariel*

We care about Sylvia Plath because of her poems, and her progress toward her last poems is one of modern literature's most exciting narratives. For her to approach the kind of rebellious confidence she finally developed required not only immense learning and experimentation in her writing, but a newly defined sense of herself as artist, as well as a more personal philosophy of art.

As has been evident throughout this book, Sylvia Plath's process of coming into her own voice was at least in part the process of erasing – or perhaps muting – some segments of her earlier knowledge. We have seen the kind of education Plath had mastered at Smith and Newnham College;[1] we have learned, as she did, how little suited to her own poetic expression much of that traditional literary knowledge was.

What we have not yet looked at closely is the way Plath moved Ted Hughes into the hallowed place she had earlier reserved for formal education. Repeatedly, in her letters and her journal, Plath praises Hughes' learning: "his mind is the biggest, most imaginative, I have ever met."[2] She raves about his command of poetry to be recited, the repertoire of lines he calls up to test her knowledge of poetry and poetics, his deep learning in areas of literature that were less familiar to her (and which she appears to think are in some way superior to her own areas of expertise simply because they differ). She wrote to Aurelia, "Ted is probably the most brilliant boy I know. I am constantly amazed at his vast fund of knowledge and understanding: not facts or quotes of second-hand knowledge, but an organic, digested comprehension which enriches his every word."[3] "We drink sherry in the garden and read poems; we quote on and on: he says a line of Thomas or Shakespeare and says: 'Finish!' We romp through words."[4] After their marriage, her praise continues, "We read, discuss poems we discover, talk, analyze – we continually fascinate each other. It is heaven to have someone like Ted who is so kind and honest and brilliant – always stimulating me to study, think, draw and write."[5]

It may be that Plath repeats herself so exuberantly because she is truly thrilled at Hughes' learning, or it may be that she has created

a metaphor of Hughes the perfect husband as *teacher* rather than go
into details of what she sees as their physical, sexual compatibility.[6]
Coded as perfection, Hughes can therefore be identified as the
source of her further education – a characterization her mother, a
student who married her professor, would surely approve – as well
as, or instead of, the source of physical pleasure. Her emphasis on
his erudition not only makes him a worthy spouse; it places him in
the family tradition of Otto Plath, the learned and stable educator.
Sylvia, accordingly, begins to play Aurelia's role as the learned
man's mate – and she does so with enthusiasm.

Ted Hughes' and Sylvia Plath's areas of information are, in fact,
quite different. When a college woman at Smith, Plath studied
modern poetry with the authoritative Elizabeth Drew, who wrote
widely read introductions to the subject and was considered a
premier teacher. It was through Drew that Plath got her personal
audience with W. H. Auden, who visited the Smith campus each
spring, giving a reading and talking with a few chosen students.
Although Plath felt that he was not enthusiastic about her poems,
she at least had an interview with him – and her reputation on the
Smith campus, and in the area, was as a leading writer. Had it not
been, and had she not been considered a brilliant student in Drew's
class, she would not have been chosen to meet with Auden.

Auden's position in American poetry of the 1950s equaled that of
T. S. Eliot. Both in a chameleon-like stage of national allegiance,
their work marked the apex of New Critical form – ironic, allusive,
carefully metered and shaped. Few improprieties (such as the existence of any recognizable personal voice) marred their current
writing, or their past reputations. Poems to model the work of
young writers on – these were the legacy of Eliot and Auden. And
to deal with such writers, Plath and her contemporaries were
indeed asked to model, to copy. As we have seen in much of Plath's
college poetry, the well-turned phrase, the attention to an exacting
formal pattern, and ingenuity with end rhyme and internal asso-
nance insured her winning college prizes, and some publication in
national magazines. At this stage in her work, however, there was
little in her work that could be identified as a Sylvia Plath voice.

Although Hughes is British, and therefore might be expected to
proffer even quicker allegiance to the Auden–Eliot nexus, he prided
himself on being an outsider to the Cambridge community.[7] After
two years of being a literature major, he studied social anthropology
at Pembroke, and his literary leanings were – by his design – much

more ribald, rougher, idiomatic, and much less allusive than the poetry that was then acceptable. Or perhaps his allusions were to different kinds of knowledge, references to other than classroom literary study. As one of his contemporaries wrote, "Ted had sized up Cambridge early and rejected most of it, the Englishness, in the precious and public school sense."[8] Hughes's work after graduation was in a rose garden, or a warehouse, or the film industry; once he had saved some money at those jobs, he returned to Cambridge and lived with friends as he wrote and talked poetry at the Anchor, a pub on the Cam. Neither were his friends likely to be the well-trained literary products of elite British schooling; they were more often outsiders to that tradition – "Scots, Welshmen, Irishmen, Northcountrymen, and jazz musicians,"[9] as one of Hughes' American friends recalled.

It was this group of students and recent graduates who published the one-issue literary magazine *Saint Botolph's Review* that was the occasion for the party at which Plath and Hughes met. Suitably, it was a tough iconoclastic little magazine – hardly a predictable product of Cambridge-educated men. The rebelliousness of it was part of its attraction for Plath, who had in her year at Newnham already made herself the topic of gossip because of her tall beauty, her easy sexuality, and her writing of low-brow fashion articles. Something of an oddity, she was far from being considered an interesting poet. Too derivative, too highly schooled, too timid – although rejection slips used more polite phrases, she had trouble convicing the Saint Botolph literary scene that her work was of any importance. To begin with, of course, she was a naive American. The second mark against her was that she was female; the group of poets who produced *Saint Botolph's Review* consisted of Daniel Huws, Danny Weissbort, David Ross, Luke Myers, and Ted Hughes, aided by the American history student Bert Wyatt-Brown.[10]

Ted Hughes's work in the *Review* struck Sylvia like a voice from within her own psyche. Of the four poems, three were untitled, but the force of their direct language made the reader attend to their unannounced themes. The fourth poem, which opened, "If I should touch her she would shriek and weeping/ Crawl off to nurse the terrible wound," shows the dour life of the woman persona who "goes to bed early, shuts out with the light/ Her thirty years, and lies with buttocks tight."[11] (Later, in Plath's poem "A Life," a woman who might be the victim of this demonic touching does crawl away to lead a ruined existence.) Different from his blunt poem about men on the battlefield, this one treats subject matter not usually considered poetic – the non-heroic (and female) existence. In the titled poem, "Fallgrief's Girl-Friends," he used the same terse language to create varied stanzas which eventually modulate to the speaker's admission, "he meant to stand naked/ Awake in the pitch dark where the animal runs/ Where the insects couple as they murder each other..."[12] There was no question that Ted Hughes' voice was authentic.

As some of these defiant poems tried to suggest, the Hughes–Huws–Myers crowd was also freer in manner because it was lower classed. For all the Hugheses' later superciliousness about Sylvia being from a family of (only) teachers,[13] Ted Hughes and many of his close friends had few pedigrees, whether those were based on education or on wealth or birth. The "Northcountry" crowd was in many ways remote from the core of Cambridge. It made sense that the knowledge it valued was different from the traditional.

Sylvia Plath saw these new bases of knowledge as challenges; she was, even after her illness and the electroconvulsive shock treatments, a quick study. What memory loss she had experienced during the summer and fall of 1953 had been largely disguised with her subsequent study at Smith and Newnham. And so from Hughes and his friends she learned contemporary Irish poetry, shamanism, the occult, astrology, D. H. Lawrence, Eastern religion, African art, the bestial, the mystic, and, among other things, Robert Graves' white goddess.[14] Keith Sagar notes that Hughes's most important effect on Plath was "to supply her with a fully worked out belief in the poetic mythology of Robert Graves' The White Goddess."[15] Plath wrote her mother, "no precocious hushed literary circles for us."[16] She learned the underside of formal education, the province that had always existed without the stamp of university approval. Folk beliefs superceded Auden and Eliot, and the irony was that even though Eliot's The Waste Land had popularized myth criticism, the poem veered firmly away from any real understanding of Frazer.

In her own writing, however, Plath was far from breaking into new freedoms of either thought or expression. Perhaps she did not know that freedom was what she wanted, because most poetry in the United States was not yet privileging the voice-rhythm line. By the late 1950s, Plath liked to read the then-unfamiliar William Carlos Williams, but Hughes found him much less interesting than John Crowe Ransom. More a matter of content and theme than rhythms,

the really new in poetry was growing increasingly more sub
even personal. But Plath's poems were not.

In fact, even after she and Hughes moved back to the States to
live, Plath found it difficult to write American poems. She still
sounded like a well-educated ambitious poet, but a poet of no
specific nationality, gender, or age. The stylistic peculiarities of
"The Other Two," "The Lady and the Earthenware Head," "On
the Decline of Oracles," and other longer 1957 poems echoed what
she thought of as her most successful pre-Cambridge poems.

'Two Lovers and a Beachcomber by the Real Sea," once selected
to be the title poem of the collection that later became *The Colossus*,
is representative of this phase of Plath's writing. A poem more
about the poetic imagination than the two lovers of the title, this
six-stanza work is abstract. It gains what strength it has by being
shaped around clear, cogent statements: "We are not what we
might be; what we are/ Outlaws all extrapolation..." Plath's
didactic phrasing here contrasts with a more customary reliance
on metaphor; for example, the poem opens, "Cold and final, the
imagination/ Shuts down its fabled summer house" and then
proceeds through a series of scenes – one even including the
beachcomber – that are meant to erase any romance the summer
might have engendered. The end of romance is signalled by her
phrase, "No sea-change," and her recognition in the last stanza
that "No little man lives in the exacting moon/ And that is that,
is that, is that."[17]

While in this poem Plath has used some comparatively daring
slant rhyme, the regularity of each quatrain suggests a grim insistence. As if to hammer home the reality implied by the adjective *real*
in the title, the repetition of *is that* in the last line fails. It seems to
exist only to finish the stanza, and undercuts whatever emphasis
the poet was aiming to achieve.

Like so many of Plath's college poems, this one shows that she
can handle the formal qualities of her art. The speaking voice,
however, has nothing distinctive about it. It is, in fact, wordy and
convoluted, giving the reader the impression that the work is a
puzzle to solve rather than a replica of some spoken communication.

In compressing her language to fit the four-line stanza form, Plath
created elliptical phrases. What is the reader to think of "the sudden
shank of bone/ That chuckles in backtrack of the wave"? While one
instance of this compression does work – "Blue views are boarded
up" – most others do not lead to any wider meaning.

Nothing about the poem as it exists (and as it was published in both *Mademoiselle* and *The Best Poems of 1955*) reflects that its author is young, female, or American. Rather it comes across as a poem written as an exercise, strained into formal locutions and meters to fit its quatrain pattern. Like many of the poems she wrote as a senior project for Professor Fisher at Smith, it seems to be a typical 1950s poem, in the tradition of Richard Eberhart, Louis Simpson, or Richard Wilbur.

Her fiction, in contrast, was changing, improving; there were even a few Plath stories that had begun to sound characteristic – or to work with themes and language that were congruent: as we have seen, one could believe that Sylvia Plath had written "Johnny Panic and the Bible of Dreams" or "The Daughters of Blossom Street." She continued to write as well the slight O'Henry-type stories, like "The Wishing Box" or "The Fifty-ninth Bear." Quasi-autobiographical, these latter stories serve as reminders that Plath continued to see herself as competing with Hughes. Marriage aside, one British writer vs. one United States writer – and to this point in the later 1950s, the British writer was far ahead.

Envious of her spouse's seemingly bottomless wellspring of imagination, Plath wrote the crabbed and sometimes crabby stories that described his effortless dreams – and the writing he did based on them. In "The Wishing Box," Agnes "smoldered in silence" as she looked at her husband's "beatific, absent-minded expression" over his breakfast. Launching into a detailed account of his night with William Blake, Harold assumed his usual role of a man who rightfully hobnobbed with celebrities, even if only in his dreams. For Agnes, jealous and bereft of all but the most prosaic night wanderings, his exhilaration drove her to insomnia. Her doctor prescribed sleeping pills. The abrupt ending of the story finds her dressed in her favorite evening gown, dead from the pills but smiling as if "in some far country unattainable to mortal men"[18] she had triumphed at last over Harold's dream existence. In "The Fifty-Ninth Bear," it is the husband who dies as the competitive wife wins the bet about how many bears they will see. As Luke Myers recalled, "In the summer of 1959, they drove across the country and in Yellowstone Park played a Teddish game of counting bears: who sighted the most won the game. The theme turned up in a story Sylvia wrote and published in the *London Magazine* the next year. She had the couple counting bears and the last bear, the fifty-ninth, killing the husband. I found the story unsettling...I was surprised she made a story of the killing of a husband for her husband and their friends to see."[19]

Gathering the scattered poems Plath was publishing would have been difficult for anyone who wanted to chart the thematic arc of her writing, but observers such as Myers would have found those same aggressive plots and comments embedded in some of her poetry as well. If the writer who was coming into her own was now capable of criticizing her beloved husband, viewed by the literary world – and seemingly by herself – as the superior writer, she was indeed making changes. But Plath's journals from these years offer very little context for the animosity expressed in "The Fifty-ninth Bear" or "Zoo Keeper's Wife." Instead her journals are filled with lacerating comments directed at herself: She has writer's block. She cannot stay with her writing; she has no energy, no discipline.[20] Her poems are artificial and unbelievable, and her dissatisfaction with them becomes the topic of both "Poems, Potatoes" in which she complains that the word "muzzles"[21] instead of liberating, and "Stillborn," which opens, "These poems do not live: it's a sad diagnosis."[22]

On March 4, 1956, just a week after Hughes hears that his poem collection, *The Hawk in the Rain*, has won an American poetry contest and will be published in the States, Plath admits, "I am stymied, stuck, at a stasis. Some paralysis of the head has got me frozen... Mail doesn't come. I haven't had an acceptance since October 1st. And I have piles of poems and stories out."[23] Although she has a moment or two when she affirms her own worth as a poet ("My writing is my writing is my writing")[24] most of the time her outlook is grim. Calling her earlier poems "too fancy, glassy, patchy and rigid,"[25] she writes that she is trying to change both her approach and her finished product: "I am splitting the seams of my fancy terza rima."[26]

Perhaps what she does makes sense. Just as from the beginning of their relationship, she has accepted Hughes's hypnotizing her[27] to help her sleep, to help her write, to help her be happy, she cajoles him into giving her ideas for her writing. One must wonder at the irony of their living in the States, in the center of the mecca of organic form, of literary shape stemming from theme and content, always intent on reflecting, if not re-shaping, the mood of a work, yet Sylvia thinking she could borrow an integral part of any piece of writing. If Hughes thought that the moor in moonlight would make a good poem, he should be the person who attempts to write that poem. But for several years – perhaps as many as four or five out of the six years of their marriage – Plath labored diligently to write on subjects and titles Hughes listed for her. Much of the time, the labor was all too evident.

Hughes's lists are frequently thoughts rather than single-word items.[28] "The grasshoppers in your new property, the rooms," for example, asks her to explore aspects of the Court Green space and grounds. Other items include "A London plane tree's monologue at 6 A.M.," "Longings for the sea-depths," "Being examined in front of a class of students," "The weight of things," "Dialogue with a bird," "Finisterre – the ancient church that looks to have been built by survivors on their way up from the sea," "Leaves as dead souls falling and fleeing." And there are also more limited suggestions, "Ants," "Woman opening a letter," "White cave and full moon," "Waves as a witch's crystal," "Single old shoe on moor," "Indian's ghost revisits Wellesley," "Who's pushing? Birth of Frieda," "The orange's ignorance of the apple," "Old woman at 6 a.m.," "Midnight." A few of the titles seem more characteristic of Ted's work than Sylvia's, as for instance "Bloody-mindedness of the amoeba," "Gulls, coming into Southampton," or "The clock, death of the fox, baying of hounds – tick, tick."

Some of the items, meant to provoke thought, could therefore leave Plath to make her own choices: "It is now nearly a month since you left London – day by day you feel yourself cleaning and purifying," "Drop a penny in the Atlantic," "Catching nothing in Winthrop Bay," "To sunbathe, and become a sea-beach." Hughes calls items on another list "starting points": "To undo the tangle of roads," "To find yourself imprisoned in a certain part of your past," "Little jobs as being a process of petrification, till you become a stone heroine on a tomb," "Fertility as a final God for sceptics, especially to find your own body overpowering you in order to show its fertility," "Metaphor each 3 lines long, for Frieda as a little paradise fountain, etc."

Among Plath's papers at the Smith Rare Book Room are a number of these listing sheets, all undated, so reconstructing the process of the interplay between Hughes and Plath is difficult. Did Plath keep the sheets and draw from them for months, even years? Did Hughes help her decide which theme to work on at a specific time or was the key to any successful use of an idea her process of free associating from a simple "starting point"? (On one of the lists, for example, Plath has added in handwriting three items that seem appropriate to her – "Candles," "Night-feeding," and "The moon's round O-mouth of sorrow.") Did their sometimes mutual hypnosis influence either of their choices for subjects for their writing?

Included on Hughes's lists are some topics that Plath did choose to write about because the effective poems that resulted are among her published work, poems such as "Surgeon at 2 A.M.," "Lament of the earthen ware head," "The Beast," "Witch-burning," "Moon and Yew," "The Pheasant," "Rabbit Snares," "Owls," "A Cricket on the Mojave Desert," and "Mushrooms, that think they are going to take over the world." In the case of the last, titled "Mushrooms," Plath creates a near-comic poem that moves quickly, stays limited in small forms, and comes to a close with an ironic maxim. It is one of her first poems to use the mocking comic voice that will dominate her October poems in 1962. It opens, "Overnight, very/ Whitely, discreetly,/ Very quietly" and after building the first stanza entirely from adverbs (in a kind of run-on construction that any English teacher would "correct"), the sentence continues, "Our toes, our noses/ Take hold on the loam, acquire the air." Just as the last line of the poem comments on the fungi's persistence – "Our foot's in the door" – so the remaining nine stanzas describe the arrival. The comment on the earth as their inheritance comes at the end, "we are meek,/ We are edible,...We shall by morning/ Inherit the earth."[29]

Quite different in tone is her adaptation of "Pheasant," where she pleads with someone for its life – "Do not kill it...Let be, let be" –[30] and this image of kingly beauty she also connects with the elm which is to be so important to her last year of poetry. The elm and the yew tree, facing each other across Court Green and therefore in different positions in regard to the moon, form one axis for Plath's late mythology.[31] In this regard, it could be said that Hughes's giving her as topic "The Moon and Yew" crystallized much random imagery for her.

Yet, psychologically, casting herself as Hughes's student or apprentice only forced Plath into a secondary – even a tertiary – role as poet. The self-motivated Hughes could write under the least productive circumstances: he could huddle in the doorway area of their tiny Chalcot Hill apartment, focus on his writing, and thereby close out the crying of the infant Frieda, perhaps because all parts of his work were his. He needed only to begin and he could write. As she nursed the baby and berated herself – always harshly – for her failures of imagination and will, Plath was driven to even greater envy by her spouse's evident powers of concentration. This, for

example, was not a productive time: after Frieda's birth in April
1960, Sylvia wrote only a handful of poems during the rest of the
year. Ted, in contrast, wrote plays for the BBC, books for children,
enigmatic but vivid short stories, and many of the poems for his
second book.

Even though Hughes's list-making had to have been invasive to
Plath's process of writing her own poems, he evidently saw it as yet
another means by which he could show the extent of what he called
their "sympathetic" relationship. As he said on the BBC program
"Two of a Kind," a series devoted to married couples who did the
same kind of work which was taped January 18, 1961, it was as if he
were "a medium"[32] for Sylvia's thoughts. He told the interviewer
that he believed in such telepathic bonds, and that he felt sure he
could write about Sylvia's experiences just as well as his own.

A few months later, Plath is interviewed by playwright Marvin
Kane on another BBC program, this one a half hour feature of her
comments about her poems, with readings of her work. As if to set
the record straight about whose poems are whose, Plath insists that:

> a poem, by its own system of illusions, can set up a rich and
> apparently living world ... [my poems] attempt to re-create, in
> their own way, definite situations and landscapes. They are, quite
> emphatically, about the 'things of the world.'
>
> When I say "this world," I include, of course, such feelings as
> fear and despair and barrenness, as well as domestic love and
> delight in nature. These darker emotions may well put on the
> masks of quite unworldly things – such as ghosts, or trolls or
> antique gods.[33]

Her aesthetic in a nutshell, Plath's description of moving between
William Carlos Williams' insistence on "No ideas but in things" and
possible vehicles for conveying "darker emotions," ghosts or trolls
or antique gods, brings the reader into alignment with her poetic
premises. She does not mention her spouse, or the fact that he is a
poet. And her comments are particularly apt for the first poem she
chooses to read, "The Disquieting Muses." In her prefatory comments, Plath gives the reader a way to understand her use of the
muses – comparing them with "Other sinister trios of women – the
three fates, the witches in Macbeth, de Quincey's sisters of madness."[34]

She also reads what she calls "landscape" poems, "Sleep in the
Mojave Desert" and "Suicide off Egg Rock." The latter was a poem

she had written for Robert Lowell's poetry workshop in Boston, and had been disappointed when he didn't see its strengths. She is reclaiming that work now, by directing her listeners to imagine "one of the sooty, ocean beaches just north of Boston . . . a backdrop of salt marshes and factories." As she points out, "The landscape is ordinary enough, but it is seen here through the eyes of a man about to drown himself."[35] While the poem begins with a description of that ordinariness, it quickly moves to a line that will be a touchstone for Plath's later writing:

> Sun struck the water like a damnation.
> No pit of shadow to crawl into,
> And his blood beating the old tattoo
> I am, I am, I am . . .[36]

While Plath will more often use the repeated "I am" line to signal the choice of life, in this poem the persona walks into the "forgetful surf."

Her comments on "Parliament Hill Fields" also stress that she is representing an individual speaker's view of the London landscape, a speaker "overwhelmed by an emotion so powerful as to color and distort the scenery." The two poems have this method in common, then, though they are written in different periods of her poetic development. She continues about the woman persona, "The speaker here is caught between the old and the new year, between the grief caused by the loss of a child and the joy aroused by the knowledge of an older child safe at home. Gradually the first images of blankness and absence give way to images of convalescence and healing as the woman turns, a bit stiffly, and with difficulty, from her sense of bereavement to the vital and demanding part of her world which still survives."[37]

Coming to the close of her reading, she chooses "You're" ("one of a growing series, about a baby . . . simple and small") and "Magi" ("I imagine the great absolutes . . . gathered around the crib of a newborn baby girl who is nothing *but* life"). Her final poems are "Medallion" (which she gives the shortest description to, "a dead snake through a magnifying glass") and "Stones," the last part of "Poem for a Birthday." As commentary on this richest, most autobiographical, work, she notes, "the speaker has utterly lost her sense of identity and relationship to the world. She imagines herself, quite graphically, undergoing the process of rebirth, like a statue that has been scattered and ground down, only to be resurrected and pieced together centuries later. Her nightmare vision of waking in a modern hospital gradually softens, as she recovers, and accepts the frightening, yet new, ties of love which will heal her and return her, whole again, to the world."[38]

Finally, as part of the persona's return to the real world, Plath the poet includes the love of her spouse – though not specifically and not by name. What is most emphasized in her comments is the process of rebirth, the persona's struggle, the persona's return from being "utterly lost...scattered and ground down." It is a resurrection that lies at the heart of "Stones," and of nearly all of Plath's late work. As she insists on what this image of rebirth means, she begins to develop the authoritative tone, and position, that takes her to the powerful achievement of her later writing. It was not until the autumn of 1993 that Ted Hughes attempted to acknowledge how surprising Plath's progress to that achievement was. As he then explained, "My notion was always that it's the one thing you don't do: you don't write about yourself. The shock of Sylvia's writing, when she really began to write, was that she was doing the very opposite of what she would normally have considered a proper thing to write about...What she'd done was to reclaim her entire psychology."[39]

9

Plath's Poems about Women

Even while the reader can find in Hughes's lists some themes that would feed into Plath's poetry, the discrepancy between those collective lists and the poems she began writing, and continued to write, starting in 1959 is noticeable. Whereas most of Hughes's ideas for subject matter were historically or geographically based, with a strong component of trees, animals, and natural scenes, many of the poems Plath wrote during these years were about women – women either achieving or non-achieving, and particularly women either fertile or barren. Working directly from Frazer's premise in *The Golden Bough* that pregnant women bespeak fertility, she crafted poems that glowed with positive imagery about both pregnancy and about babies. And working just as directly from the polar opposite concept in the same source, that a barren wife "infects" her husband's garden with her own sterility, she wrote repeatedly about barren women who were unfruitful by their own doing: a woman who had had abortions became, for Plath, the Other. (Nothing is simple here: we have Plath's comment in her college journal that "I do not want primarily to be a mother,"[1] and biographer Paul Alexander contends that Plath had aborted their first child, a few months after her marriage to Hughes.)[2] As a corollary to the barren women theme, Plath also wrote several poems that criticized the artifical ways women maintained their beauty (e.g., "Face Lift," "The Rival").

A systematic emphasis on physical beauty was inherent in this set of poems, for the 1950's privileged the thin, the emaciated, the ill-nourished. Because of her height, Plath could carry somewhat more weight than the Twiggy model-thin women who starved themselves to be fashionable; at the time she delivered Frieda, her weight – usually 135 to 137 pounds – had climbed to 155; when Nicholas was born in January, 1962, Plath weighed 170 pounds. Although she remained attractive in her pregnancy (one of Ted's friends wrote that as the time neared for Frieda's birth Sylvia was "a woman blazing with life and good spirits"),[3] her use of the adjective "cow-like" in several of her poems about babies and mothering reflected the way she knew society would view her large, nursing, body. It was a new problem for her, one that stemmed entirely from maternity and its processes.[4]

From early childhood, Plath had been a "good eater." As her journal entries and letters to her family show, she finds food – and eating it – interesting. She grew up very conscious of the cost of things; knowing that the Sunday roast cost $0.41 a pound made her feel as if she were eating pennies. Similarly, her childhood letters from camp are hardly more than descriptions of what food has been served at each meal, and the comment that she ate it all.[5] As a college woman, her life was still ruled by necessary economies (one has only to look at the accounting of what she spent in each year at Smith to see the way she tracked minute amounts of, for instance, $2 for postage stamps, or $1.50 for cleaning).[6]

Chary about any spending, Plath would not invest money in food and then leave it on her plate. Because she and Hughes had so little spendable income, especially during the early years of their marriage, her habits of accounting for every dollar were reinforced. She loved the luxuries – London's "sour cream and cream cheese"[7] not to mention the Fortnum and Mason chicken pies – but she knew they were just that, luxuries. It also seems plausible that the fierce argument she had with her sister-in-law occurred over the fact that Plath was usurping a daughter's place, perhaps by eating too much.[8]

To a surprising extent in Plath's later poems, this dichotomy of the thin, mannequin styled woman set against the comfortably well-fed motherly female is played out. In a 1961 poem, "Heavy Women," she describes the "Irrefutable, beautifully smug/ As Venus ..." women settling in "their belling dresses." Their pregnancies bring such satisfaction that they smile to themselves, listening "for the millennium,/ The knock of the small, new heart." Nature blesses them too, in other ways, as Plath writes that "Over each weighty stomach a face/ Floats calm as a moon or a cloud." Hooded in "Mary-blue," these women live happy and contented lives among their "Pink-buttocked infants." At a distance, "far off, the axle of winter/ Grinds down."[9]

Written just a week earlier, "Morning Song" re-creates the joyous mothering occasioned by the infant who wakes during the night. Although the mother-persona describes herself as "cow-heavy and floral/ In my Victorian nightgown," her significant quality is her ability to hear, to sense her newborn's need. "I wake to listen: A far sea moves in my ear.// One cry, and I stumble from bed ..."[10] Disdainful of what fashion-conscious observers might think of the motherly body, the persona knows that her love for the child is the essential characteristic.

During that same week, Plath writes the poem titled "Barren Woman," and it interestingly reverts to the intricate images of some of her earlier poems. The opening word is "Empty" and the structure the poet then envisions is museum-like, echoing, "blind to the world." Even the flowers here, which are forbidding lilies, "Exhale their pallor like scent." A place of deadness, the space that the barren woman represents is the site not of celebration but a place where "nothing can happen."[11] For a short poem, "Barren Woman" consists of a great many images, all underscoring the notion of being barren, fruitless.

"Face Lift," which Plath admitted was about Dido Merwin's plastic surgery (and about which Dido later recalled Plath's curiosity),[12] extends the themes of the measures the barren woman will take to enhance her beauty. Written in the voice of the woman who has had the surgery, the poem recounts her much-married history, the easy anesthesia, and the secrecy of the hospitalization: "For five days I lie in secret,/ Tapped like a cask, the years draining into my pillow./ Even my best friend thinks I'm in the country..." The net result is, as the persona says with elation, "I grow backward. I'm twenty." In the last stanza of the poem, addressing her former self as "Old sock-face, sagged on a darning egg,"[13] she wishes that self dead. Although the persona has been reborn, the irony of the poet's tone undermines her self-congratulation.

Plath wrote to friends late in 1962, after Hughes had left Court Green to live in London with Asia Wevill, "the woman he is with is on her third husband and has had so many abortions she can't have children. She is part of this set of barren women... that I am glad to get rid of. I guess I am just not like that..."[14]

Wrestling with the fact that her sister-in-law had accused her of being selfish and piggish, Plath wrote a poem about the beautiful Olwyn titled simply "The Rival." In draft, the poem consists of three sections, but only the first appears in *Ariel* and *Collected Poems*. Although Plath never saw her sister-in-law again after the argument of the 1960 Christmas in Yorkshire,[15] she knew that the closeness that existed between Ted and his older sister was not going to be diminished by physical absence – that her beautiful sister-in-law was, in fact, a rival.

The poem is filled with vivid yet metallic images of the invasive woman, "Ticking your fingers on the marble table, looking for cigarettes...dying to say something unanswerable."[16] Given to debasing people, "making stone out of everything," preying on everyone ("No day is safe from news of you"), the rival remains her exquisite self. It is in this 1961 poem that Plath reinforces the pattern of identifying the moon with coldness, with inhuman responses; yet when the rival is compared with the moon, the rival is even less human. This is the poem's decisive opening: "If the moon smiled, she would resemble you./ You leave the same impression/ Of something beautiful, but annihilating."

Part 2 of the poem contrasts the aloof beauty with the speaker, a woman "corruptible as a loaf of bread," whose virtue is that she has "a baby you like." The rival sits beguilingly in a distant room, while the young mother "crawled on all fours,/ A sow or a cow" to play with the smiling child. Living away from England, the rival now writes to them "with loving regularity," her letters – typically filled with "dissatisfactions" – are "expansive as carbon monoxide."[17]

Part 3 describes the persona's longing to escape from the force of the rival's personality. Her home is filled with the killing gas of memory; the horizon is preoccupied with the rival, and the sea "keeps washing you up like an old bone." The truth is that the rival is as indestructible as a diamond. Yet because the diamond is such a valued object, the persona will wear her at the center of her forehead, marked forever as a victim.

In the corner of the first page of the draft, Plath has listed other poem titles; "The Rival" comes first, followed immediately by "Face Lift." In a pattern strangely prescient, Plath has set up the contrast that she will write about and around almost to the time of her death. Late in 1962, with "Mary's Song" she returns to the mother theme, but this time the mother persona is obsessed with the possible harm the world may do to her child. For all its crystalline beauty, the poem "Child" also echoes with tones of worry and fear; its closing image leaves the reader with "this troublous/ Wringing of hands, this dark/ Ceiling without a star."[18] As Plath had written in "Winter Trees," her life is now absorbed by "Memories growing, ring on ring/ Knowing neither abortions nor bitchery,"[19] and therefore, "Truer than women."

Closely related to "Winter Trees" is Plath's poem "Brasilia," the manuscripts of which show the kind of intertextual borrowing that occurs in many of the very late poems. (Lines deleted from the center of "Brasilia" become the opening stanza of "Childless Woman," a different kind of contrast – sharper, bloodier, dominated by the blood-letting spider which utters "nothing but blood – / Taste it, dark red!")[20] The watchful mother in "Brasilia" who swims under the defenseless child is herself a prehistoric fish, an "old coelacanth... Out-of-date and bad luck to the fisherman/ Nearly extinct." Once she too dies off, the child will be "one of the new people/ motherless, fatherless."[21] What he awaits will be the destruction she sees on the horizon.

One of Plath's most moving poems, "For a Fatherless Son," also draws from imagery of destruction, trees that carry death rather than life, and the core image of the child's life, the absence of his father. The shifts of focus and mood in the poem's opening lines lead the reader through the simple statement of loss, intensifying in the "death tree" metaphor. The contrast of the baby's grabbing the mother's nose – emphasized with unexpected words such as "dumb" and "stupidity" to suggest his voicelessness – brings the reader back to normalcy, but only for a time. Quickly into stanza three, the poet describes the way the child will "touch what's wrong."[22] As if she cannot pull back herself from the edge of her realization, she lists in a crabbed series three surrealistic images: "The small skulls, the smashed blue hills, the godawful hush." Replete with the -s linkage – small, skulls, smashed, hills, hush – the poet takes the reader away from the *l*'s in the first image, drawing the poem to the hush of its ending. The turn of the last line cannot counteract the assonantal mood of quiet sorrow, of absence both literal and metaphoric.

While in these manuscripts, the mother has also left the child, the finished poems give the woman a living identity. In the poem "Childless Woman," forbiddingly, the woman "achieves" a body that is "ivory,"[23] bloodless, as she becomes herself a rose – and, significantly, not a live woman. In "Amnesiac," Plath points to the pretended forgetfulness of the husband/father, the man who has left his family, so that he can "travel, travel, travel" with "the red-headed sister he never dared to touch." Here she fuses the barren woman of the affair with his forbidden sister (emphasizing for the reader, "Barren, the lot are barren!"), and turns the poem into a comedy as the two travel with "scenery/ Sparking off their brother-sister rears."[24]

In "The Fearful," Plath is even more direct: she accuses the woman in question of hating "The thought of a baby – / Stealer of cells, stealer of beauty – // She would rather be dead than fat,/ Dead and perfect, like Nefertit..."[25] And the protagonist of "Lesbos" also suffers from having "blown your tubes like a bad radio/ Clear of voices and history."[26] The reader is not surprised when this woman suggests to her friend, the poet-persona, that she get rid of both her kittens and her small daughter.

A long poem, "Lesbos" includes a number of unexplained references, but the last section describes the persona-mother's reaction to the woman who continually advises her: "Now I am silent, hate/ Up to my neck,/ Thick, thick./ I do not speak./ I am packing the hard potatoes like good clothes,/ I am packing the babies,/ I am packing the sick cats . . ." Persisting in her only real ambition – to be a good mother to the children she has borne – the persona has to leave the sterile woman, relinquishing her offer of friendship, wiping her out of her consciousness.

In March of 1962, all the knowledge Plath had acquired about pregnancy and childbirth, and social attitudes toward both, came to fruition in her magnificent – and radical – radio play about three women in a hospital maternity ward. Because Hughes had made both good money and important literary contacts through the BBC productions of his radio plays, Sylvia was eager to become one of their playwrights. Douglas Cleverdon was a talented, earnest producer, responsible for airing Dylan Thomas's *Under Milkwood*, a work Plath had long admired. To know Cleverdon would be exciting, she thought, and the subject matter of the unique "Three Women" was certainly near to hand – and her own. She had only birthed Nicholas Farrar a short six weeks earlier.

What Plath achieves in choosing three different kinds of pregnancies – one miscarriage, one full-term delivery in which the unmarried mother would give the baby up for adoption, and one delivery in which the mother would take the child and raise it – is the canvas for a spectrum of physical experiences and attitudes. The bereavement of the woman who miscarries is poignant, separated as she is from her husband and the men of the office in which she works. Male behaviors here are truly obtuse, and metaphorically, men's bodies are described as flat. Or in the monologue of the woman, "That flat, flat, flatness from which ideas, destructions,/ Bulldozers, guillotines, white chambers of shrieks proceed,/ Endlessly proceed . . ."[27]

It is the Third Voice that has no place for the child. Surprised by her pregnancy, she repeats, "I wasn't ready." Angry at the smug male doctors who deliver these children, wanted or unwanted, she contends, "what if they found themselves surprised, as I did?/ They would go mad with it." Her anger subsiding, she watches her "red, terrible girl," "crying," "furious," Scratching at my sleep like arrows,/ Scratching at my sleep, and entering my side." Her leave-taking is an amazing poem. Packing the clothes "of a fat woman I do not know," she is surprised – now – at how vulnerable she has become: "I am a wound walking out of hospital./ I am a wound that they are letting go." Pained and hollow, she realizes that "I leave my health behind. I leave someone/ Who would adhere to me: I undo her fingers like bandages: I go."

The heart of the long poem rests in the solemn happiness of the First Voice, the woman who gives birth to a long-wanted child. As she speaks before delivery of her time ("I am slow as the world. I am very patient"), she brings the gentle humor of fulfillment into the juxtaposed tones of the work: "When I walk out, I am a great event./ I do not have to think, or even rehearse./ What happens in me will happen without attention .../ Leaves and petals attend me. I am ready."

When her pains begin, fear overtakes her equanimity; the "calm before something awful" is shattered. "A seed about to break," she feels the first tug of the "cargo of agony ... inescapable, tidal." After the long labor,

> There is no miracle more cruel than this.
> I am dragged by the horses, the iron hooves.
> I last. I last it out. I accomplish a work ...

Hard-earned satisfaction suffuses the mother's reaction as she sees the boy. She hardly notices the "red lotus [that] opens in its bowl of blood;" rather, she croons to the angry infant:

> What did my fingers do before they held him?
> What did my heart do, with its love?
> I have never seen a thing so clear.
> His lids are like the lilac-flower
> And soft as a moth, his breath.
> I shall not let go.
> There is no guile or warp in him. May he keep so.

Amid the two other women's complaints, this lullaby of the First Voice continues, almost to the end of the poem. One of the most beautiful lyrics in twentieth-century poetry occurs toward the end of "Three Women," in the passage of the loving mother which begins, "How long can I be a wall, keeping the wind off?/ How long can I be/ Gentling the sun with the shade of my hand ..."

Never predictable because of the juxtaposition of the three voices, speaking at very different emotional places and tempos, "Three Women" conveys women's reactions to childbirth or miscarriage with more variety than the uninitiated might expect. Sheer hatred darkens the speech of the Second Voice, the woman who has miscarried again and again. Her vengefulness takes in the patriarchal world, including her husband. She is hopelessly self-centered: "I am bled white as wax, I have no attachments./ I am flat and virginal, which means nothing has happened . . . It is I. It is I – / Tasting the bitterness between my teeth. The incalculable malice of the everyday."

The vacuity after the pain of leave-taking saddens the reader. Will the Third Voice ever come to be human again? The birth of her child is only a fast-fading memory: "I had an old wound once, but it is healing./ I had a dream of an island, red with cries./ It was a dream, and did not mean a thing."

The secure joy of the First Voice, as she watches her son sleep, both begins and ends the poem. "I am reassured. I am reassured . . . I am simple again. I believe in miracles." Her blessing for her child is that he be normal, not exceptional. Wanting to protect him, feeling powerless to keep him innocent, the voice explains, "It is the exception that interests the devil. It is the exception that climbs the sorrowful hill." Rather, her wish is that he be common, "To love me as I love him,/ And to marry what he wants and where he will."

A strange ending for the First Voice, so soon recovered from the ordeal of childbirth: would she be worried about her son's marriage, unless she were haunted by thoughts that her husband's family does not love her, and perhaps that her family does not think she has made a suitable match either. Or perhaps the persona herself worries about the suitability of that match, fraught as it is with angry fights and physical brutality? As focused as the text manages to be on the three child-bearing women and their poetry, their responses to the life events that are handed to them, fated for them, elements of Plath's own life at the time manage to creep in. While she keeps the woman who miscarries from being objectionable in herself, recasting her as a sympathetic woman rather than an intentionally barren one, she clearly favors the pregnant woman who takes her child home to care for. Women who give birth assume a lifetime of responsibility, with love to leaven the weight of that care. There could be no equivocation about that responsibility – or about that love.

To be considered along with these autobiographical emphases is the pattern Sandra Gilbert finds that connects "Three Women," or

"Three Voices" as it was originally titled, with the three women characters in Virginia Woolf's novel, *The Waves*. With some remarkable similarities between the language of Susan, Rhoda and Jinny and Plath's three speakers, and with knowledge of the fact that she much admired and loved Woolf's work, Gilbert's point is plausible.[28] It also is comforting to see that a woman writer would turn to another women writer for imaginative help in creating effective and poetically real female characters. As a composite of Plath's hospital experience, her reading life, and her own emotional understanding of becoming a mother, "Three Women" is the most impressive long poem Plath had written, or would write. It was also a powerful precursor to the later works that also evolved from her conceptualization of a single idiomatic voice. Here, the voices are largely calm and sympathetic. But the stridency and despair of the Second Voice will soon become all too familiar.

By the late fall of 1962, the time of "The Munich Mannequins" (a poem which was earlier titled "The Bald Madonnas"), Plath becomes more autobiographical as she assigns a German cast to the beautiful, heartless barren woman. (Because of the distinctively ethnic name of Hughes's new lover, Assia Guttman Wevill, Plath chose to describe objectionable things as German in many of her late poems; she also takes onomatopoetic jabs at the sibilance of "Assia.") After its revealing title, this stark poem opens, "Perfection is terrible, it cannot have children."[29] The poem is loaded with metaphors of coldness, poisonous gas, sterility, snow, and nakedness (and the sibilance of the *s*'s in *sulfur loveliness, smiles, sacrifice* and *snow*, used three times in key positions to signal death). Spreading like a poison gas, the mannequin's inhumanity infects her male companion; together, in "Munich, morgue between Paris and Rome," the two lovers are pictured as "Naked and bald in their furs,/ Orange lollies on silver sticks," but – because they have frustrated the life force – 'Intolerable, without mind.'

This poem connects subliminally with another written in January of 1963, called enigmatically "Totem," a recitation of various kinds of killings that seem to take place in Smithfield. The killings go beyond hog butchery, however, and include the killings of children as well as the rabbits that have become Plath's own totem for innocence. As the persona notes tersely, "There is no mercy in the glitter of cleavers."[30] As might be expected in the context of her other writing, "Totem" contains abortion imagery, as well as a litany of sacrifice ritual from Radin's African folktales. The Anansi spider returns, mirrors chart events, cobras hypnotize the viewer, and death seems inescapable.

In several of Plath's February poems, among the last half dozen she composed before her suicide, the dichotomous imaging of good-mother, not-mother disappears. Absorbed into a less angry and less tenuous way of looking at the world, Plath's categories meld into larger notions of calm. In "Kindness," the poet cryptically describes the acts of the good godmother caring for the children, "Sweetly picking up pieces!," and bringing the persona "a cup of tea/ Wreathed in steam."[31] Caring for equates with the *tenderness* that Plath has long used as a positive description in her writing. Even without the intertextual response to Hughes's BBC play about dead rabbits and the rabbit killer carrying two roses to his new lover, "Kindness" rings a different chord in her gallery of women's por-traits. As the concluding line of the poem emphasizes, it is Dame Kindness who proffers her beloved children to the persona: "You hand me two children, two roses." That this line is given the closing position, one of sure emphasis, undercuts the importance of the previous two lines, which are often quoted, "The blood jet is poetry,/ There is no stopping it." In effect, the presence of the two children does stop that blood loss, or at least blunts it. If the persona were in a position to choose, the structure of the poem – with its ending line restatement of "two children" – makes clear what her choice would be.

"Edge," the last poem attributed to Plath before her suicide is also about a mother and her children. Drawing from the opening line of "The Munich Mannequins," that "Perfection is terrible," here the persona shifts her lens. Terrible it may be, or perhaps it is "terrible" in the sense of creating terror as a parallel to "awful" as a means of inspiring awe, but the poem opens with a sentence that has a clearly positive effect, "The woman is perfected."[32] A significant change occurs in the composition of this poem from draft stage to final version: in the draft, the perspective is of viewers high above the scene, looking down on the body of a dead woman. At that time the poem was titled "Nuns in Snow" and the observers are nuns, travel-ing as if on a pilgrimage to view the dead woman. From that per-spective, the later countless images of a woman's being nunlike, being pure, coalesce in the impact of this tautly crafted work.

Critic Mary Kurtzman notes that Plath relied on her knowledge of the Tarot cards (a Western Tarot based on the Hebrew Cabala, repli-cating the 22 paths on the Cabalistic Tree of Life, each standing for a "state of consciousness and spiritual unfolding") throughout her last years of writing, using the pack as an organizing principle as early as the chapter arrangement of *The Bell Jar*. She attributes the positive effect of "Edge" to the fact that its details and form suggest that Plath was drawing on the High Priestess card as model, and the role of the High Priestess was to experience the "highest possible union with the Goddess or God (Tarot divinities are both female and male)." Such union is labeled "Isis perfected" and Kurtzman notes that someone wrote ISIS on the final typescript of the poem "Edge."[33]

She also speaks to the choice of the word "illusion" and concludes that Plath was explaining that, although the Scorpio sign which was her astrological marker might suggest a fated suicide, such a link was illusory: Kurtzman then reads the poem's last four lines as the reason for the suicide, which may well have been chosen to avoid another hospitalization, complete with its terrorizing electroconvulsive shock. As the blacks "crackle and drag" in the treatment, the woman would lose the heart of her life – both the full creative powers of her mind, and, as a socially mandated result, the custody of her beloved children. In the poem, the woman has protectively folded her children back into her body – from which they came.

The poem's imagery suggests that her symbolically taking the children back is as natural as a rose closing its petals at night; her act is part of that necessity that mother's lives are governed by. Had the poem been longer, had the woman persona been given speech before her death, she might have echoed the moving lines from the "Three Women's" First Voice:

> How long can my hands
> Be a bandage to his hurt, and my words
> Bright birds in the sky, consoling, consoling?
> It is a terrible thing
> To be so open: it is as if my heart
> Put on a face and walked into the world.[34]

If only the child could be spared that world, if only the poem's persona could have been spared it. But, if Kurtzman is correct about the symbology of "Edge" (and other of Plath's late poems), the persona here has "accomplished" what she set out to do, find a mystical unity with the spiritual world, and she has thereby finally escaped – by journeying to the edge of the known world – that world that so increasingly frustrated her, and her writerly ambition.

10

Plath's Triumphant Women Poems

Sylvia Plath would have been the first to admit that there were multiple roles for women during the 1960s besides mothering or not mothering. In the age of professionalism, of incipient careerism, a woman would have been expected to have identities other than her status as a bearer of children. Just as so many of Plath's journal entries dealt with her future work, and the conundrum of which work a talented woman writer, artist, and teacher should take up, so many of her poems deal with the varieties of achieving women. It is also clear in her journals that she was intentionally searching for women writers to emulate. She regularly mentions Virginia Woolf, Emily Dickinson, Stevie Smith, Willa Cather, Lillian Hellman, Louise Bogan, Adrienne Cecile Rich (often with some asperity, since Rich was her contemporary and by having won the Yale Younger Poets competition, already headed toward an important career as poet).[1] In fact, Liz Yorke has concluded that the journal entries "make it clear that Plath made a self-conscious decision to study women. Her critique of the ideology of the feminine; her critical consciousnes of women's emotional, erotic and economic loyalty and their subserviance to men can be shown as developing continuously from this time [1958]."[2]

Unfortunately, by the time Plath had freed herself from her apprenticeship modes and was writing in what seemed to be her true voice, she was obsessed with rage at what she saw as the betrayal of their life together – and her opportunity to become a good writer – by her husband. It was barely possible to scrape out time to write during these years with two very young children, yet Plath had. She had finished *The Bell Jar* and "Three Women," she had worked on several short stories that satisfied her, and many, many poems. Writing within a family household was possible, if difficult. But she was accustomed to difficulties. Plath was not so oblivious to how hard maintaining her writing schedule was, however, as to believe she could write effectively if there were no other adult in that household. The years had made her a pragmatist.

Just as we have seen that she created a mythic structure from her comparison of her own fertile womanhood with the barrenness of other more fashionable women, so it seems plausible that she would emblematize the realm of patriarchal power that not only minded babies but accepted poems, scheduled BBC readings, and wrote reviews as a man of a certain type. For the "old boy network" that was determining her fate as a writer, particularly in England where she had no connections except through her still-outsider husband, she had only anger and even contempt. Her quasi-flirtation with Al Alvarez was prompted at least in part by his power both to accept her work and to review it, and there was frequently a sexual element in her dealings with other established literary men on the British scene. In some ways, the fact that Hughes had begun an affair – while enraging on its own terms – also may have been catalytic in freeing her to express her deep-seated anger against the controlling and male-dominated literary world. Again, York sees the male presence in so many of what can also be read as Plath's "strong woman" poems as more indefinite than the figure of a disloyal husband: "Hatred against men begins to fuel the vitriolic stance of many poems."[3]

Two situations illustrate her frustration at being a woman writer in the British literary world. The first is the narrative of her meeting Alvarez in 1960. *Lupercal*, Hughes's second poem collection, had just appeared. Admiring it greatly, Alvarez phoned and suggested that he and Ted take their infants for a walk, thereby having a chance to talk about poetry. When he arrived at the flat, Alvarez recalled that Mrs. Hughes struck him as "briskly American: bright, clean, competent, like a young woman in a cookery advertisement, friendly and yet rather distant." He pays small attention to her. But as Hughes is getting the baby's carriage out, Plath turns to Alvarez,

"I'm so glad you picked *that* poem," she said. "It's one of my favorites but no one else seemed to like it."

For a moment I went completely blank; I didn't know what she was talking about.

She noticed and helped me out.

"The one you put in *The Observer* a year ago. About the factory at night."

"For Christ's sake, Sylvia *Plath*." It was my turn to gush. "I'm sorry. It was a lovely poem."

"Lovely" wasn't the right word, but what else do you say to a bright young housewife? ...[4]

The apparent inability to equate "housewife" and "young mother" – not to mention, perhaps, "American" – with "poet" created little more than a minor social gaffe here, but Plath's life was filled with occasions when she was the quiet American to her husband's ever-growing reputation as one of England's brightest rising stars. At a Faber & Faber cocktail party, she is called out into the hall to witness Hughes's having his picture taken in the company of Stephen Spender, T. S. Eliot, Louis MacNeice, and W. H. Auden. There was no question that Auden would remember having a brief conference with the Smith coed Sylvia Plath, yet now he is standing only six feet from that girl's poet spouse. As the five men look into the camera, sherry glasses in hand, there is an air of self-congratulation that Plath would have found difficult to stomach.[5]

As he recounted that first meeting, Alvarez had the conscience to admit, "I was embarrassed not to have known who she was. She seemed embarrassed to have reminded me, and also depressed."[6]

Faced with the issue of role, Plath knew her place was to be the help-meet, the alert and sensitive supporter to her husband and his burgeoning career. One imagines that when the Hugheses are invited to T. S. Eliot's home for dinner, Plath is hardly a participant in the conversation; she would certainly not talk about how many poems she had recently published. Australian poet Charles (known as Mike) Doyle remembers being invited to Ted and Sylvia's Boston apartment for dinner the year before, and having no idea that Plath also wrote poetry. He recalled her cooking a chicken dinner and then clearing the table and washing dishes, while he and Ted sat for hours reading and commenting on their poems in manuscript. Charles Doyle remembers it as being a long evening of talk about specific poems – the men's poems. He concludes, "Nothing was said about her poetry."[7]

A second situation is the years-long period of interaction with Peter Davison, a poet and editor of Harvard University Press (and other presses subsequently) with whom she had had an affair during the summer of 1955, just before she sailed for her Fulbright year in England. Davison writes in his memoir that he felt "used" after Plath broke off the sexual relationship, and summarized their later contact, after he had become Poetry Editor of *The Atlantic*, by saying, "she sent me some of her last poems for *The Atlantic*."[8] The truth of the statement is that Plath beseiged that magazine, sending both her poems and Hughes's to it regularly. It was prominent and it paid well: poets who published there were known, and notable.

She had published in *The Atlantic* before Davison was connected with it, and seemed always to be treated a bit high-handedly. For instance, the magazine kept a large group of her poems for months and then, on April 18, 1955, sent her a check for $25 and told her to revise "Circus in Three Rings."[9] Perhaps they will include it if she can get the first or third stanzas up to the quality of the second, which someone wrote was "a perfect beauty," and then use as title either "The Tamer" or "Lion Tamer." Over Edward Weeks' unsigned but typed name, the quasi-acceptance cheered the Smith co-ed on: the letter concluded, "do a revision which will win us completely. I am confident that you can."

Plath replied politely and sent Weeks the revision and five new poems, saying she would not cash the $25 check until she heard from him. (*The Atlantic* printed "Circus" as it had been submitted originally, despite the revision Plath sent them.) The interchanges continue. In the spring of 1956 they accept "Pursuit," the poem she wrote about the possibility of meeting Hughes, although they comment that it seems too long. Then Weeks asks if he can see her poem "Two Lovers and a Beachcomber by the Real Sea," which was shown to him by a friend. Ironically, that poem had been included in the batch of work that had originally prompted the $25 check and the patronizing encouragement.

In September of that year, Plath hears from Davison, who has just joined the staff. Her reply to him is enthusiastic and overblown, and – even though she and Hughes have already married – she describes Hughes's work to him with the comment that she has become his "agent." She closes that she is eager to know the details about his job, and wants to keep in close touch with him while she remains at Newnham for the year. She also tells him that she and Ted will be married next summer in Wellesley.

Davison's reply is cordial, and he is encouraging about Hughes's poems. But Plath notices that, whereas she had already been published in *The Atlantic*, and although her poems were appearing in *Poetry, The Spectator, The Nation, London Magazine, Granta, Partisan Review, New Yorker, Harper's,* and a number of other good places, neither she nor Ted found ready acceptance at *The Atlantic* once Davison was there. She comments on this in letters home and in her journal; and there is a comic scene of Davison – now married to a former housemate of Plath's at Smith – taking her and Hughes out to dinner and talking throughout the meal about little except his own poetry. Finally, Plath submits their work directly to Edward

Weeks, and acceptances begin again. In the autumn of 1960, her poem "The Manor Garden" appears, and in 1961, "Words for a Nursery."

Davison is right, Plath did send what she called "this rather alarming wad of new stuff"[10] to him November 16, 1962, telling him she was both eager to have his opinion and eager to have any payment. He returned most of the poems but kept six, and noted on her letter – as he passed the poems to Weeks – that "In the Bee Box" was his favorite. He replied to Plath on November 20, saying that the poems were "quite extraordinary," and that the bee poem hummed with "fright.' Although the letter began 'Dear Sylvia," his reply was addressed to "Mrs. Ted Hughes."[11] Even at the peak of her finest production, Plath could not gain recognition for herself, or for her work, on her own terms.

Plath would have smiled grimly at the set of editorial responses appended to a copy of Davison's letter in the *Atlantic* file. Although one reader commented on "Terrific vitality, color and originality," even that most enthusiastic responder went on to complain that the emotions in the poems seemed to be "contrived." The four readers could not figure out what was going on. One wrote, "I think she is overdoing these bees." Another noted, "She certainly is queer for bees. Too much buzz and not enough sting in most of these."[12] (*The Atlantic* did accept both "Bee Box" ["The Arrival of the Bee Box"] and "Wintering," eventually, and they saw print in April 1963.)

Considering these representative anecdotes from the six years that Plath served as 'agent' for Hughes's work – not to mention typist, arranger, and record keeper – simultaneous with her offering to do the same for Luke Myers,[13] while trying to develop as a writer herself (and serve as agent, typist and record keeper for her own work), Professor York's assessment that in her late poems Plath was finally speaking out for her feminine/feminist rights is credible. York insists that Plath's late work "presents us with the spectacle of femininity in crisis. It symbolizes the aggressive return of the repressed through a dramatic poetry of mythic formulas, plots and patterns – in which the stage is set for the poet/woman to introduce her shrieks, her suffering, her anguish, her murderous fury, her disruptive *disorder* into the well-regulated, gendered codes of conventional patriarchy."[14]

Plath's neatly-typed letters throughout her marriage are illustrative of that well-regulated behavior. Whether she was writing to Theodore Roethke about a possible teaching post for Hughes, even though it was Plath herself who was so moved by Roethke's poetry,[15] or to John Lehmann with submissions for both of them to *London Magazine*,[16] or to Brian Cox about *Critical Quarterly*,[17] she appeared to be the tidy and competent secretary she had so feared becoming. Unfortunately, as we have seen, some of her earlier poems gave off the same aura of starched neatness – with any recognizable emotion kept at a distance. The truly dramatic changes between those college-era poems, like "Circus in Three Rings" and "Two Lovers and a Beachcomber by the Real Sea," and such late poems as "Applicant," "Purdah," and "Lady Lazarus," were both shocking and inexplicable. That comparatively few of the very late poems were accepted by the first magazine Plath submitted them to was partly because of this wide discrepancy between what a Plath poem had often been, and what editors were reading as Plath poems in the autumn of 1962.

All three of these later poems show the persona moving from her conventional state of social acceptance to the flourish of triumph, no matter how unconventional her behavior has become. In "Applicant," the woman appears to be applying for the job of marrying some man, any man; in "Purdah," she is a reluctant member of a man's harem; and in "Lady Lazarus," she is a woman who readily defies death to taunt the society that would contain, and constrain, her. The tone of the voice interrogating the applicant in that poem is clearly haughty, probably British, and condescending; if one is not "our sort of person,"[18] nothing can be done. Being "our sort of person" sets up sexual classes as well as economic ones. Calling the woman "sweetie," as did the aggressor in the Johnny Panic story, this voice insults her with regularity: an empty head, a naked body, a scenario right out of the Hallmark anniversary charts, this woman does not even merit the dignity of a feminine personal pronoun. Instead, she is an "it" in the lines near the conclusion: "It can sew, it can cook,/ It can talk, talk, talk." These repetitive sentences balance with the repetition in the concluding line, "Will you marry it, marry it, marry it."

In "Purdah" the question is not of marriage, it is of the man's ownership of the woman, who smiles, enigmatic, watching the sun polish her shoulder. Yet the warning occurs early: even as she plays her usual role, the woman is changing, "shifting my clarities."[19] With unbelievable swiftness, the woman attacks her lover, unloosing "The lioness" (the power of her self), "The shriek in the bath" (reminiscent of that most famous of murders, Clytemnestra's of

Agamemnon, which results in "The cloak of holes"). A poem of vengeance, "Purdah" adds a surreal chapter to the anguished punishment the persona metes out in "Burning the Letters," as she destroys her beloved's writing. A key metaphor in that poem is, "The dogs are tearing a fox. This is what it is like – / A red burst and a cry / That splits from its ripped bag and does not stop..."[20] To kill a fox, when one of Hughes's best-known early poems was "The Thought-Fox," speaks pointedly, even if metaphorically.

Polite anger is one stance; explosive rage that does not end is another. Plath's use of the word "shriek" throughout these poems, whether or not the persona is herself doing the shrieking, signals the reader that what she has to tell cannot be told in a normal pitch. Ideally, the poem is a means of voicing all kinds of states, yet it cannot express the volume of rage (or, it cannot express rage in the volume of sound) that the poet or her created persona would think appropriate.

Merely murdering the powerful man responsible for the female persona's state is not enough. (The reader will see the intricacy of a possible ritual death in the poem "Daddy.") Instead, in the brilliantly titled "Lady Lazarus," Plath uses the metaphor of Lazarus returning from the dead, changing him into a woman (and a woman of some social power) so as to reverse the gender of that miracle. Throughout the poem there is no mention whatever of the biblical origin, or of whatever god might have been responsible for Lazarus's resurrection. Instead, Plath's Lady Lazarus is under the command of her own superior will. Superior in all respects to the general population, and to her former beloved, the persona can even out-do her competition in killing herself. She does this with no personality change: "I am the same, identical woman."[21] Even as she is martyred by the male patriarchy – what can be more representative of that power but the German title "Herr" and the various manuscript designations of "Herr Professor," "Herr Doktor," "Herr God," "Herr Lucifer," and finally the direct name of "Enemy"? – the woman does not remain dead. From the pile of ash, she becomes the uncontained and mystic phoenix, rising from the carnage that men have created for her, and of her. Her final act, always phrased comically, is to "eat men [in the plural] like air."

Critic Susan Van Dyne, in her meticulous work with the many manuscript drafts of Plath's late poems, points out here that the audience for what she calls Lady Lazarus's *performance* is not a single adversary, but the world of men – a world for which the persona has only contempt ("the peanut-crunching crowd"). "What Lady Lazarus suffers is not male brutality but the gendered asymmetry of her relationship to power in which her role is always defined as dependent and defective: to male professor she is student; to executioner, criminal; to priest, sinner; to doctor, patient." And yet, by her addition of comedy to this shriek, Van Dyne notes, Plath sidesteps the trap of sentiment: "Her burlesque of suffering both confesses the damage of gender and uses it as a weapon...The persistent double consciousness of 'Lady Lazarus' is not the split self of alienation that marks Plath's other poems of rage but a strategy for control."[22]

Who are the antagonists in Plath's late poems like "Lady Lazarus"? Sometimes her persona's own self, but more often men – husbands, fathers, power figures at large – or, as she begins to suggest here, filaments of airy stuff that have no substance. If even the physical strength of men, a strength they customarily vaunt over weaker women, is subterfuge, where does their superiority lie? In manuscripts for the poem, Plath includes lines that show the protagonist's ordinariness, and her recurring purity: "Yes, lady, I'm like you,/ I have a child or two.// Yessir, yessir Though the doctors say it's rare/ Each time I rise, I rise a blooming [bloody] virgin." The mark of a woman's successful life – up to a point – being her virginity, there is a tonal difference between the two words Plath bracketed in the draft. While both might be slang, "blooming" reinforces the glowing incandescent skin this exuberance warrants, whereas "bloody" must have more sinister connotations.

Again, the woman persona can stand alone. Yet as long as she has to do battle with men, readers have been tempted to read these poems as autobiographical, as poems about the battles – literal and figurative – between Sylvia Plath and Ted Hughes. Realizing this, Plath turns to poems about women who separate themselves from such adversarial men – this is her route to "Ariel," and it is probably the reason she chose *Ariel* as the title for the collection she planned to publish from her late poems.

For in "Ariel," the woman persona is completely alone. Her mind is free from the canker of hatred for her husband; her spirit is coming into a newly fruitful phase as she leaves human discord behind. Fusing her human identity with the animal spirit is itself a kind of transcendence, and recalls Robert Graves's insistence in his *White Goddess* (a book that was a kind of Bible for Ted Hughes) that the spirit of that fiery female goddess often appears as a mare, tigress, owl, sow, serpent, she-wolf, female spider, snake, or queen bee.[23] (Of these, the serpent and the racehorse are holy animals, as is the lion.)[24] Reading Plath's poems retrospectively, from this vantage point, shows how thoroughly she was mining Graves's philosophy.

In "Ariel," the persona, and the reader, is on a ride into the unknown, into a world that may be natural or spirit, real or imaginary, physical or emotional. What is known only is that the persona and God's lioness, either as mythical or spiritual identity, are united, fused, into one. Reminiscent of a sexual image, here Plath denies the bodily detail: all the viewer sees is berries, shadows; all she hears is the child's cry in the morning dawn. What has happened is a transfiguration. Leaving behind "Dead hands, dead stringencies"[25] [and in draft, the phrase is "dead men"], finding herself empowered to move forward – perhaps for the first time, alone – the persona does not fear what may be ahead.

Literally, "Ariel" is said to be the name of Plath's horse, but surely we are made fools of if we read this evocative poem so simply. As the poem says, "Something else // Hauls me through air –" This poem is Plath at her metaphysical best; we are hesitant to recognize that theme because we have noticed it so seldom. (Our reading of Plath's poetry has been stymied because there have always been interesting ways to read her work – if not from the technical appreciation perspective, or the autobiographical, then from the feminist.) The literary associations with the name "Ariel," however, lead us to the metaphysical. Whether we are with Prospero in *The Tempest*, or with Prospero in W. H. Auden's *The Sea and the Mirror*, his verse commentary on Shakespeare's play, we must grant the excessive power that Ariel commands, even in the face of the whole British kingdom. Small and slight, gendered both sexes and neither, Ariel is the all-knowing – and achieving – sprite any writer would wish to be. Particularly a woman writer. Although the name Ariel sounds feminine, at least in contrast to the adversarial Caliban, it is not womanly: it is the best of the spirit world, the best of imaginative power.

In the gendered narrative of Shakespeare's play, the shaman Prospero, thinking he has been able to protect his innocent daughter Miranda, finally breaks his staff and rids himself of his "rough magic." As he does this, he frees Ariel from his control. With close attention to the way the shaman can relinquish his magic powers, Plath may be suggesting that the self-styled shaman in her life, her controlling husband – controlling in the province of art if less so in the domestic – no longer has power over her creative spirit, the Ariel in Plath.

Auden creates his dialogue between Prospero and Ariel so that wisdom is expressed throughout it. Prospero defines magic as "the power to enchant that comes from disillusion," and continues that the wise man is one who has learned to tell "the difference between moonshine and daylight." In her customary intertextual way, Plath may be assuming the mantle of one who has been disillusioned, and has now grown past that angry despair. Particularly apt is Prospero's farewell comment to Ariel. He blesses the spirit, saying "Ages to you of song and daring."

There is little question that Plath knew that her late poems, which she characteristically saw as songs or lyrics, were superior to any she had ever written; and that they were so clearly superior because of their great daring. Part of that daring was inherent in the poems – they would take on the subtle hints of meaning that had first surprised her when she wrote "Tulips" and parts of "Three Women." They would grow from the slightest suggestion of an image, forgetting to follow rational coherence, and they would take on new themes in the process of following those scatty images. Like "Cut,"[26] images and metaphors run out of gaps, cracks, flaps, and they do so unchecked because the poet, at last, is willing to be known as "Dirty girl." For it is, finally, the misbehaving no-longer-tidy Plath who has taken control of her art. The freedom to find this new voice has been given to her through her willingness to leave behind all the studies, all the knowledge, all the tutoring – by Hughes as well as by Kazin, Fisher, Krook, and countless other well-intentioned professionals – so that she might come to bedrock.

For Mary Kurtzman, and to some extent Timothy Materer in his book *Modernist Alchemy*, that bedrock is comprised in large part of Plath's Cabalistic beliefs that grew stronger with each month of the poet's last years. Luke Myers lends credence to Kurtzman's readings as he notes that Hughes had been well-versed in those elements for some time.[27] Kurtzman's reading of "Ariel" depends, line by line, on those beliefs as generated from Tarot card 14, Art or Temperance, on which a black-white woman is doing alchemical work over a cauldron, with a lion and an eagle at her feet. Associated with this iconography is the number 60, the Hebrew letter S, the sign Sagittarius, the God Jupiter, the Goddess Diana, the color blue, the horse, the Arrow, the hips and thighs, the Centaur, and the Path of union with one's Higher Self or Holy Guardian Angel, symbolized by the Sun. Considering how brief the poem "Ariel" is, the fact that so many of these symbols occur in it lends weight to this critic's detailed reading (see *Centennial Review*, 32, 1988). As she concludes, "Knowing the spiritual meaning of 'Ariel' – [the word as translated from the Hebrew means 'God's lioness'] – helps one avoid some critical pitfalls."[28]

The speaker, says Kurtzman, "is Plath, a persona neither suicidal nor insane. She is a mystic using her own, always idiosyncratic, version of the ancient language of mysticism. Like H.D., she renames the patriarchal myths, reclaiming Ariel as feminine and declaring her independence from the 'hooks' of male definitions of woman. She becomes the Goddess of the cauldron of poetic inspiration – autonomous, creative, fertile, the very voice of the Angel Ariel."[29] Card 14 also, as Kurtzman notes, is the basis of the major ritual of the Golden Dawn, the mystic society that was so important to W. B. Yeats, and it is in Yeats' house that Plath lived the last few months of her life.

Originating from a number of complex sources, the late Plath voice is, truly, unique. There was no way she could have learned to use it by modeling her poems after those of other poets. There was no way she could have practiced finding it by writing poems on subjects her husband set out for her, as if she were a little tired monk, burrowing away in some chilly monastery. There was no way she could have released herself from the "oughts" and "shoulds" of her superior education, with its classist emphasis on taste, on what the right sort of people read and liked. What could have released the poet from the well-educated Wellesley girl was the right to experience unfeigned passion.

Naked (i.e., "White/ Godiva, I unpeel"), visionary (surrounded with darkness yet capable of sight), and incredibly fast ("foam to wheat"), the poet persona has never experienced anything like this loosening, this unburdening, this flying apart. In some perverse echo of Eliot's *The Waste Land*, Plath's "Ariel" shows the validity of shoring fragments against ruin. Here, her act of fragmenting saves her. She has known enough to take action, she has finally overcome Mrs. Willard's curse that she recounts in *The Bell Jar*, and she has herself become the arrow, complete with its vindicating speed and straightness, rather than remaining in the suitable womanly space, the place from which the (male) arrow shoots off.

And why should she not? Isn't this the vision of a woman of enormous ambition? Where in her thirty years had Plath ever settled for less than a superior rating, a first prize, even a husband to beat out all former suitors? Why should she not aim for that complete transcendence as she becomes a part of the natural world, losing herself as she looses herself in the cauldron of morning? Reaching that kind of nirvana left no room for mourning.

"Ariel" also serves as a culmination for another set of themes Plath had worked with earlier, when she was first learning about Robert Graves' particularly feminized mythology. In 1958 she had written an intricate syllabic poem about a run-away horse named Sam; the elegant long lines of "Whiteness I Remember"[30] might appear very different from the terse shape of "Ariel" but the description of the rider's consummate power, her union with the powerful – and mythic – horse, foreshadows what Plath accomplishes in the later poem. "Whiteness I Remember" is one of the poet's first attempts to evoke the persona's sheer fright; it is a kind of ur-text for "Ariel," where the persona no longer fears either riding or going past the physicality of riding into some new metaphysical region. In the 1962 poem, the rider is in control throughout the ride because the human being fuses with the animal, and begins to understand the source of its power. There is another similarity between these two poems, and that is the speed at which Plath wrote them; she comments in her journal that "Whiteness" is a "book poem," but that she should have taken longer to write it. In her words, "I write my good poems too fast...."[31] By 1962, she had learned not to question the way poems came.

As has been mentioned, Sandra Gilbert links the voice of many of Plath's late poems with the women's voices in *The Waves* (in connection with Plath's imagery of ascent she describes Rhoda's "ascending" images, for example, and that character's notion of becoming "incandescent"), but she finds a more significant correspondence between Plath's work and the late poems of Yeats, particularly his "To Dorothy Wellesley." There he writes of Wellesley being no "common" woman but rather one awaiting visitation of the "Proud Furies each with her torch on high." Gilbert also cites Yeats' poem "He and She" as a possible source for Plath's repeated phrase "I am I," quoting the lines

> She sings as the moon sings:
> "I am I, am I;
> The greater grows my light
> The further that I fly."[32]

The finishing lines of that sexain – "All creation shivers/ With that sweet cry" – are in the poet-persona's voice rather than the

woman's. The woman artist, so intent on extending her reach as she
confirms her self identity, prompts the imagery of both ascent and
light, and suggests some possible reinscription on Plath's part in her
poem "Fever 103°."

A pair poem to the riddle of mystery that, in its fragmentation,
"Ariel" has been, in the blunt "Fever 103°'" Plath creates a gloss on
the notion of "dirty girl," the sexual and sexualizing naughty woman
who will not stay decorously in her place. But rather than accept the
barbs of jealous (and still male-dominated) society, the persona here
declares her purity. Whether she is strangled like Isadora Duncan (or
like Plath in the scene Paul Alexander recounts on the Spanish hill-
side during her honeymoon),[33] or killed by radiation, or wrung
completely out of life by the raging fevers her body was subject to
during this torturous and torturing autumn, the persona is so intent
on her purpose and her direction that she succeeds. Wryly, she asks
her tormentor, "Does not my heat astound you. And my light./ All
by myself I am a huge camellia/ Glowing and coming and going,
flush on flush."[34] Sexual innuendoes aside, the persona insists, All by
myself. *All by myself.* This combustible being, willing herself to rise in
order to escape the dross of life, the boorishness of some parts of
British life in particular, the crass weight that some human beings
pile on to the fragile spirit, finally sings out in the triumph she has
been working toward: "I/ Am a pure acetylene/ Virgin" and, as
such, unattended and surprisingly cavalier about who or what is no
longer necessary in her existence, the woman persona overcomes all
odds. Amazingly, she rises – and "To Paradise."

Suitably, as the last stage in her metaphoric lift-off, she sees her
"selves dissolving" and names them "old whore petticoats." The
social forms disregarded, the petticoats, slips, and modest under-
garments trashed, the entirely pure woman, alone, recognizes that
the way she has whored her path through life has been to accept
roles she did not ever want, only because society coerced her.
Knowing herself, whether she follows that injunction from Emerson
or from Confucius, has enabled the pure persona to reach her vision
of Paradise. In that place she is reunited with the personae of those
sister poems, "Lady Lazarus" and "Ariel." And these women
protagonists now have no use for anything that remains of their
earlier lives.

As this persona says clearly, in a voice that now cannot be mis-
taken, "I am too pure for you or anyone." It is, truly, the Plath voice.

11

Getting Rid of Daddy

The triumphant woman is, of course, also the murderer of the "Daddy" persona, whoever (or how many whoevers) that figure is interpreted to represent. In her creation of her widely based poetic mythology, Plath anthropomorphized the powerful white male who has lied to her, betrayed her, spent her money, and/or abandoned her – all the while expecting her to perform the household tasks, however menial; a variety of sexual services; and the bearing of, and caring for, his children. She did not have to use her imagination to create this persona. As she wrote to her beloved college roommate Marty a month before her suicide,

> I have been so utterly *flattened* by having to be a businesswoman, farmer – harvesting seventy apple trees, stringing all my onions, digging and scrubbing all my potatoes, extracting and bottling my honey, etc. – mother, writer *and* all-round desperado that I'd give anything [to be alone]. I feel like a very efficient tool or weapon, used and in demand from moment to moment by the babes... Since he's [Hughes] never paid a bill or figured income tax or mowed the lawn, etc., he's no notion of what it takes...[1]

Her long years of correspondence with Marcia Brown give credibility to her honesty here. In 1956 when she wrote her former roommate that she had become involved with Hughes, she did not try to romanticize him but rather told her confidante that he lived in a "condemned slum" and had no money. After they were married and living in Cambridge, she complained about England's "grim" winters ("Nothing ever gets dry or clean" and called herself "a shivering housefrau waging a day to day battle against cold and dirt"). Reminiscing about the luxuries of Smith College, she remarked, "I have lived in the most unlikely dumps and on so little it often stuns me."[2]

In the January 2, 1963, letter quoted above, Plath told Marty that she had lost twenty pounds, run 103° fevers, and "almost died of the flu this summer."[3] The day before, on New Year's Day, her London physician Dr Horder had ordered a chest X-ray for her, fearing tuberculosis.

Plath could probably have stood much of the physical work at Court Green, but the fact that she was ill made those tasks seem insurmountable. Her refrain in all her letters – to Ann Davidow, another close college friend, and to a more recent acquaintance, Ruth Fainlight – is that her weariness suffuses her life; it is as if she is trying to find a reason for her illness in her state of utter fatigue.

What she writes to Marty on February 4, 1963, however, not a week before her suicide, expresses the emotional heart of her physical fatigue. "Everything has blown and bubbled and warped and split," she begins, but her imagery is used less to complain than to explain: "I am in limbo between the old world and the very uncertain and rather grim new."[4] Part of her unhappiness, she tells Marty, is that she is "cut off from my dearest friends and relatives." She continues,

> I long to have somebody really play with and love the babies – it is still a fantastic shock to me that they are so beautiful and dear and will have, in effect, no father. Ted comes once a week like a kind of apocalyptic Santa Claus and when I'm in the country I guess half years and years will go by without him seeing them at all.[5]

This letter, one view of Plath in extremis, is controlled and orderly. Is this the true tone of her acceptance of her new life, one that would lull some observers to contend that Plath could not have killed herself; even during the bleak winter of 1963, even living a lonely and terribly burdened life, some friends said, she was filled with light, with purpose, with plans?[6] We have seen that her metaphoric representation of her emotions, within her late poems, is more extravagant, more highly colored, more distanced in some ways – to use Van Dyne's word, more "performative." We know full well that we cannot read the artful poem as simple autobiography, particularly Plath's late and most artful poems. But the last years of that most significant resource, her journal, in which she wrote until very near the end of her existence, is no longer available. When the severely edited journals from Plath's earlier years were published in the US (no edition has ever appeared in England), the book was prefaced with comments by Hughes; in that "Foreword" he gave the only explanation known for the disappearance of the journal entries which Plath wrote during the last three years of her life: "Two more notebooks survived for a while, maroon-backed ledgers like the '57–'59 volume, and continued the record from late '59 [about the time of their arriving in England to stay] to within three days of her death. The last of these contained entries for several months, and I destroyed it because I did not want her children to have to read it (in those days I regarded forgetfulness as an essential part of survival). The other disappeared."[7]

Most critics have used Plath's published journals as a reasonably accurate expression of her darker feelings, and have set those entries against her more consistently cheerful letters "home" to Aurelia and to her brother, Warren. The poems from all but the last three years of her life, then, benefit by being contextualized between these very different expressions of mood.

Because the reader does not have access to Plath's late journals, a few (unpublished) excerpts from her letters to her mother, to whom she usually presented a composed facade, show the depth of her anger during the autumn of her husband's betrayal, the period of time when she was coming to understand that she had, in fact, lost Hughes – that the children would "have, in effect, no father."

Written on September 23, 1962, in what appears in *Letters Home* to be a happy recounting of her vacation in Ireland, in the uncut version of the letter Plath tells the real story, that Hughes left her alone in Ireland to come home with the heavy baggage, "and when I returned I found a telegram from London saying he might be back in a week or two. I realize every week the elaborate tissue of lies he had invented while I thought I was leading a real true life."[8] The next day she continues her lament to Aurelia: she has discovered that he was also "spending, I now find on checking our bank statements, checks he never entered in the book in addition to the large sum listed, plus his insistence on coming home about once a week and making life utter hell and destroying my work plus living off my novel grant...He is not only infantile, but dangerously destructive, and I feel both the children and I need protection from him, for now and forever."[9]

Both her September 23 and 24 letters include a sorry tale of Hughes's supposedly watching the baby, and telling Sylvia that he had strapped Nick in his pram. But when the baby fell out and Plath ran down to rescue him after hearing his terrible scream, it was not his father but the housemaid who was picking him up from the concrete floor. The earlier letter continues, "He [Ted] tells me now he never had the courage to say he did not want children. He does like Frieda, she flatters his vanity, as this woman he is living with has had so many abortions she can't have children. I think he would try to get Frieda from me. He has been trying to convince Dr Webb I am 'unstable.'"[10] The Sept. 24 letter goes on at some length, as Plath vents her real anger: "I am furious. I threw everything of mine into our life without question, all my earnings, and now he is well-off...He is a vampire on my life, killing and destroying all."[11] Two days later she writes that she thinks Ted is "possessed," but she knows he is "utterly gutless. Lies, lies, lies."[12]

By October 9, she has faced the fact that divorce is more likely than separation: "Ted is glad for a divorce, but I have to go to court, which I dread. The foulness I have lived, his wanting to kill all I have lived for six years by saying he was just waiting for a chance to get out, that he was bored and stifled by me, a hag in a world of beautiful women...I have been so shamed and degraded it has almost killed me."[13]

The root of her shame lies in her own misjudgment of her colossus-like husband, the man who had seemed so perfect and yet was capable of using her and their resources, lying to her, even hating her. "I've had shock after shock, as Ted has fed me the truth, with leer after leer. The husband [Wevill] chased him with a knife, then tried to commit suicide...Ted just gloats...laughs at me, insults me, says my luck is over."[14] In her October 16 letter she admits that Ted and Assia "have already wistfully started wondering why I didn't commit suicide, since I did before! Ted has said how convenient it would be if I were dead, then he could sell the house and take the children whom he likes. It is me he does not like."[15]

It is amazing that Aurelia Plath would remain in the States when her daughter is clearly being threatened and undermined psychologically. Perhaps Sylvia knew her mother well enough to realize she would distance this pitiful cry for help, for on October 18, she wrote Warren with essentially the same story – but this time she included Olwyn as one of the participants: "they would descend, the charming Olwyn in advance, and literally try to do me in. The most sordid thing is Ted's playing on my nervous breakdown, and telling me how convenient it would be if I were dead...He'll just have to learn he can't kill what he's through with, namely me and the babies."[16]

If Plath is finally able to write revealingly to her family, one can only imagine the kinds of narratives she was confiding to her journal. Lacking that material, we can read what she had written there four years earlier when she feared that Hughes was involved with a Massachusetts coed: "No, I won't jump out of a window or drive Warren's car into a tree, or fill the garage at home with carbon monoxide and save expense, or slit my wrists and lie in the bath. I am disabused of all faith and see too clearly. I can teach, and will write and write well."[17] Her anger then, and in the autumn of 1962, is the kind of response a strong woman would have.

By late December and early January of 1963, however, she wrote pitifully to Olive Higgins Prouty and to the Huwses, that "the desperate mother in me...is so saddened at losing the children a father."[18] Here, the voice is similar to that of the just-married Plath of her 1957 journal entries, in which she describes the way "he sets the sea of my life steady, flooding it with the deep rich color of his mind and his love and constant amaze at his perfect being...yang to ying."[19]

The difference between Plath's anger toward Hughes during the fall of 1962, when she is writing most of her strong women poems, and what seems to be her lamenting nostalgia for their marriage here in 1963 is frightening. It is as if she has forgotten her very real physical fear of him,[20] fear that had, whether or not consciously, kept her from ever rousing him to complete anger.[21] Even as she told her mother in September that she was afraid of him, she brainwashed herself past those fears. All she can remember now, in his absence, is his perfection. Given these January reactions, perhaps there is credibility to Hughes's claim in a letter to Aurelia after Plath's suicide that they were going to go away together on the week of her death, working toward reconciliation. He wrote Mrs. Plath in that March 15, 1963, letter, about "madness" on both their parts, saying that Sylvia's "proud hostility and hatred" stood in her way of forgetting about the divorce, "the one thing in this world she did not want."[22]

Steven Gould Axelrod describes what he calls Plath's "knot" of emotional involvement with Hughes, analyzing his attraction for her in Freudian terms: "Plath attempted to unite with a man who possessed both the controlling imperatives of her mother and the fearsomeness of her father." Above all, Hughes was valuable to her because he, too, was a writer, and she saw his success as a route to her own. As Axelrod continues, "she associated authorship with both paternal privilege and maternal creativity."[23] And because she fused areas which were usually kept separate, her work and her marriage, determining her motives is difficult.

The sense of Plath doubling herself, undermined by her almost constant self doubt, seems clear to Axelrod (he points specifically to her early sexual jealousy of Hughes, which might – or might not – have been imaginary). "It was less a man that she attempted to marry, less the voice and flesh of the other, than her own sense of herself as a poet, her own egotism compromised by low self-esteem ... Dr Beuscher's questions that Plath tried so long to evade return to haunt us as they must have haunted her: 'Would you have the guts to admit you'd made a wrong choice?' and 'Does Ted want you to get better?'" Axelrod suggests that in being married to Hughes, Plath was more or less "married to her sickness, and just as her anger reflects the degree to which the marriage did not meet her needs, her repression of the anger reflects the even greater degree to which she was unwilling and afraid to change."[24]

Compromising her judgment by staying in her marriage, and – perhaps worse – by pretending it was healthy, Plath at the end of the six years of being Mrs. Ted Hughes was already thoroughly angry with her spouse (and with herself). For *him* to leave *her* was a culminating insult to those six long years of her investing everything she had, emotionally and materially, into their partnership. Within her poetry of the previous year, however, Plath is systematically if unconsciously beginning to question her love for Hughes; this questioning starts before the Wevills come to stay the weekend in Court Green. In a poem as innocuous as "An Appearance," she asks "Is this love then, this red material?"[25] When in "Little Fugue" she describes the vile behavior of a father figure (whose voice, "Black and leafy, as in my childhood, [is]/ A yew hedge of orders, /Gothic and barbarous, pure German"), she notes that – in early April, 1962 – "Now similar clouds/ Are spreading their vacuous sheets." The numbed and fearful woman persona can do little but wait and, hopefully, "survive ... Arranging my morning. These are my fingers, this my baby."[26] "Crossing the Water" portrays that same repressed woman and her lover, described as "cut-paper people ... the spirit of blackness [is] in us."[27]

What has become a narrative of a disintegrating relationship continues through the intermediary poem "Pheasant," which opens "You said you would kill it this morning," a memory that quickly evokes the wife's plea, "Do not kill it."[28] Struggle between the husband and wife marks each of these poems, and comes to more overt (but still disguised) expression in the poem Plath wrote April 19, 1962 – the surprisingly rich "Elm." Embedded within that work is the rumbling of "dissatisfactions," the threat of madness. The poem's core is the description, "Love is a shadow./ How you lie and cry after it/ Listen: these are its hooves: it has gone off, like a horse." The persona, "terrified" by her fears, says, with apparent exhaustion, "I am incapable of more knowledge."[29]

Most critical explication of Plath's poems of suspicion begins with accounts of Hughes's affair with Assia. "Event," written the day the Wevills left after their weekend at Court Green, May 21, 1962, was originally titled "Quarrel," but here the speaker also identifies the problem as being less the spouse's lust for another woman than "A groove of old faults, deep and bitter."[30] Dismembered by their anger, however, the couple can only "touch like cripples." When the husband does reach out to his wife, his touch "burns and sickens." (Hughes comments to the Merwins about his separation from Plath and about his inability to write during the last months they were together, although as he writes, "Marriage wasn't entirely to blame... there were other troubles, which may now be over. Anyway, I'm finding it much easier to write.")[31]

More pertinent to the happenings of the affair are Plath's July poems, "The Other" and "Words heard, by accident, over the phone." When these poems are followed with the enigmatic "Poppies in July," which speaks of undisclosed pain, and "Burning the Letters," which describes Plath's exorcism of burning Hughes's writing, the narrative is running as swiftly and predictably as a detective fiction.

To read autobiographically, as we have suggested, is in many cases to miss the artistry Plath demands of her writing, and often achieves in it. The pairing of "Event," an almost perfect set of tercets which culminates in the single-line concluding stanza, with a poem Hughes did not choose to include in *Ariel* – "The Rabbit Catcher" – is to see how deft her sense of structure was. "Event" is grounded by the persona's acceptance that what occurs between the couple can be said only by "Intolerable vowels." The distance cannot, yet, be expressed. A poem ironically about speechlessness, "Event" grinds into the reader's consciousness the icy separation of physical distrust: "Love cannot come here."[32] The image of a small maggot represents a small soul, and the persona's disgust at it keeps her from accepting any sexual closeness.

Enigmatic in a finished version, "Event" in draft was poignantly clear. Included in the early version are a number of tellingly direct lines: "I do not believe in anything./ I walk with an absence." Later the persona says, tersely, "I am iron, resolved,/ my limbs heavy."[33] "Event" also gains from being read with "The Rabbit Catcher," a poem which also begins with speechlessness, "the absence of shrieks," but here the silence results from violence: "The wind gagging my mouth...Tearing off my voice..."[34] Malignity, simmering paths, a trek in the fields in search of what the snares have caught: this is the poem's narrative. Reluctant to go, and most assuredly reluctant to find the rabbits, she is aware only of "a hole in the hot day, a vacancy."

Yet for the male partner who waits to kill those animals, "those little deaths...excited him." The last stanza comes into the kind of direct speech that marks so many of Plath's late poems, as she moves from the hunting story to focus on her marriage, announcing "we, too, had a relationship." As attention shifts from the trapped rabbits to the couple's love, the ending lines chart the woman's discomfort. In the midst of "Pegs too deep to uproot," the "constriction" of their competing minds will kill her.

In finished form, "The Rabbit Catcher" seems inevitably neat; clearly the poem has been heading for this revelation about marriage all along. But worksheets for the poem show how many different themes Plath was trying to express from the beginning; parts of those worksheets end up appearing in her later poem, "Getting There." Stretches of long-lined stanzas describe the snares (as "Zeroes, shutting on silence') and especially "the hands of the man behind them/ And his mind, loving its alley of looped wires.../ Fashioning the doors of silence, strong, ingenious." In some of the discarded lines, the man's hands are wringing throats or muffling "me" like gloves. Another segment describes that "me" persona, moving as if "on wires,/ A flat personage in the gorse/ Dragged and chastised..."[35] If the finished poem seems to segue unexpectedly to the relationship, in draft Plath was working through the issues of a troubled marriage in many more parts of the poem.

Jacqueline Rose devotes much of a chapter in *The Haunting of Sylvia Plath* to this poem, discussing it as an example of Plath's ability to masculinize her feelings, and to value that gendering. The bedrock of the best Plath poems, according to Rose, is her ability to mix "Fantasy and identity (linguistic and sexual)" so that the reader comes away acknowledging that such states as "victimisation and transcendence, accusation and apotheosis are the reverse sides of the same coin" and the "twin poles of reading" many Plath poems.[36] Rose also links "The Rabbit Catcher" with "Event," and goes on to say that "There is a sense in which the poems in *Ariel* have to be read in relationship to each other – not only in terms of the order Plath proposed for her own collection (which would put 'The Rabbit Catcher' back into *Ariel*, where it belongs), but also in the sense of the way she wrote them... the division between poems is almost arbitrary."[37]

Where Plath goes after the suggestiveness of "Event" and "The Rabbit Catcher" is into the more explicit, if guarded, "Apprehensions." Written May 25, this poem began as a series of outspoken images: the persona admits that she will have to carve out a new life for herself, "now I am deserted." Amid the bloody and "sour" imagery, she states in draft that she is fearful of "scorching to death from you," perhaps because "Steel and flame are my bad angels." The last stanza in the early version has the persona stating calmly, "What happens will happen./ Separations repeat themselves: I am shaken." Yet just a few lines above, she addresses some unidentifiable birds on the wall, asking the person who has deserted her, "Is it you they are waiting for?/ Is it you they mark in their book."[38] Referring to occult methods of knowing, which she seldom does so directly, adds as much interest to the early version of this poem as do her forthright comments about being deserted. In this poem, like "The Rabbit Catcher," Plath's changes from draft to final version disguise what she is feeling, and fearing.

Besides "Apprehensions," she writes several differently focused poems, seemingly oblique to the worry that was eating away at her power to write. The long soliloquy for Percy B. upon his dying, the beautifully poignant "For a Fatherless Son," and the purposefully mysterious "A Birthday Present" lead to the first of her directly spoken autumn poems. In "The Detective" (early titled "The Millstones") Plath vents her anger at the confinement her marriage, and her controlling husband, has forced her to endure. Disintegrating as the female persona has through the years, once she has officially died, "There is no body in the house at all."[39] Vaporized, as Plath wryly explains, the mouth went first, because speaking frankly was forbidden. The breasts went next, though they were needed for nursing the children. The vagina was not mentioned by name by the super-sleuth Holmes and his assistant Watson, but it too had become only "dry wood." Living in the valley of death as she did, she disappeared so easily that no one even thought to call the police: "This is the smell of years burning, here in the kitchen/ These are the deceits, tacked up like family photographs."

Its pair poem is "The Courage of Shutting-Up," and true to Rose's observation, the two poems were written just a day apart. Here the wife takes it upon herself to be quiet (the early title for this poem was "The Courage of Quietness") even as the abusive spouse provokes her. All she can think of, in her restraint, are "the accounts of bastardies./ Bastardies, usages, desertions and doubleness," and the refrain becomes a physical mark, almost as if it is tattooed on to her skin.

To be sure she stays silent, the hunter-husband eventually cuts out her tongue ("The things it has pierced in its time," the persona comments) and hangs it in his library with his other trophies, "the fox heads, the otter heads, the heads of dead rabbits."[40] But he lets her keep her eyes, because he believes she will censor her vision herself.

Plath takes another complex detour in mining her autumn experiences as the betrayed wife; here she works through what becomes a series of five bee poems. Remarkable for their cohesive themes and varied tonal effects, these poems only indirectly rehearse the gender war Plath and Hughes have embarked on. To be a queen bee, and to be served by hundreds of drones, is to reverse the pattern of patriarchal power and controlling sexuality. It is also to draw on Robert Graves's privileging of that insect, her father's profession, her own summer of 1962 experience with keeping bees, and her need to find apt metaphors for the female supremacy over the male. The Hawthorne-like mystery of the "meeting" poem, the explicit anger in others, and the quiet beauty of "Wintering" show the versatility of Plath's art here in the autumn of 1962. Because of the very recent excellent work of Karen Jackson Ford, Susan Van Dyne, Jacqueline Rose, and a number of other critics, I refer the readers of this study to their commentaries.[41]

But the poet soon returns to the theme of the problem that has darkened what feels to have been her entire life, coping with the man in her household who has ruined her idyl – whether that man be her father or her husband. On October 12, 1962, Plath wrote the poem that has immortalized her, and in "Daddy" voiced what were at least six years of frustration. Aurelia Plath sometimes said that her daughter failed – i.e., had no "ego strength."[42] What "Daddy" explains is the way living with a man of formidable, and cruel, ego can wear another person's identity away, like water dripping slowly on rock. Anger less at her husband's affair than at the waste of her own self – that is the theme of "Daddy" as Plath carves out her intricate chant of rage.

"Daddy" mixed the sexual with the familial, the physical with the emotional, the father with the husband in a rhythmic swirl of energized language that set form in opposition to content for the utmost in ironic effect. Having learned through some other of her late poems how dynamic the use of repetition (particularly of words not usually repeated) can be, Plath began this poem with the repeated "You do not do, you do not do" and thereby gave her persona control of the men's actions. Hearing a command like this, no one argues, especially when the male persona or personae seem to be guilty as sin. Not that the persona has not been complicit – she too has "a love of the rack and the screw"[43] – but that she has gotten more control than even she had bargained for.

That she wrote the poem the day after she finished "The Applicant" makes a kind of apt poetic sense: "Daddy" is the answer to the obsequious, fawning voice that wants a job, that wants to be married. In this poem the speaker turns away, as rudely as possible, from the powerful male force that had dominated her life. Now it is she who gives commands. Now it is she who plans the way life is going to go, even down to making the problem people in that life disappear. Yet the female persona involves her community in enacting her justice; the villagers gather around her, and it may be the villagers who actually kill the father-husband persona: the stake in his "fat black heart" appears, the persona does not strike him, and the villagers then celebrate his impaling by "dancing and stamping on" him. After all, as the poundingly ironic voice has narrated, even if she killed him, it was only returning an eye for an eye. He had, in one guise or another, "bit [her] pretty red heart in two."[44]

Plath makes the transfer from father to husband in the last four stanzas of the poem. Pulled from the sack of her failed death, the persona, "stuck [me] together with glue," finds "a model of you,/ A man in black with a Meinkampf look."[45] Wearing his predictable black, the clothing Hughes had adopted as part of his poet-facade, her spouse also assumes the haughty and brusque and even fear-inspiring control that mimicked Otto Plath's manner. The literal reason for the persona's insistence on the powerful male being German – Otto's ethnicity – is less important than the Germanic privileging of the male, the genetic, the anything-but-the-non-Germanic – or, worse, the feminine (the "gypsy," the Jew, the sane). By naming her persona Jew and gypsy, Plath locates her in the most contemptible categories, but also the most intellectualized and the most sensitive. For this persona to become the avenging angel, the killer, is an unimaginable reversal of power: that is the scaffolding on which "Daddy" builds.

Her revenge through naming culminates in her calling the husband "vampire." Drinking his wife's blood as an analogy for using her money, her energy, her love, her own poetic talents dominates the last stanzas, and it is in the penultimate verse that spouse becomes daddy. Shape-shifting is easy for vampires, and even as he drank her blood – for the year, or for seven years – this vampire "who said he was you" was only living on what she could give him. When all her resources were exhausted, he would move on to another host. It is because the husband has never really existed as a person that the persona addresses the poem, throughout, to "Daddy." In naming her antagonist and her confidant as her parent, she extinguishes the husband's power entirely: he has been, vampire-like, fantasy.

But the guilt the child has accepted for the past two decades, since the time of the actual parent's death, runs alongside her anger: "If I've killed one man, I've killed two." That, she recognizes at the close of her vituperation – which is also her psychological coming through to the validity of her self, is what finally getting rid of her father will allow her to put to rest. No longer haunted by the thought that she had something crucial to do with Otto Plath's dying, now the empowered persona will know that she was responsible for his demise, in one way or another. Fittingly, "The Beekeeper's Daughter" has learned how to empower herself as poet in the process of crafting the bee poems. It could well be more literal than ironic that the tools Otto Plath had himself formed, his authoritative comments about bees, were, finally, his own undoing. And the undoing of his double, that vampire husband, as well.

Although it can be read rationally, "Daddy" was intended to strike the reader as illogical, as a frenzy (which it is, rhythmically). In some ways, it continues the movement of Plath's August poem of ritualized anger, "Burning the Letters." There at the end of the ceremony, as the wife persona – wearing a modest "housedress" as emblem of her passive and powerless role – explains that she has burned his cardboard carton of papers, "Holding in its hate," she gives a similar explanation of the righteousness of her anger: "And I am no criminal. I am killing a photograph./...As it blackens, I grow tall.// And I am not subtle."[46]

The empowerment the persona allows herself to have as a result of her ritual is the foregrounded text of "Daddy," but that later poem plays ironically with her last line here, agreeing with the male speaker that she is not, probably, "subtle." What is most subtle about "Daddy" is that it nowhere refers to the husband's act of betraying her, of taking another lover. By not naming his powerful action, the poem reduces him to an insignificant part of the tale, little more than the father's clone. The true narrative is the wife's vengeance.

A last spit of rage fuels Plath's October 17 poem, "The Jailer." As the title indicates, the husband has now assumed full responsibility for the role of controlling, manipulative man. The sexualization of the male figure in "Daddy" is completed here, in his role as rapist, abuser, liar, and murderer – as well as captor. His sexual torture of the persona leads to her announcing, sadly, "I am myself. That is not enough."[47] (In draft, this refrain line occurs throughout the work.) His amnesiac stance – that he does not remember loving her or wanting to marry her – offends her, even as his evasion makes her into a criminal. She counts the various ways she can die: "Hung, starved, burned, hooked." These are murders, not suicides, and they approximate what her body in its anxious terror has been doing – running high fevers, losing weight.

In the manuscripts of the poem, there is another actor in the drama – the mother-in-law. As the persona curses him with impotence, she completes her fantasy by including his mother in the equation: "I imagine him/ Distant and impotent as thunder/ Called away by a letter or a sick mother/ In whose shadow I have eaten my ghost ration." The complicit mother (who might also appear in "Medusa," as the figure who watches the lovers have sex) adds to her isolation; as she has written early in the poem, though he has seemed to be a part of their family ('He is bringing me emptiness in a silver tureen'), he has always remained a part of his own. To please that unit, the persona herself has been "Chained to a plank of impossible [stupid] duties/ My lungs in rags!" She, in turn, in an unused line from "Burning the Letters," has written accurately, "there was nobody for me to know or go to."[48]

It comes as no surprise when the persona says calmly, "I wish him dead or away." Yet even as she makes the wish, and hopes for its power to affect change in her dim life, she realizes how impossible such a change – "That being free" – is. At a loss as to how this story will end – because in "The Jailer" the persona deals directly with the betraying husband, and that story has not yet ended – the poet falls back into the use of sometimes effective repetition. Taking the "I said I do, I do" line from the heart of "Daddy," Plath writes an accurate, though less effective, ending for "The Jailer": "what would he/ Do, do, do without me?" The crux of Hughes's leaving her was not only that he betrayed her love; he also usurped what she had assumed was her equal power in the relationship. She was the partner who had done what looked to her to be most of the work, most of the accomplishing; she was the "do-er" of the two. As she had written in a draft of "The Jailer," "I am necessary...what would he be, without me, without me?"[49]

12

Sylvia Plath, The Poet and her Writing Life

The temptation to do little but re-create Plath's biography through readings of her work – and, implicitly, to try to unearth the complex reasons for her tragic suicide – overtakes the most focused reader. What happens as one studies Plath's *oeuvre* is that the vivid humanness of her narrated experience becomes overpowering. Too often, the mere establishment of intellectual boundaries, some means of separating the work from what appears to be the story told in it, proves ineffectual. For Sylvia Plath to be valued as the magisterial poet she was, readers must accept a number of her writerly principles as guides for their absorption of her work.

After years of apprenticing herself to writers and critics she considered important, including her husband Ted Hughes, Plath had arrived at a tranquil if complex prolegomenon for writing at her best. During the last year and a half of her writing, she knew what she was trying to achieve, and *The Bell Jar* and "Three Women" were starting points for that accomplishment. The late poems, and sporadic single poems written from 1959 through the end of her work as well, proved to her that she could achieve the miraculous – art that both lived on its own terms, and as demandingly skillful work, and yet spoke for some common, and real, need within people's consciousness.

In reviews through the late 1950s and 1960s, Plath had written about the responsibility of the modern poet, which she saw as creating new worlds from old. The poet might draw from arenas of existing myth but then be obligated to "transform the material . . . make it freshly his own and ours."[1] She is explicit about the way the poet should work: the mythic material must appear to be organic to the new poems, not just added in or – worse – "pointed at, rather than realized in the poems" shape and texture." The poet will probably use metaphor to achieve all this. If so, he must keep in mind that "The metaphor-moral is intrinsic to the poem, working back and forth on itself, not expressed prosaically at the close, like the moral in a fable."[2]

One of her fullest statements of what the American poem in 1963 might be occurs just a few weeks before her death, when she records the BBC program that has as its nucleus *The New American Poets*, Donald Hall's anthology of contemporary poetry (in which Plath did not appear). While Ted Hughes makes clear that he looks askance on the turmoil of the new in the United States poetry scene, in one letter to W. S. Merwin warning him to stay clear of the influence of William Carlos Williams,[3] Plath was always enthusiastic about poetry in the States. She began the January, 1963, broadcast by asking, "Is it a coincidence that so many American poets should all at once cast off the old, stiff suits of early styles? – Lowell, Simpson, Adrienne Rich, Anthony Hecht, W. S. Merwin..." Plath calls the new mode "this new surrealism...fullblown if slightly manic" and attributes some of its presence to the fact that many of the poets Hall includes are also translators of such world poets as Pasternak, Montale, Neruda, and Trakl. Not that there is anything imitative about the United States poems; the new voice is "uniquely American, that's where it lives."[4]

Plath then warns about the employment of this "freer sort of poetry" when there is no intense feeling, or "when the feeling is lacking or forced or suspect": then, she says by discussing the work of William Stafford, Howard Nemerov, Reed Whittemore (whose poems she finds "over exposed") and Richard Wilbur ("curiously bloodless"), "the poem fizzles like a wet squib."

It is as if she is playing critic to her own late writing, some of the best poems of which she called "light verse" to underplay their fantastic rhythmic effects and weird rhymes. She takes a line from Galway Kinnell's poem, "Flower Herding on Mount Monadnock," to show "what's been happening in a lot of American poetry." The line reads, "And the dimension of depth seizes everything."

Her only negative criticism is that Donald Hall has omitted the work of Anne Sexton, particularly her writing in "her remarkable second book *All My Pretty Ones*." Plath correctly ties Sexton's work to that of W. D. Snodgrass, who is included in the anthology, though in comparison to Sexton, Plath calls Snodgrass's seemingly personal poems in *Heart's Needle* "watercolors...The voice is quiet, colloquial, laconic, wry. As often as not, it's the voice of the solilpsist," and she quotes from Snodgrass, "I myself am hell; Nobody's here." By emphasizing the work of the poets who would come to be called "confessional," Plath draws the listener back to the newness of what she terms the "inwardness of these images, their plummeting subjectivity." Using a dramatic image, she explores the way the best of these poems work as they give the reader "the uncanny faculty of melting through the leaves of the wallpaper through the dark looking glass into a world one can only call surrealistic and irrational. The analyst's couch has played its role here, I think – that important and purgatorial bit of American literary furniture." What such poems achieve in their technique of using "startlements of free association" is, Plath comments, the "claustrophobic flow of nightmare."

Linking poems she finds interesting with film, Plath expands on the way "the juxtaposing of images, without editorializing" provides "images [that] jostle and touch. The spark that springs – horror, tenderness, whatever – is the response of the viewer. I say viewer, because so much of this poetry is visual."

She discusses work by Robert Bly, James Merrill and James Wright to show how it is possible for the poem to achieve "this *in*-feeling, this identification with light, treees, water, *things* – this is another aspect of the new poetry... There's no sure objective ground." As the reader moves from the documentary effect, particularly in Wright, he or she might find that the works "drift into something at once subconscious and archetypal."

Robert Lowell's poetry, and his shift from early ("as fine and wild and rich and still as the animal room at the Vatican") to later modes (poems which are "walking the tight rope of the psyche naked"), represents all dimensions of this change, what Plath calls the "new spirit... Whatever it is, has been happening, like breathing, quietly and spontaneously among individual poets for some while now.

Plath was more than a competent critic of the new. Not only had she just written enough of these new style and very American poems for her own major book, but two years before, during the winter and spring of 1961, she had edited a comprehensive collection of recent American poetry for the British journal, *Critical Quarterly*. Published in the autumn of 1961 as a booklet, in an edition of 10,000 copies, *American Poetry Now* included the work of nearly all the poets she singled out for mention in her broadcast, as well as a substantial number of poems by writers Donald Hall had excluded.[5] The two poems by her Boston friend Anne Sexton, "Kind Sir: These Woods" and "Some Foreign Letters" show the quieter side of that flamboyant poet, whose classically psychological explorations had first won Plath to see what was possible in poetry while the women were students in Robert Lowell's poetry seminar at Boston University. In class, Sexton had read for discussion her remarkable poems

"You, Dr. Martin" and the sequence poem, "The Double Image" (as well as her poignant prose narrative "A Story for Rose"). Plath drew on Sexton's confidently voiced poetry for inspiration – and many readers have found reason to think that, had Sexton not sent Plath a copy of her first book, *To Bedlam and Part Way Back*, Plath might never have grown into the style of her late poems.

Sexton also sent Plath her next collection, the one Plath referred to as "her remarkable second book, *All My Pretty Ones*,"[6] on Hughes's birthday, August 17, 1962. (This was the time when the two Hugheses were in London to spend a day and a night with Mrs Prouty, pretending that their marriage was intact so as not to alarm the woman who had been Plath's mentor for more than a decade. [Mrs Prouty was not taken in.] It was on his birthday that Hughes bought for Sylvia, and signed, a copy of American novelist Joseph Heller's *Catch-22*.) When Plath wrote Sexton to thank her for the second book, she repeated much of what she had written earlier, that Sexton's poems were "terrific" and that the book was "blessedly unliterary," and perhaps most important "womanly in the greatest sense." Plath said flat out that she was "absolutely stunned and delighted" by Sexton's poetry.

Although she included poems by Denise Levertov, Barbara Guest, Adrienne Rich, and Sexton in her small collection, the fact that she did not include work by more women spoke to the actual situation: there were few women publishing poetry in the States – or in England – early in the 1960s.[7] One of the reasons both Sexton and Plath had such immense readership very early in their careers was the hunger of women readers for work that spoke to their experiences and needs. (That their poems also had a raft of male readers goes without saying: what both Sexton and Plath were accomplishing was entirely new, more dramatically done, more seemingly personal than the corresponding personal, confessional poems by Snodgrass, Lowell, and, a bit later, John Berryman.)

Plath's choice of poems by women shows her trying to ferret out the new. Of Levertov's work, Plath used "The Five-Day Rain," a lyric description of laundering clothes in Mexico that turned into a personal lament; of Guest's, a prose-like poem that also lamented the lack of color in the female persona's life; and of Rich's, several that Adrienne evidently sent to Plath which had not yet been published as well as the sexual fantasy "Living in Sin" from her book, *The Diamond Cutters*. Rich's work seems more like the three poems of William Stafford's which Plath uses, in that it is restrained and yet – somewhere – smoldering. The abrupt statement in Rich's "The Evil Eye" that brings the poem into personal focus is "I knew beyond all doubt how dead that couple was" and the same kind of effect builds in her "Moving in Winter" as another couple carries pieces of their life – "collapsed like unplayed cards" – from one space to another. When Stafford speaks in that quiet voice, it is less personal, usually describing events both natural and human.

Of the poets represented in *American Poetry Now*, Robert Creeley speaks for the laconic new, the terse offshoot of the William Carlos Williams school that Hughes warned Merwin about; Edgar Bowers speaks for the traditionally formal. The George Starbuck poem which Plath chooses – this, like the early poem by E. Lucas Myers and the selection by Anthony Hecht, reflecting ties of friendship – works with the Creeley poem in its use of direct, humorous idiom; and that may be what attracted her to the two poems by Nemerov. To reflect her college-age attraction to Richard Wilbur (and her interviewing him for *Mademoiselle*), there is a Wilbur poem but no Eberhart, no Bishop, no Roethke, no Shapiro, no Ignatow, no Bly, no Duncan, no Logan, no Ferlinghetti, no Ginsberg. (Plath noted that she had wanted to use work by Gregory Corso but could not get permission[8] – she was aware of the Beat activity on the Pacific coast.)

Plath's admiration for the poetry of W. S. Merwin colored her selection for the supplement to some extent. Merwin had been Poetry Editor of *The Nation* (to which Plath had subscribed during 1961), and several of the poems she included had been published there; these were so new that they had not yet appeared in collections. But the greatest effect on Plath was that of Merwin's own poems, and in this supplement she chooses three very different works of his. "The Native," a grotesque portrait in an intricate syllabic form, had already appeared in his book, *The Drunk in the Furnace*. Ostensibly about "He and his, unwashed all winter," Merwin's poem also works with the biblical maxim that the meek shall inherit the earth. The shorter poems, one from *The New Yorker* and one from *The Nation*, were more characteristic of his later work. The wry irony of the surreal "Another Year Come" was typical of Merwin's indelibly distinctive voice. The poem begins, "I have nothing new to ask of you,/ Future, heaven of the poor./ I am still wearing the same things." Moving quickly from recognizable irony, the poem moves to the surreality of the poet persona, "Eating the same stone" and realizing that "the hands of the clock still knock without entering." In much of the correspondence from Hughes to Merwin, Hughes often tells him how much he and Sylvia admire his new poems.[9]

As we have seen, Plath's personal journey into understanding the intricacies of the fully voiced modern poem, the work that had to reach beyond the traditional (for how many times could one imitate Eliot, Pound, or even Yeats) and into some as yet unimagined linguistic construction, was torturous. Being able to recognize good and innovative poetry was not the same as being able to write it. Critical as she had been in that earlier review, aware that metaphor could not just be added to a poem, she still needed practice in achieving the effects, and the totality, of poems she intellectually understood that she wanted. And the process was complicated because Plath was a perfectionist. She would not settle for anything that was untrue to her developing voice, or anything that was not pushing the boundaries of art as she had come to know it in the literary world. To be visionary was Plath's aim, but she often found herself buoyed down, rather than up, by the literalness of the ideas and words Hughes assigned to her as subjects.

It may be, in part, this difficulty that led her to continue writing so much fiction. As she had explained in a late 1950s journal entry, "Prose sustains me. I can mess it, mush it, rewrite it, pick it up any time – rhythms are slacker, more variable, it doesn't die so soon."[10] During 1961 and 1962, besides stories, essays, and *The Bell Jar*, there was one novel at least partly finished that was to commemorate the Hugheses' great romance. This is part of the material she burned in the ritual pyre of July, 1962, although she had planned to give it to Ted on his August birthday. And there was evidently a third novel being written during the fantastically prolific autumn, one she described to Mrs Prouty in November of 1962 as the exposé of a man who was all pretense (called *Double Exposure*). That novel has, like her journals from the British years, disappeared.[11]

In one of her BBC essays in 1962, in the midst of her writing both prose and poetry, Plath described the distinction between the genres. Beginning with what was becoming her easy broadcast commentary voice, Plath announced, "How I envy the novelist!" The gist of this essay which is almost a prose poem itself is that the novelist has room, space, to give the details of life (represented here by a toothbrush) full accommodation – and, therefore, life. As she often does, Plath begins with a narrative: "I imagine him – better say her, for it is the women I look to for a parallel – I imagine her, then, pruning a rosebush with a large pair of shears, adjusting her spectacles, shuffling about among the teacups, humming, arranging ashtrays or babies, absorbing a slant of light, a fresh eye to the weather and piercing, with a kind of modest, beautiful X-ray vision, the psychic interiors of her neighbors – her neighbors on trains, in the dentist's waiting room, in the corner teashop. To her, this fortunate one, what is there that *isn't* relevant!"[12] In contrast to the inclusiveness of prose, the poem – what she describes as "the smallish, unofficial garden-variety poem" – takes "about a minute...a door opens, a door shuts," and in between there is the glimpse of the subject's heart, which the poem must record.

Quoting Ezra Pound's "In a Station of the Metro," Plath illustrates her premise, that "a poem is concentrated, a closed fist" and that it contrasts vividly with the novel, which is "relaxed and expansive, an open hand: it has roads, detours, destinations; a heart line, a head line; morals and money come into it." She closes her beautifully phrased piece with the comment that, whereas of course the novel has a shape and must be exclusionary to some extent, the door of the poem, still in contrast, shuts with "manic, unanswerable finality." Her comments foreshadow what will be the process of writing many of her autumn poems, when her earlier worries about how fast she writes the good poems have been stilled by the remarkable repetition – morning after morning – of her ability to achieve effects she had not even dreamed of.

There is some sense in which the fact that Hughes published a collection of her short stories and essays, with his long prefatory introduction, has been limiting. He indicates that Plath's ambition to write short stories for both *The New Yorker* and *The Ladies' Home Journal* baffles him; the tone of his essay about her fiction writing suggests that he is also baffled by her even wanting to write prose.[13] But he does not give enough credence to the fact that Plath's continuing model for prose was the fiction of Virginia Woolf, that most poetic of modernists. (As she had written in her journal several years earlier, "What is my voice? Woolfish, alas, but tough.")[14] For Plath, as for Woolf, there was little difference between a prose paragraph or a long-lined poem stanza. The integrity of the work's rhythm remained the determining principle for organization.

Limited as the writer's words about the act of writing are, the reader must demand Plath's words rather than be guided by interpretations about her work set forth by her then-estranged spouse, interpretations that at times tend to obscure some of her themes. For example, in a 1995 essay, Hughes considers several of the slight poems this text has read – "Crossing the Water" and "Pheasant." He too sees them as transitional poems, leading to the powerful "Elm" which is the focus of his interest. Yet as he summarizes the poems, as well as commenting about "Elm," he does not mention the elements that relate to the widening gulf between husband and wife. He reads "Crossing the Water," for instance, as the description of her "being rowed across a lake of dark heaven."[15] His gloss on "Pheasant" is that it "describes a pheasant that Sylvia Plath herself flushed from the narcissi...the actual bird flew up into the actual Elm." Both poems take part, he notes, in an air "charged with the business of rebirth." He concludes his discussion with the sentence, "It is certain that the poet herself saw no particular continuity in this series of poems, as she wrote them."[16]

A central critical issue has become the way Hughes rearranged the manuscript for her *Ariel* collection which Plath had left, complete, at the time of her death. Marjorie Perloff and Steven Axelrod, among other critics, have explained the differences between the book as Plath had organized it (which poems were included, and their preferred order) and the version of *Ariel* which Hughes saw to publication two years after Plath's death, in 1965.[17] Prefaced in the US edition by a somewhat patronizing essay by Robert Lowell,[18] *Ariel* has become the route into Plath's poetry for most of her readers. The gist of the detailed analyses is that Plath left a book that she saw as a positive statement of the ability of the woman writer, the spirit linked to the mystical Ariel of *The Tempest*. Through her art, coupled with her physical fecundity which gave her children, the woman writer could make a fulfilling, happy statement about life and its gifts. Beginning with "Morning Song," a lyric about her newest child, and ending with the bee sequence, so that the elevating ending of "Wintering" would close the entire book, Plath's *Ariel* would renounce the petty neuroses and self-sabotaging unease of the would-be writer of Plath's journals and *Letters Home*. *Ariel* was to be a consummate statement of the woman artist's potential for greatness – of *Plath's* potential for greatness.

By omitting some of the strongest of her last poems (among these, "The Rabbit Catcher," "Purdah," "The Jailer," "The Detective," "The Courage of Shutting Up," "Amnesiac," "The Other," "Barren Woman," "Magi," – and the more biographical though flawed "A Secret" and "Stopped Dead"), Hughes tailored the collection to make it much less autobiographical. Perhaps these generally angry poems fell outside his criteria for successful art; whatever his rationale, his *Ariel* was quite different from Plath's intended collection.[19]

His substituting her 1963 poems, which were of a decidedly different tone and style, for these omitted 1962 poems of anger, changed the character of the collection considerably. By adding "Edge," "Contusion," "Mirror," "Paralytic," "Totem," "Words," "Little Fugue," and other poems – some of which, like "The Hanging Man," he went back to 1960 to find – to the book, and placing them at the end of the collection, Hughes suggested that Plath's work ran backward, from the point of her suicide. This strategy kept even the bee sequence, which Plath saw as a positive ending to her *Ariel* but which now appeared just past the center of the collection, from being read as positive.

The ironies of here leading readers to read from the suicide back replicates what happened to *The Bell Jar*. Published in the States only years after Plath's suicide, the novel argues against its own positive ending of rebirth: American readers – like readers around the world, given its countless translations – found the novel, and read it, because of the tragic biography of the brilliant poet. There was no way the cure at the end of the novel could maintain its stability as cure, given what people knew about Plath's fate. Perhaps unintentionally, then, the poem collection *Ariel* seemed to parallel her novel.

It might be that his version of *Ariel* would have been even more truncated had not *The Review* published many of the late Plath poems in the October after her death. In a supplement edited by A. Alvarez titled "The Last Poems of Sylvia Plath" appeared "Daddy," "Lady Lazarus," "Fever 103°," "Ariel," "Poppies in October," "Nick and the Candlestick," "Brasilia," "Mary's Song," and "Lesbos," along with Alvarez's edited transcript of his BBC talk on Plath. All the poems published here except "Brasilia," which had not been included in Plath's manuscript, do appear in the Hughes's collection of *Ariel*. As the poems are printed in this first publication, they are peppered with exuberant punctuation,[20] including a great many exclamation marks and ellipses. All that has disappeared by the time of the poems' appearance in *Ariel*, with periods replacing almost every stronger mark (those were probably used to indicate the vehemence with which the poems should be read).

Nearly twenty years after Plath's death appeared the long-promised volume of her collected poems. The sluggishness of this process – which allowed for many years of small, limited editions of Plath's unpublished poems to be printed and sold, often by presses owned by members of the Hughes family – led to some of the misconceptions that have tracked the poet's important work. It was not until the appearance in 1981 of *The Collected Poems of Sylvia Plath*, which won the Pulitzer Prize for Poetry in 1982, an award seldom given posthumously, that people understood what had happened to Plath's original *Ariel* manuscript. As a way of clarifying the differences between the collection she had left on her desk, and the book he had published, Hughes printed the two tables of contents in the appendix of *The Collected Poems*.

For all his critical commentary about Plath's writing, Hughes has said comparatively little about the furious crystallization of her poetic abilities in the late poems.[21] Given that he was presumably the only person who read the last three years of her journals, Hughes had information available to no one else about what Plath *thought* she was achieving in the last months of her writing. Aside from the excited acclamations she wrote to her mother ("I am a writer...I am a genius of a writer; I have it in me. I am writing the best poems of my life; they will make my name..."),[22] the Plath voice is heard – now – only in the work itself.

The reader, then, is forced to turn repeatedly to that work. Having access to the manuscripts of early versions of Plath's poems is inordinately helpful. It is as if Plath the critic speaks through her own revision (and revisioning) process. The way the poem "Ariel" fits into the nexus of angry women poems, particularly "Lady Lazarus" and "Fever 103°," for example, is evident largely through comparison of the early drafts of "Ariel" with the other poems. There Plath includes the lines

> I rise, I rise, now
> I am the arrow. I am the ram [sow] that flies
> In the cauldron of morning
> One white melt, up flung
> To the lover, the plunging
> Hooves I am, that over and over...[23]

What is now a stripped-down and seemingly essential part of the ending of "Ariel" was placed earlier in the poem and figured the persona as another of Plath's ascending women protagonists.

A later section of the poem in draft repeats the "I/ am the arrow" but prefaces it with "O bright beast," an apostrophe which makes the reality of the horse clear. There is also much more information about horses in the poem's opening. After "how one we grow" comes the lines

> Crude mover whom I move and learn to love
> Pivot of heels and knees, and of my color
>
> Opens before us the red furrow,
> The dull rump runs, ...

Lacking the elliptical concentration of the finished poem, this descriptive opening assures the reader that "Ariel" is, in many ways, a poem about the horse whose name means, according to the title on one early version, "Lioness of God." ("Ariel" first saw publication titled "Horse.")

Another of Plath's more enigmatic late poems, "The Couriers," fits better into the cluster of mystical-religious poems once a few words from its draft version are noted. The second stanza in draft reads "Acetic acid. A ring on this? In a sealed tin? not wine? vinegar [?]'[24] Positioning the reader for a crucifixion image with the reference to Jesus's being given vinegar rather than wine as he hung on the cross, Plath also – with her mention of "acetic acid" – takes the reader back to her description in "Elm" of "the sound of poisons" as "tin-white, like arsenic."[25] By then moving the brief mention of the ring from this stanza, she creates the central image of the poem, the gold wedding ring which now represents only "Lies and a grief." To the concluding line, the draft version adds the persona's ownership: "Love, love, *it is* my season!" As this replicated line shows, "The Couriers" is one of the poems in which she used plentiful exclamation marks; once those indicators are removed, the poem's somberness overshadows its mystery.

Another way of learning to read Plath's late poems more accurately, despite the absence of useful explication on her part – i.e., journal entries – is to work intertextually. Surmising that she was studying St. Augustine's *Confessions* during that troubled autumn leads the reader to one of the passages she marked there – "The Letter killeth, but the Spirit giveth life"[26] – in reading "Words," one of the last half dozen poems she wrote. "Words dry and riderless'[27] can be read as the poet's Prospero-like renunciation of her art. But in the spirit of *Confessions*, the phrase becomes just an accepted exchange – the letter for the resonance (i.e., "echoes") of spiritual knowledge. Broken free from the detritus of her life, the persona, with a metaphor that recalls the Kafkaesque axing of the frozen seas within, can experience sap welling "like tears," much like running water trying to return to a place of natural stability.

The closing lines of "Words" can also be read in a meaningful intertextual way with the St. Augustine. He admits that after he "recovered from his belief in astrology,"[28] he was free to undertake his real spiritual tasks. Plath echoes his release, implying that simply because she was born under a particular sign, she is not fated to do any particular thing.

Intertextuality works, too, with many of the other words and phrases Plath seems to emphasize in her late poems. The last line in draft of "Burning the Letters," for example, "And I am not subtle," may refer to one of the highest states of spiritualism as described by G. R. S. Mead, the "Subtle" or "Radiant Body,"[29] the body of light achieved. States of purification always join with degrees of light, so Plath's repeated images of ascent into brightness may signal achievement on her spiritual quest.

That the woman persona has red hair as she rises, or as she is reborn or transformed from ash, may also indicate she has attained the stage of "the rubedo." Whitening is the first goal of an alchemical process, and white is the color most people connect with being redeemed. After it comes silver and gold, and finally red, "the result of raising the heat of the fire to its highest intensity." The fire itself is both "healing and purifying."

The sacrilization of the soft blue of Mary's robe also connects with the occult. A residue of "faint blue violet" accrues from the process of transforming ash into nothingness; ideally no ash would remain in any transformation because everything would have been consumed. As Timothy Materer points out in his recent book, the real goal of alchemy process is not to transmute less precious metals into gold or silver, but to transmute the self. He reads Plath's poems, beginning with her "Dialogue over a Ouija Board," as her charting her spiritual trek through occultism to achievement, saying that her "ability to alchemize a poetic vision from occult sources...rivals Yeats'." From a more pragmatic perspective, Materer insists that Plath's "occultism helped to liberate her creative energies."[30]

Even if a reader resists seeing Plath's symbology in her late poems as stemming from occult beliefs (some of which she could easily have found represented in Yeats' late poems), a number of her recurring images lend credibility to Materer's readings. Bald and stone-like surfaces may suggest the ovoid shapes that, with the sphere, represent life patterns; funnels and stairs, the gyre and vortex. The moon seems omnipresent in Plath's late work, changing tonally with its "phases," in Yeats' term. Serpents, crystal and crystal balls, magicians, even the wise men (who occur somewhat frequently in the work of a poet who says she is not religious) can easily be related to occult symbology. (In the case of the wise men, Materer points out, they were originally "astrologers from the East,"[31] but Christianity gave them more prestigious roles.) The image of the babe sitting in the lotus is the symbol for the purest possible suicide, one who is so innocent that going directly to buddhahood will be possible. (We recall the inscription Hughes placed on Plath's gravestone, "Even amidst fierce flames the Golden Lotus can be planted,"[32] and – sobered – we reread three of her last poems, "Years," "Paralytic," and "Mystic.")[33]

Perhaps what grips the reader most about Plath's poetry is this immense range of suggestivity. From so many perspectives – including these archetypal, occult ones – her work opens out, gives back to the reader a rich set of images that quickens the imagination without confining it. So truly has she followed her own precept, that the metaphor must *become* the poem rather than being superimposed on it, that her poems seem almost otherworldly. As if writing in a language marked by the swiftness of non-verbal exchange, Plath opened what had been her painfully studious method of composing to the true wildness of her imagination at its unfettered best.

That imagination was, however, never ungrounded or unstable. It was set firmly in place on the foundation of more than twenty-five years of reading, of writing, and of a mystical kind of yearning to become the great poet. Plath set out on her journey nervously, without benefit of moneyed friends or truly encouraging family. The world she lived in gave lip service to respecting the arts, but it almost conspired against her ever becoming a writer: her American world was too conscious of what society would think, of allowing her – or any woman – to rise only to become respectable and married. Hindsight shows, however, that Sylvia Plath seemed to need very little encouragement. The triumph that colors that proud poem, "Letter in November," was hers through much of her life. As she wrote there, "This is my property./ Two times a day/ I pace it.../ And the wall of old corpses./ I love them./ I love them like history..../ Nobody but me..."[34]

We must remind ourselves that the life of the great writer is unlike most people's lives. That is, in fact, what one means by "the literary life."

13

The Usurpation of Sylvia Plath's Narrative: Hughes's *Birthday Letters*

When Plath's *Collected Poems* won the Pulitzer Prize for Poetry in 1982, that award re-established the importance of her writing and helped to cut through the sense of legend that the first publication of *Ariel* in 1965, two years after her suicide, had initiated. Those *Ariel* poems, important as they were, were so immediately, so intimately, tied to her death that readers found it difficult to comprehend such poems as "Lady Lazarus," "Daddy," "Words," "Edge" and the others without remembering her end.

The same phenomenon occurred after her novel, *The Bell Jar*, was published in the States in 1971. (The novel had appeared in England, under the signature of "Victoria Lucas," just a few weeks before Plath's death in 1963 – to good reviews and many comparisons with J.D. Salinger's *The Catcher in the Rye*; it was republished in England under Plath's name in 1966.) The delay of its US publication, however, made it something of a cult book. *The Bell Jar*, the novel that Plath thought ended happily, with Esther Greenwood's leaving the mental institution to return to college – recovered, well, herself again – also gained a last and final chapter in readers' imaginations: Plath's suicide had irrevocably rewritten that happy ending, and readers found the fictional character's recovery to be only a sad whistling in the dark, a keen reminder of the fragility of the human psyche.

In some respects, Sylvia Plath's recognition as a supreme twentieth-century poet was most visible immediately after *The Collected Poems* appeared in 1981 and then won for her work the 1982 Pulitzer Prize for Poetry. In the near-ebullience of the favourable reviews, in the first light of seeing her poetic *oeuvre* systematized, with poems dated and arranged chronologically, her readers could see the logic of her developing voice, narrative and craft. In the panorama of her art, there was less room for the haunting of her suicide.

As Katha Pollitt wrote in the influential *Nation* review, reading Plath's *Collected Poems* let one see "that Plath's was one of those rare poetic careers – Keats's was another – that moved consistently and with gathering rapidity and assurance to an ever greater daring and individuality. She was always becoming more distinctly herself, and by the time she came to write her last seventy or eighty poems, there was no other voice like hers on earth."[1]

For poet Dave Smith, reading her *Collected Poems* is every bit as fulfilling, but he speaks honestly about the emergence in these 224 adult poems of what he calls a "new" Sylvia Plath, the writer who "had learned to write her poem, the poem that was unlike any other . . . the Ariel poem. I like it that this poem takes the name of her horse, the horse she is hell-bent on in a pre dawn ride that is all fluid feeling . . . ."[2] Canadian critic Michael Kirkham agrees, that reading *this* Plath "calls for a new way of looking at her craft."[3] Even the sometimes chary William H. Pritchard recanted the often expressed notion that if Plath were to be kept in anthologies, it would be as "an interesting minor poet."[4]

Such an effulgent chorus did a great deal to establish Plath's prominence in any consideration of mid-century American poetry. Whereas before her *Collected Poems*, critics tended to delineate Robert Lowell and W.D. Snodgrass and perhaps John Berryman as the influential confessional poets, adding in either Anne Sexton or Plath for a feminist voice, now attention moved from Sexton to Plath and – besides her – often only Lowell was included in the confessional paradigm. Plath's *Collected Poems* brought a visible re-ordering to any discussion of modern American poetry. For a time, the book left Plath balanced there on some ephemeral top rung of the world of recent poetry.

Perhaps her then-estranged husband, Ted Hughes, who had edited the collection, also benefited. Although readers were disturbed at the editorial changes he had made in creating the published book *Ariel* from Plath's ordered *Ariel* manuscript, a collection she left ready for publication at the time of her death, the consensus was that Hughes's editing of the poetry was sensible and accurate. In 1984, Hughes was named Poet Laureate of England, a sinecure he held until his death in 1998.

Plath's achieved prominence led to the publication of half a dozen biographies and even more expert critical studies – as well as hundreds of conference papers, essays, memoirs and poems. There was a film made of her novel, *The Bell Jar*; and there is the film in progress at the time of writing of a fictionalized Plath herself. Her journals, which had appeared in a partial edition in 1982 (and only in the United States), were published in 2000 as *The Unabridged Journals of Sylvia Plath*, in both the United Kingdom and the United States. And in 2001 Emma Tennant's novel, *Sylvia and Ted*, appeared, a book in which Assia Wevill appeared as a third character in a year that resembled 1962.

So much activity had occurred since the *Collected Poems* and its reception that many scholars who had devoted their careers to Plath were feeling almost complacent. Almost. The right to study and to teach Plath had been hard-won; complacency never seemed an appropriate mode. As Plath had herself written in her 1958 journal, "My one want: to do work I enjoy . . . My odd publications here & there argue writing is no vain dream, but a provable talent."[5] Five years later, viewing the vast development of her art – structure created to not only enhance but to create voice – Plath was scarcely more confident. We critics could be no more sure of her position in the academy than Plath herself had ever been.

Early in 1998, with hardly any advance notice or preliminary reviews, Ted Hughes published the 88 poems of *Birthday Letters*. Poems about Plath, or written in response to her writing, this collection included only a few poems which had been previously published: it was a secret hoard – perhaps a secret missile – and from its title to its contents, seemed conceived to infuriate Plath readers. To begin with, the title of the book, Plath's birthday was 27 October 1932. The publication of *Birthday Letters* in February seemed instead to memorialize her suicide day, 11 February 1963.

There was little question that the book felt like an affront: within its covers Hughes had written poems built on Plath's most famous works. He had argued with the narrative her poems had created; he had set himself the task of correcting the story her writing had told. In a flat and literal voice, he had created a reasonable narrative intentionally unlike the exuberance, the intensity, the comedy of Plath's late voice.

Given that Ted Hughes had gained some position in contemporary letters by being a good editor of Plath's work, this strange and unexpected collection felt like a betrayal. For 20 years, the literary world had allowed Hughes to be Plath's best critic, the caretaker of her art. Now, these poems argued against our relinquishing that role to Hughes. They, literally, took the words out of Plath's mouth, and her art. Not only did Hughes's poems usurp the authority of Plath's narrative; they nearly erased her voice.

For instance, one of the critical *foci* of Plath's poetry was her use of both "Ariel" (the title poem of her most important collection) and "Whiteness I Remember," her re-creation of the run-away horse Sam, a poem that I have called the Ur-text for "Ariel." The latter poem was included in her first published book, *The Colossus*; and she had once thought she might use "Whiteness I Remember" as that book's title. *Birthday Letters* includes Hughes's versions of both of these key poems, "Night-Ride on Ariel" and "Sam."

"Sam" is a comparatively subtle recasting of Plath's intricate, syllabic verse about her near-death experience with the runaway horse. The three stanzas of "Whiteness I Remember" evolve to a twelfth line in the last stanza, the true closing for the poem entire, "[all colors] Spinning to still in his one whiteness."[6] A tapestry of animal power and the rider's fear, the poem settles into its voiced telling with control and energy: it is a poem about much more than Sam's rider.

When Hughes recasts the poem, however, it becomes a self-excusing prologue to other of his poetic accounts about his being right and Plath's being wrong – somewhat ironically, since the experience that led to the poem about Sam occurred before Plath knew Hughes. One of the most prosaic of the poems in *Birthday Letters*, "Sam" spends the first 80% of the poem retelling Plath's experience, albeit sometimes undermining what seems to be her straightforward expression. Hughes gives Sam his deity – "the white calm stallion" – and pictures Plath "an upside-down jockey" caught in "bounced and dangling anguish / Hugging what was left of your steerage." Abruptly, in the last four lines of Hughes's poem, with no transition from the riding Sam experience, Hughes changes himself into a horse and becomes Plath's victim:

> When I jumped a fence you strangled me
> One giddy moment, then fell off.[7]

The source of this scene is thin air. That the closing two lines which follow leave Plath dead after she has tripped the Hughes figure doesn't add any clarity to the image, or to the poem. The closing sentence, after her death in the closing line, is "Over in a flash." Bewildered, the reader cannot ferret out where the carnage in the closing stanza originates, or why its truncated and distorted expression is used. After all, Plath's poem "Whiteness I Remember" is carefully honed syllabic verse which builds to its metaphorically logical closing. "Sam" has none of those qualities. It has very little to do with either this Plath poem or with any of her poems. But its title, and its inclusion in the book, mandates that the reader figures it out.

Circumstances are much clearer with Hughes's revision of Plath's "Ariel." In "Night-Ride on Ariel," he opens the poem with a declaration of war: "Your moon was full of women."[8] Long known for her use of the moon as mystical and not always kindly mentor, Plath relied in part on mythic associations for womanly and goddess attributes – but she seldom included the roster of older women who had befriended her in her poem figures (she used those women, uncomfortably, within *The Bell Jar*, a novel which was a constant source of embarrassment for her mother because of her satiric treatment of these helpful, real women). Hughes here lines up recognizable women, from her teachers, her Smith benefactor, her mother, and maliciously describes each of them. He also uses their real names. Implicit in his listing is his attributing Plath's death to the pressures these women had created for her – for instance, the Smith teacher who secured Plath's lectureship for her is described: "She propped you/ On her lectern, / Lecture-timer."[9] The most offensive charges are levelled against Mrs Plath, in what becomes a litany of blame for Otto Plath in the role he chose not to play in Sylvia's life, and her Boston therapist, a woman Hughes describes as "Twanging the puppet strings / That waltzed you in air out of your mythical grave . . . ."

The unifying image for these mean caricatures is the thread of Plath's suicide on Monday morning. The poem ends, again, abruptly, with the two-word line: "That Monday." The inevitability of Plath's suicide, suggested by the recurrence of the moon watching over that day of the week, never rises to become the poem's theme, although that was probably Hughes's intention. What remains is the ridiculing line-up of women who cared about Sylvia Plath.

There are several dozen poems in which Hughes begins with a poem that readers of Plath would recognize, and then rewrites her text so that nothing sensible remains of her original work. Creating conundrums was probably less his aim than erasing the blame that had followed him since her death in 1963 – keeping him from giving many readings of his own work, because of shouted accusations as well as mute hostility from audiences; keeping him busy moving Plath's gravestone because the name "Hughes" (from "Sylvia Plath Hughes") had once more been chiselled off; keeping him irritated with yet another version of why his wife had died, whether in biography or memoir or scholarly essay.

One of the most interesting rewritings in *Birthday Letters* occurs in his recasting of a poem that he, as editor, had omitted from the 1965 *Ariel*, even though at one point Sylvia Plath had not only included the poem in that collection, but had named the collection for it, rather than *Ariel*. "The Rabbit Catcher" is the title in both books.

In Plath's "The Rabbit Catcher," she begins with a scene on a remote English moor, and finds the rabbit traps, snares "shutting on nothing."[10] In an atmosphere of "malignity," of killing, she jumps to a consideration of what kind of person traps rabbits, what kind of person kills. But it is only at the end of the poem, the last two stanzas of five lines each, that she eroticizes the killer – "those little deaths! / They waited like sweethearts. They excited him." Stanza six opens and makes the transfer to personal meaning, "And we, too, had a relationship –"[11] Nothing unclear about the progress of Plath's consciousness in this poem; she continues to speak what feels like truth when she announces that she is as much harmed by the snare-like constriction as the rabbit. "The Rabbit Catcher" becomes an accusatory poem, its flinty import aimed directly at her husband.

When Hughes rewrites this poem, his version almost triples the length of Plath's poem. First, he sets the scene with great detail. While, he assumes, the reader will understand the need for a relatively poor country boy to trap rabbits, he heightens the drama of Plath's finding the snare and tearing it up – "the sanctity of a trapline desecrated."[12] But he has prepared the reader to discount her invasion of the hunting ground by giving a highly charged description of why the two of them were out on the moor in the first place, their edges bared, in his terms. The speaker's wife is described as "Inaccessible / In your dybbuk fury, babies / Hurled into the car . . . ."[13] We already see how fragile is the woman's control, according to the long-suffering spouse ("I simply trod accompaniment, carried babies.").

The innocence of the country man, practicing his heritage's customs in trapping and hunting – "Filling a Sunday stewpot" – parallels the innocence of the "baby-eyed / Strangled" rabbits.[14] The turn at the end of this very long poem is to charge Plath herself with the murder, a self-murder of her "doomed self, your tortured, crying, / Suffocating self." Remote from whatever her passion was in this exploration, the hunter, complete with bloody hands, feigns an utter lack of comprehension at her wild anger. In Hughes's poem, "The Rabbit Catcher" remains that. His placidity unwrites the text of Plath's poem of that title.

One last example of the way Hughes's poems in *Birthday Letters* recast those from the Plath *oeuvre*. Her simple description in 1959 ("Man in Black") of Hughes dressed in "Black coat, black shoes, and your / Black hair till there you stood"[15] was never hailed as a great addition to her body of work. But when Hughes writes his version of the narrative, titling it "Black Coat," he sees his wife's observation as only threatening: he calls her "the paparazzo sniper" who attributes to him the qualities of her dead father. Along the ocean shore, again the innocent, the Hughes figure tries to come to terms with the power of the Atlantic. Instead, in the foreground, Otto Plath crawls from the sea and, in the wife's scrutiny, "slid into me."[16] Confused as Sylvia Plath had shown herself to be in that great poem "Daddy," she here is explained as some misguided, and thoroughly sinister, figure with the power to change her innocent British husband into the man who had mortally wounded her, her father. Relating himself to Otto Plath, and describing his wife's memorializing of her love–hate for the father, is a pervasive tactic in Hughes's poems from *Birthday Letters*.

Not every one of the 88 poems is skewed. There are the nostalgic commemorations like "Fulbright Scholars," although that poem too plays on Hughes's poverty in the closing lines about his eating a peach. The two daffodil poems ("Daffodils" and "Perfect Light") are truly re-creations of a great love, and include their daughter – "Like a daffodil / You turn your face down to her, saying something. / Your words were lost in the camera."[17] "The Blue Flannel Suit" attempts to understand the inexplicable fears that, in Hughes's backward view, twisted Plath's self-confidence. But for the most part, critics were right to make assumptions that the poems were not Hughes's best work, that they were motivated by either guilt or the process of excusing himself. As Janet Burroway noted, the book suffered from "the grim celebrity that Hughes rolled before him like Sisyphus' rock . . . . In *Birthday Letters*, Hughes reads the portent and the damage of failed marriage back into that time, reads the viper back into the rag rug, the coffin lid in the table top."[18]

Most of the reviews of *Birthday Letters* were negative. For Katha Pollitt, hardest to comprehend was Hughes's depiction of "himself as a passive figure, a stand-in for Daddy in Plath's lurid psycho-drama." In the best poems, she finds the mix of an "emotional, direct, regretful, entranced" tone effective.[19] For Calvin Bedient, the poems of *Birthday Letters* cannot compete with what he calls Plath's "verbal genius, the steel needle that flew so unerringly." Here, instead, Hughes's work seems dull, marred by his "big-handed, cuffing, slack paraphrases."[20] Jack Kroll finds the most offensive part of the book Hughes's lack of any "deep self-examination" even as he "subjects Sylvia Plath to the most searching examination from myriad angles." Rather, what we get from *Birthday Letters* is "Hughes's retroactive self-defence against the dark team of Sylvia and her father, who represent the death wish against Hughes's clean, country bid for life."[21] Only for Michiko Kakutani does the collection seem "remarkably free of self-pity, score-settling and spin."[22]

Had critics known that Ted Hughes's decision to publish *Birthday Letters* in February rather than waiting until October, to suit its title, was prompted in part by his own illness, perhaps the chorus of criticism would have been ameliorated. But most of the sense of insult stemmed, at least in part, from the role Hughes had played during those 35 years after her death in taking care of Plath's work – writing numerous essays about both her prose and her poems, selling her collection of manuscripts and books (and pieces of furniture) to the Smith College Rare Books Room, guarding the rights to reproduce her work with an almost fanatical eye. Some of the bitterness of those 35 years comes through in Hughes's poem "The Dogs Are Eating Your Mother," with its sharp admonition, "Protect her / And they will tear you down / As if you were more her."[23] As if in answer to her now-absent father, Frieda Hughes describes in her *Wooroloo*, in a poem called "Readers," the desecration of the woman writer's body. It is a dialogue with Hughes in his poem, repeating details of Plath's burial, of her short life. Almost unbearable, the poem includes the image of the readers who "bit away her tongue in tiny mouthfuls / To speak with her voice."[24]

The voice is the reason we revere the work of Sylvia Plath. It is the reason we are angered by the use Ted Hughes made in his volume, *Birthday Letters*, of her own accomplished *oeuvre*. Recognized as a major poet, Sylvia Plath deserves to be swept along in a steady stream of appreciative criticism, scholarly accuracy and newly loyal readers. May the twenty-first century bring her work a truly lasting resonance.

Notes

1 The Writing Life

1. Aurelia Schober Plath, introduction to *Letters Home by Sylvia Plath*, p. 5. Much of the information about the Plath and Schober families is drawn from interviews with, and from letters and annotated pages of manuscript from, Aurelia Plath. See also her 'Letter Written in the Actuality of Spring' in Alexander, *Ariel Ascending;* her introduction and headnotes to *Letters Home;* and her interview in *The Listener* (April 22, 1976), as well as her 'Authors' Series Talk' (Smith College archive). The biographies by Paul Alexander (*Rough Magic,* 1991), Anne Stevenson (*Bitter Fame,* 1989), and Linda Wagner-Martin (*Sylvia Plath,* 1987) and the 1988 essay by Plath's cousin, Anita Helle, in *Northwest Review* provide much of this information; they are supplemented by this author's interviews with Wilbury Crockett and Perry Norton. Max Gaebler's memoir (unpublished) also provided new information.
2. Aurelia Plath, introduction to *Letters Home,* p. 13.
3. Ibid., p. 16.
4. Sylvia Plath, "Ocean 1212–W," *Johnny Panic,* pp. 124–25.
5. Sylvia Plath, "Heat," unpublished; used with permission of Lilly Library, Indiana University, and Olwyn Hughes.
6. Sylvia Plath, "The Brink," unpublished; used as above.
7. Sylvia Plath, "The Dark River," unpublished; used as above.
8. Sylvia Plath, "East Wind," unpublished, used as above.
9. Aurelia Plath, "Letter Written," *Ariel Ascending,* ed. Paul Alexander, p. 216.
10. Ibid., p. 217.

2 Creating Lives

1. Aurelia Plath, letter to Wagner-Martin, March 27, 1988, p. 1.
2. Anita Helle, "Family Matters," *Northwest Review,* 1988, pp. 155–6.
3. Sylvia Plath, "The Colossus," *Collected Poems,* pp. 129–30.
4. Steven Gould Axelrod, *Sylvia Plath: The Wound and the Cure of Wounds,* 1990, p. 25. Axelrod sees much of Plath's career as motivated by her ambivalence toward her father, including her choice of an Honors thesis topic. As well as focusing on the double characters of Dostoevski, the thesis treats Ivan Karamazov, who consistently desired his father's death (pp. 28–9). See also Lynda K. Bundtzen, *Plath's Incarnations* (1983).
5. Sylvia Plath, *The Journals of Sylvia Plath,* p. 35.
6. Ibid.
7. Ibid., p. 62.

8. Sylvia Plath, "Among the Bumblebees," Lilly Library, Indiana University; published posthumously in *Bananas* 12 (Autumn 1978), pp. 14–15 and republished in the third edition – and the United States edition – of *Johnny Panic* (1979).
9. Sylvia Plath, "The Day Mr. Prescott Died," *Johnny Panic*, p. 46.
10. Ibid., p. 51.
11. Plath, *Journals*, p. 128.
12. Ibid.
13. Ibid., p. 25.
14. Ibid., p. 123.
15. Ibid., p. 143.
16. Sylvia Plath, "Lament," *Collected Poems*, pp. 315–16.
17. Sylvia Plath to her mother, *Letters Home*, p. 87.
18. Sylvia Plath, "Sunday at the Mintons'," *Johnny Panic*, p. 154.
19. Ibid., p. 165.
20. Sylvia Plath, "The Christmas Heart," unpublished, The Lilly Library, Indiana University.
21. Sylvia Plath, "In the Mountains," *Johnny Panic*, p. 174.

3 Creating the Persona of the Self

1. Sylvia Plath, "Mary Ventura," unpublished, The Lilly Library, Indiana University. The metaphor of the train suggests Plath's very late poem, "Getting There."
2. Sylvia Plath, "Mary Ventura and the Ninth Kingdom," essay appended, "Teen-Agers Can Shape the Future," unpublished, The Lilly Library, Indiana University, p. 1 of essay.
3. Ibid.
4. See Wagner-Martin, *Sylvia Plath, A Biography*, pp. 185–91.
5. Sylvia Plath, "Stone Boy with Dolphin," *Johnny Panic*, p. 174.
6. Ibid., p. 175.
7. Ibid., p. 188.
8. Sylvia Plath, "The Smoky Blue Piano," unpublished, The Lilly Library, Indiana University.
9. Sylvia Plath, "housewife," unpublished, The Lilly Library, Indiana University.
10. Sylvia Plath, "Song of the Wild Geese," unpublished, The Lilly Library, Indiana University.
11. Alice Miller, *For Your Own Good*, pp. 255–56. Elaine Martin's 1981 essay (*French American Review*, pp. 24–47) reinforces the analysis, as she points out that the achieving mother represents "anxious pressure" to conform to the patriarchy, particularly in the absence of the father. The middle-class value system, which makes little sense to a developing young woman, causes madness; and sexual acts are really overt acts against the repressive mother.
12. Miller, p. 257.
13. Ibid.

14. Sylvia Plath, "The Disquieting Muses," *Collected Poems*, p. 75.
15. Aurelia Plath, "Letter Written in the Actuality of Spring," *Ariel Ascending*, ed. Paul Alexander, p. 215.
16. Sylvia Plath, "The Disquieting Muses," *Collected Poems*, pp. 75–6.
17. See Anita Helle, *Northwest Review*, 1988, and Max D. Gaebler, 1983 interview, Smith College Rare Book Room.
18. Pat Macpherson, *Reflecting on The Bell Jar*, 1991, p. 61. For more discussion of this mother–daughter symbiosis, see Barbara Mossberg, "A Rose in Context: The Daughter Construct" in Jerome J. McGann, 1985; Anita Helle, 'Family Matters,' *Northwest Review*, 1988; and Mary Lynn Broe, "A Subtle Psychic Bond: The Mother Figure in Sylvia Plath's Poetry" in Cathy N. Davidson and E. M. Broner, 1980. Also by Broe, 'Enigmatical, Shifting My Clarities' in P. Alexander, *Ariel Ascending*, 1984.
19. Aurelia Plath to Sylvia Plath, November 13, 1954 and December 4, 1962, Smith College Rare Book Room.
20. Sylvia Plath, "Aerialist," *Collected Poems*, pp. 331–2.
21. Sylvia Plath, "April 18," *Collected Poems*, pp. 301–2.
22. Sylvia Plath, "Morning in the Hospital Solarium," *Collected Poems*, pp. 332–3.
23. Sylvia Plath, *Journals*, p. 169.
24. Ibid., p. 166.
25. Ibid., p. 169.
26. Ibid., p. 172.
27. Sylvia Plath, *Letters Home*, p. 323.
28. Sylvia Plath to Warren Plath, *Letters Home*, p. 112.
29. Ted Hughes, "Introduction," *Johnny Panic*, p. 18.
30. Jacqueline Rose, *The Haunting of Sylvia Plath*, 1991, p. 127.

4 Recalling the Bell Jar

1. Aurelia Plath, "Letter Written in the Actuality of Spring," *Ariel Ascending*, ed. P. Alexander, p. 216.
2. Sylvia Plath, *The Bell Jar*, p. 197.
3. For more about the complexities of the situation, see Patricia Hampl's "The Smile of Accomplishment: Sylvia Plath's Ambition," *Iowa Review*, 1995, pp. 1–28.
4. Ted Hughes agrees in his 1995 essay, intended as the introduction for an edition of *The Bell Jar* bound with Plath's *Collected Poems*. See "Sylvia Plath's *Collected Poems* and *The Bell Jar*," *Winter Pollen*, 1995, pp. 466–81.
5. Stan Smith provides the most comprehensive defense of Plath's use of Jewish/holocaust personae and themes in his *Inviolable Voice*, 1982, pp. 200–25. He explains what he sees as the reciprocity between Plath's "intensely private" poems and their ability to record "so profoundly and distinctly the experience of living in history" (p. 202). "It would be wrong to see Plath's use of the imagery of the concentration camp simply as unacceptable hyperbole, in which a merely private anguish is inflated to the proportions of global atrocity. Rather ... Plath has seen

the deeper correspondences between the personal and the collective tragedies, their common origins in a civilisation founded on repression at the levels of both the body politic and of the carnal body" (pp. 218–19). Jerome Mazzaro had spoken to the wider scope of Plath's political interests in his ground-breaking essay, "The Cycles of History: Sylvia Plath (1932–1963)" in his *Postmodern American Poetry*, 1980, pp. 139–66. More recently, see James E. Young's "'I may be a bit of a Jew': The Holocaust Confessions of Sylvia Plath" (*Philological Quarterly*, 1987), pp. 127–47.

6. Sylvia Plath, *The Bell Jar*, p. 3.
7. Ibid.
8. Ibid., p. 4.
9. Ibid., p. 5.
10. Ibid.
11. Ibid., p. 33.
12. Ibid., p. 69.
13. Ibid., p. 93.
14. See Rose Kamel, "'Reach Hag Hands and Haul Me In': Matrophobia in the Letters of Sylvia Plath," *Northwest Review*, 1981, in *Sylvia Plath, The Critical Heritage*, ed. Linda W. Wagner, pp. 223–33; Marilyn Yalom's *Maternity, Mortality, and the Literature of Madness*, 1985; and Pat Macpherson's *Reflecting on The Bell Jar*, 1991. The latter states that the novel can be read "as a daughter's case of matrophobia [Plath's fear of becoming her mother] ... Esther's fear and hatred of her mother entrap her within a misogynist version of motherhood that is potentially lethal." Macpherson also notes, "Encountering the fear of becoming one's mother is the central experience of female adolescence" (p. 59). Plath's journal entries from the period of her second session of therapy with Dr Beuscher, pp. 266–70, illustrate this emotion.
15. Sylvia Plath, *The Bell Jar*, p. 100.
16. Ibid., p. 132.
17. Ibid., p. 193.
18. Ibid., p. 119.
19. Ibid., p. 98.
20. Ibid., p. 101.
21. Sylvia Plath, *Journals*, pp. 318–19.
22. Ibid., pp. 319–20.
23. Pat Macpherson, *Reflecting on The Bell Jar*, 1991, pp. 78–9.
24. Sylvia Plath, *The Bell Jar*, p. 125.
25. Marilyn Yalom, *Maternity, Mortality, and the Literature of Madness*, 1985, p. 4.
26. Ibid., p. 20.

5 Lifting the Bell Jar

1. Sylvia Plath, *The Bell Jar*, p. 158.
2. Ibid., p. 166.

3. Ibid., pp. 193–4.
4. Ibid., p. 164.
5. Ibid., p. 173.
6. Ibid., p. 89. The most memorable nakedness in the novel is the sight of Doreen's breasts bouncing from her clothes as she and Lenny jitterbug in his apartment – a sight which, presumably, sends Esther into shock; at least she leaves the apartment and walks back to the hotel, where she cleanses herself in a hot bath.
7. Ibid., pp. 89–90.
8. Ibid., p. 86.
9. Ibid., p. 91.
10. Ibid., p. 68.
11. Ibid., p. 51.
12. Ibid., p. 56.
13. Ibid., p. 69.
14. Ibid., p. 172.
15. Ibid., pp. 62–3.
16. Ibid., p. 189.
17. Ibid., p. 190.
18. Ibid., p. 169.
19. Ibid., p. 179.
20. Ibid.
21. See Teresa De Lauretis, "Rebirth in *The Bell Jar*," *Women's Studies*, 1975, pp. 173–83; Pat Macpherson, *Reflecting on The Bell Jar*, 1991; Gayle Whittier, "The Divided Woman and Generic Doubleness in *The Bell Jar*," *Women's Studies*, 1976, pp. 127–46; and Linda Wagner-Martin, *The Bell Jar, A Novel of the Fifties*, 1992.
22. Sylvia Plath, *The Bell Jar*, p. 198.
23. Ibid., p. 199.
24. Ibid.
25. Ibid., p. 200.

6 Plath's Hospital Writing

1. Sylvia Plath, "The Daughters of Blossom Street," *Johnny Panic*, pp. 96–7.
2. Ted Hughes, "Introduction," *Johnny Panic*, p. 14.
3. Sylvia Plath, "Johnny Panic and the Bible of Dreams," *Johnny Panic*, p. 23.
4. Ibid.
5. Ibid., p. 24.
6. Ibid., p. 28.
7. Ibid., p. 33.
8. Ibid., p. 29.
9. Ibid., p. 38.
10. Ibid.
11. Ibid., p. 39.
12. Ibid.

13. Sandra M. Gilbert, "In Yeats' House: The Death and Resurrection of Sylvia Plath," *Critical Essays on Sylvia Plath*, Linda W. Wagner, pp. 204–22.
14. Sylvia Plath, *Journals*, p. 149.
15. Paul Alexander, *Rough Magic*, p. 196. This biographer also emphasizes the Hughes's interest in all forms of the occult, including Ted's reliance on astrology and hypnosis; he refers to another of Plath's now-lost stories, "The Hypnotizing Husband" (pp. 192–6). Of perhaps more interest are letters from Hughes to W. S. Merwin, housed at Emory University, in which Hughes plans poem submissions, book publication dates, and personal life events astrologically. He casts Merwin's horoscope as well, saying in one 1960 letter that Merwin should be thankful to have ♄ on his ascendant and ♃ on his moon. The latter helps with renovating the imagination. Such comments are the rule rather than the exception in this correspondence.
16. Pat Macpherson, *Reflecting on The Bell Jar*, p. 92.
17. Sylvia Plath, *Journals*, p. 149.
18. Sylvia Plath, "All the Dead Dears," *Johnny Panic*, p. 187.
19. Ibid., p. 184.
20. Ibid.
21. Sylvia Plath, "All the Dead Dears," *Collected Poems*, p. 70.
22. Ibid., p. 71.
23. Sylvia Plath, *The Bell Jar*, p. 175.
24. Sylvia Plath, "The Hanging Man," *Collected Poems*, pp. 141–2. Leonard Baskin's "Hanging Man" may have been an influence as well; see Plath, *Journals*, p. 226.
25. Sylvia Plath, "Poem for a Birthday," *Collected Poems*, p. 132.
26. Ibid., pp. 134–5.
27. Sylvia Plath, "A Life," *Collected Poems*, p. 150.
28. Ibid.
29. Marilyn Yalom, *Maternity, Mortality and the Literature of Madness*, p. 5.
30. Ibid., p. 9.
31. Sylvia Plath, *The Bell Jar*, p. 193.
32. Sylvia Plath, "Tulips," *Collected Poems*, pp. 160–2; these lines, and others quoted subsequently, are not a part of the published poem; they appear in drafts of the poem, available from The Houghton Library, Harvard University.
33. Sylvia Plath, "In Plaster," *Collected Poems*, pp. 158–60; lines from the draft (unpublished) are housed at The Lilly Library, Indiana University.

7 Defining Health

1. Sylvia Plath, "Tulips," both published version (pp. 160–2 in *Collected Poems*) and manuscript (Harvard University, Houghton Library).
2. Sylvia Plath, *Journal*, p. 164.
3. Ted Hughes, "Sylvia Plath's *Collected Poems* and *The Bell Jar*," *Winter Pollen*, p. 467.

4. Ibid., p. 468.
5. Sylvia Plath, "Mothers," *Johnny Panic*, p. 113.
6. Ibid., p. 118.
7. Ibid., p. 117.
8. Sylvia Plath, "The Fifteen-Dollar Eagle," *Johnny Panic*, p. 65.
9. Ibid., p. 69.
10. Ibid., p. 75.
11. Sylvia Plath, "Love Letter," *Collected Poems*, p. 147.
12. Sylvia Plath, "Parliament Hill Fields," *Collected Poems*, p. 152.
13. Ibid., pp. 152–3.
14. Sylvia Plath, "Whitsun," *Collected Poems*, pp. 153–4.
15. Sylvia Plath to Aurelia, *Letters Home*, p. 391.
16. Ibid.
17. Ibid., p. 405.
18. Ibid., p. 405.
19. Sylvia Plath, "Zoo Keeper's Wife," *Collected Poems*, p. 154.
20. Ibid., p. 155.
21. Sylvia Plath, "Poem for a Birthday (4. The Beast)," *Collected Poems*, p. 134.
22. Sylvia Plath, *Letters Home*, p. 388.
23. Sylvia Plath, "Zoo Keeper's Wife," *Collected Poems*, p. 155.
24. Sylvia Plath, "I Am Vertical," *Collected Poems*, p. 162.
25. Aurelia Plath, Interview with Wagner-Martin, August 27, 1984.

8 The Journey Toward *Ariel*

1. For a full discussion of Plath's academic experiences, see Linda Wagner-Martin's *Sylvia Plath, A Biography* and Paul Alexander's *Rough Magic*.
2. Sylvia Plath, *Journals*, p. 145.
3. Sylvia Plath, *Letters Home*, pp. 251 and also 233.
4. Ibid., p. 235.
5. Ibid., p. 289.
6. Ibid., p. 289; she writes Aurelia that "He is better than any teacher, even fills somehow that huge, sad hole I felt in having no father. I feel every day how wonderful he is and love him more and more. My whole life has suddenly a purpose..."
7. Comments from Daniel Huws to author, 1985, in response to an early draft of Wagner-Martin's 1987 Plath biography.
8. Ibid.
9. [E.] Lucas Myers, "Ah, Youth...Ted Hughes and Sylvia Plath at Cambridge and After," published as Appendix I to Anne Stevenson's *Bitter Fame*, pp. 309ff. In Philip Gardner's Sept. 13, 1984, letter to Wagner-Martin, he comments that he doubted whether Plath's association with Ted Hughes would have had any influence on whether or not her poems were accepted in Cambridge. In Gardner's view, Hughes "was somewhat outside Cambridge magazine life...and

I remember hearing him talked of as rather a wild man – certainly he was not a smooth member of any Cambridge undergraduate 'establishment' (p. 2).

10. Described by Daniel Huws, Luke Myers, Christopher Levenson (October 27, 1984, letter to Wagner-Martin in which he comments that he and his friends thought Plath's poems were "too tricksy, too self-consciously clever'), and Bertram Wyatt-Brown (conversation and letter of January 24, 1987. As he recalled there "Ted's friends complained of Sylvia's association with the *Granta* crowd, although they did not know her personally. David Ross, the editor, Daniel Weissbort, Luke Myers, and others told each other that her work was precious and superficial. They belittled the appearance of her poems in popular American middle-brow journals.").

11. Ted Hughes, untitled poem [later titled "Secretary"], *Saint Botolph's Review*, p. 19, (undated, but published in early 1956, only issue of the magazine).

12. Ted Hughes, "Fallgrief's Girl-friends," *Saint Botolph's Review*, p. 16.

13. Letter from Olwyn Hughes to the author, August 30, 1984, p. 2; on p. 1, Olwyn had described Sylvia as "just a student who wrote poems..."

14. Luke Myers, Appendix I, Anne Stevenson's *Bitter Fame*, p. 316.

15. Keith Sagar, *The Art of Ted Hughes*, 2nd Edition, 1978, p. 10.

16. Sylvia Plath, *Letters Home*, p. 234; Huws's comments support this.

17. Sylvia Plath, "Two Lovers and a Beachcomber by the Real Sea," *Collected Poems*, p. 327. Considering that this poem served as the title poem for one of Plath's submissions to the Yale Younger Poets competition and for the manuscript that would be published as *The Colossus*, it is hardly representative of her "Juvenilia," which is the section into which all her poems written before 1956 (the year she met Hughes) fall in this volume. The arrangement limits the reader's focus in reading Plath's poems to those produced during her last six years of writing. Few readers will turn to the back of the collection to unearth "Juvenilia," poems appearing there with no dates and no previous publication information. It is the contention of this study, however, that Plath was a serious writer throughout her college years, beginning in 1950. Many of her poems were then appearing, for good pay, in leading United States magazines. Therefore, it seems clear that her poetry should be considered "mature" long before 1956.

18. Sylvia Plath, "The Wishing Box," *Johnny Panic*, pp. 54, 61.

19. Lucas Myers, Appendix I, Anne Stevenson's *Bitter Fame*, pp. 317–18. Plath's story, "The Fifty-Ninth Bear" appears on pp. 100–11 in *Johnny Panic*.

20. Sylvia Plath, *Journals*, pp. 251, 253, 254, 260, 273ff.

21. Sylvia Plath, "Poems, Potatoes," *Collected Poems*, p. 106.

22. Sylvia Plath, "Stillborn," *Collected Poems*, p. 142.

23. Sylvia Plath, *Journals*, p. 155.

24. Ibid., p. 255.

25. Ibid., p. 221.

26. Ibid., 137.

27. Sylvia Plath, *Letters Home*, 263 and see Paul Alexander, *Rough Magic*.

28. All Hughes's lists are housed in the Rare Book Room, Neilsen Library, Smith College. They are undated, and I have drawn randomly from the lists, which by my count number ten pages of various sizes, to try to process the information for the reader.

29. Sylvia Plath, "Mushrooms," *Collected Poems*, pp. 139–40.

30. Sylvia Plath, "Pheasant," *Collected Poems*, p. 191.

31. For commentaries on Plath's poetic mythology, see particularly Judith Kroll, *Chapters in a Mythology: The Poetry of Sylvia Plath* (1976), Susan Van Dyne, *Revising Life: Sylvia Plath's Ariel Poems* (1993), and Al Strangeways, *Sylvia Plath: Poetry and Influence* (1998). There are countless separate critical essays, and readings in all the Plath biographies as well.

32. Ted Hughes on the BBC "Two of a Kind" broadcast, quoted in Paul Alexander's *Rough Magic*, p. 255.

33. Sylvia Plath, transcription of her comments on a BBC reading of her poems, Smith College Rare Books Room.

34. Ibid.

35. Ibid.

36. Sylvia Plath, "Suicide off Egg Rock," *Collected Poems*, p. 115.

37. Sylvia Plath, Comments for BBC reading, Smith College Rare Books Room.

38. Ibid.

39. Ted Hughes, Interview, *The Independent*, September 5, 1993, p. 32.

9 Plath's Poems about Women

1. Sylvia Plath, *Journals*, p. 74.

2. Paul Alexander, *Rough Magic*, p. 252.

3. Daniel Huws, Comments on 1987 Wagner-Martin manuscript.

4. Marilyn Yalom in her *Maternity, Mortality and the Literature of Madness* touches on this only obliquely; somewhat strangely, though perhaps reflective of the 1950s attitudes about maternity, Plath's letters do not mention her physical appearance during or after pregnancy.

5. Sylvia Plath, various letters from childhood and adolescence to her mother, The Lilly Library, Indiana University.

6. Sylvia Plath, notebooks, Smith College Rare Books Room archive.

7. Sylvia Plath, letter to Helga Huws, October 30, 1961.

8. Paul Alexander, *Rough Magic*, p. 252.

9. Sylvia Plath, "Heavy Women," *Collected Poems*, p. 158.

10. Sylvia Plath, "Morning Song," *Collected Poems*, pp. 156–7.

11. Sylvia Plath, "Barren Woman," *Collected Poems*, p. 157.

12. Dido Merwin, "Vessel of Wrath: A Memoir of Sylvia Plath," Appendix II, Anne Stevenson, *Bitter Fame*, pp. 329–30. I have numerous letters from Ms. Merwin written during the mid-1980s attesting to her consistent view of Plath's character.

13. Sylvia Plath, "Face Lift," *Collected Poems*, pp. 155–6. See Susan Van Dyne's discussion of this poem in *Revising Life*.

14. Sylvia Plath, letter to Helga and Daniel Huws, late December, 1962.

15. Paul Alexander makes this claim in *Rough Magic*, p. 252.
16. Sylvia Plath, "The Rival," *Collected Poems*, pp. 166–7, and manuscript drafts (of the three-section poem) from The Lilly Library, Indiana University. Quotations not from the published poem are from the manuscript.
17. The metallic imagery is reinforced with the description of the rival's "steel complexion," which connects with the inhuman "people with torsos of steel" in "Brasilia.'
18. Sylvia Plath, "Child," *Complete Poems*, p. 265.
19. Sylvia Plath, "Winter Trees," *Complete Poems*, pp. 257–8.
    In manuscript, the line is "No face-lifts, abortions, affairs." (New York Public Library, Berg Collection, poetry exhibition, 1996).
20. Sylvia Plath, "Childless Woman," *Collected Poems*, p. 259.
21. Sylvia Plath, "Brasilia," manuscript drafts in the Berg Collection, New York Public Library; final version in *Collected Poems*, pp. 258–9.
22. Sylvia Plath, "For a Fatherless Son," *Collected Poems*, pp. 205–6. In manuscript, the poem was titled "For a Deserted One" (Smith College Rare Books Archive).
23. Sylvia Plath, "Childless Woman," *Collected Poems*, p. 259.
24. Sylvia Plath, "Amnesiac," *Collected Poems*, pp. 232–3; manuscript versions, Smith College Rare Book Room.
25. Sylvia Plath, "The Fearful," *Collected Poems*, p. 256.
26. Sylvia Plath, "Lesbos," *Collected Poems*, pp. 227–30; a poem written about the same time, "The Tour," has less vitriolic imagery, but it still writhes with irritation at superior women and their attitudes.
27. Sylvia Plath, "Three Women," *Collected Poems*, pp. 176–87; individual quotations are not cited in notes. That spring Plath wrote to Olwyn that she was excited to be doing "longer stuff," and happy to be back in her study, which she calls "my poultice, my balm, my absinthe" (undated, 1962, p. l, Lilly Library, Indiana University).
28. Sandra M. Gilbert, "In Yeats' House: The Death and Resurrection of Sylvia Plath," *Critical Essays on Sylvia Plath*, ed. Linda W. Wagner, pp. 217–18.
29. Sylvia Plath, "The Munich Mannequins," *Collected Poems*, pp. 262–3.
30. Sylvia Plath, "Totem," *Collected Poems*, pp. 215–16.
31. Sylvia Plath, "Kindness," *Collected Poems*, pp. 269–70.
32. Sylvia Plath, "Edge," *Collected Poems*, pp. 272–3, and draft versions housed at Smith College Rare Books Archive. See Van Dyne, *Revising Life*, and Mazzaro, *Postmodern American Poetry*, p. 162.
33. Mary Kurtzman, "Plath's 'Ariel' and Tarot," *Centennial Review*, Summer 1988, pp. 286–95.
34. Sylvia Plath, "Three Women," *Collected Poems*, p. 185.

10 Plath's Triumphant Woman Poems

1. Sylvia Plath, *Journals*, pp. 32, 54–5, 152, 164, 186, 196, 211–12, 217, 310, 316–17, 321.

2. Liz York, *Impertinent Voices, Subversive Strategies in Contemporary Women's Poetry*, 1991, p. 66.
3. Ibid.
4. A. Alvarez, *The Savage God*, p. 8.
5. See photo in Wagner-Martin, *Sylvia Plath*, photo section after p. 104.
6. Alvarez, *Savage God*, p. 8.
7. Charles Doyle, letter to Wagner-Martin, October 20, 1983.
8. Peter Davison, *Half-Remembered*, pp. 170–1.
9. Information that follows is drawn from the file of Plath letters at *The Atlantic*.
10. Sylvia Plath to Peter Davison, November 16, 1962 (*Atlantic* file).
11. Peter Davison to Sylvia Plath, November 20, 1962 (*Atlantic* file).
12. Editorial comments, *Atlantic* file.
13. Lucas Myers, Appendix I, Anne Stevenson, *Bitter Fame*, p. 314.
14. Liz York, *Impertinent Voices*, p. 81.
15. Sylvia Plath, correspondence with Theodore Roethke, University of Washington Library Rare Books Collection.
16. Sylvia Plath, correspondence with John Lehmann, *London Magazine*, The Harry Ransom Humanities Research Center, University of Texas, Austin.
17. Sylvia Plath, correspondence with Brian Cox, *Critical Quarterly*, University of Kansas, Kenneth Spencer Research Library.
18. Sylvia Plath, "The Applicant," *Collected Poems*, p. 221–2. As a gloss on that locution, Ted sometimes addressed Olwyn in his letters as "upper class English" (The Lilly Library, Indiana University).
19. Sylvia Plath, "Purdah," *Collected Poems*, p. 242–4.
20. Sylvia Plath, "Burning the Letters," *Collected Poems*, pp. 204–5; see Van Dyne, *Revising Life*.
21. Sylvia Plath, "Lady Lazarus," *Collected Poems*, p. 244–7 and manuscript versions at Smith College Rare Books Collection. In W. B. Yeats' *A Vision*, he uses Lazarus as a kind of double; he also writes that "virginity renews itself like the moon." (*A Vision*, 1961, p. 24.)
22. Susan Van Dyne, *Revising Life*, pp. 55, 57.
23. Robert Graves, *White Goddess*, 1948, p. 12.
24. Ibid., p. xi.
25. Sylvia Plath, "Ariel," *Collected Poems*, pp. 239–40 and manuscript drafts at Smith College Rare Book Room.
26. Sylvia Plath, "Cut," *Collected Poems*, pp. 235–6.
27. Luke Myers, Appendix I, Anne Stevenson, *Bitter Fame*, pp. 320–1.
28. Mary Kurtzman, "Plath's 'Ariel' and Tarot," *Centennial Review*, Summer 1988, pp. 286–95. See also Timothy Materer, *Modernist Alchemy: Poetry and the Occult*, 1995.
29. Ibid., p. 294.
30. Sylvia Plath, "Whiteness I Remember," *Collected Poems*, pp. 102–3.
31. Sylvia Plath, *Journals*, p. 248; she realized, thinking back to the way she had written "Mad Girl's Love Song" [not included in *Collected Poems* but published in *Smith Review*, Spring 1953, and *Mademoiselle*, August 1953] and "Pursuit" [*Collected Poems*, pp. 22–3] that fluid composition might be a way into her truly creative imagination (*Journals*, p. 131).

32. Sandra M. Gilbert, "In Yeats' House," *Critical Essays on Sylvia Plath*, pp. 204–22.
33. See Paul Alexander, *Rough Magic*, p. 194.
34. Sylvia Plath, "Fever 103°," *Collected Poems*, pp. 231–2.

11 Getting Rid of Daddy

1. Sylvia Plath to Marcia Brown, January 2, 1963, Smith College Rare Book Room; see also her [undated] 1962 letter to Olwyn Hughes (The Lilly Library, Indiana University) where she comments that she needs to lift "a nose and a finger from the last 3 years... of carrying, bearing, nursing and nappy-squeezing."
2. Sylvia Plath to Marcia Brown, December 15, 1956, Smith College Rare Books Room.
3. Sylvia Plath to Marcia Brown, January 2, 1963, Smith College.
4. Sylvia Plath to Marcia Brown, February 4, 1963, Smith College Rare Books Room.
5. Ibid.
6. Correspondence between author and Clarissa Roche and Father Michael; the latter, a graphologist, in analyzing some of Plath's 1963 letters to him (they were in correspondence about his poetry), concluded, "it is inconceivable that Sylvia Plath could have committed suicide... she was emotionally perfectly steady." And see Ted Hughes's statement that there was no reason for Plath to have killed herself in his March 15, 1963, letter to Aurelia Plath, The Lilly Library, Indiana University.
7. Ted Hughes, "Foreword," *Journals of Sylvia Plath*, p. xiii.
8. Sylvia Plath, unpublished excerpt from her Sept. 23, 1962, letter to Aurelia (The Lilly Library, Indiana University); see also Richard Murphy, Appendix III, Anne Stevenson, *Bitter Fame*, pp. 348–54.
9. Sylvia Plath, unpublished excerpt from her Sept. 24, 1962, letter to Aurelia (The Lilly Library, Indiana University).
10. Unpublished excerpt, Sept. 23, 1962, letter.
11. Unpublished excerpt, Sept. 24, 1962, letter.
12. Sylvia Plath, unpublished excerpt from her Sept. 26, 1962, letter to Aurelia (The Lilly Library, Indiana University).
13. Sylvia Plath, unpublished excerpt from her October 9, 1962, letter to Aurelia (The Lilly Library, Indiana University).
14. Ibid.
15. Sylvia Plath, unpublished excerpt from her October 16, 1962, letter to Aurelia (The Lilly Library, Indiana University).
16. Sylvia Plath, unpublished excerpt from her October 18, 1962, letter to Warren Plath (The Lilly Library, Indiana University).
17. Sylvia Plath, *Journals*, p. 233.
18. Sylvia Plath to Helga and Danny Huws, late December, 1962.
19. Sylvia Plath, *Journals*, 165. Similar comments are represented by this: "I am married to a man whom I miraculously love as much as life" (Ibid., p. 195).

20. See Paul Alexander, *Rough Magic,* p.194; Linda Wagner-Martin, *Sylvia Plath, A Biography,* p. 154.
21. Sylvia Plath, *Journals,* pp. 134, 140, omitted lines, housed at Smith College Rare Books Room.
22. Ted Hughes, letter to Aurelia Plath, March 15, 1963, The Lilly Library, Indiana University. Hughes's analysis continues, making their separation the only reason for Sylvia's death: "when all she wanted to say simply was that if I didn't go back to her she could not live."
23. Steven Gould Axelrod, *Sylvia Plath,* pp. 178–9.
24. Ibid., p. 184.
25. Sylvia Plath, "An Appearance," *Collected Poems,* p. 189.
26. Sylvia Plath, "Little Fugue," *Collected Poems,* pp. 187–89.
27. Sylvia Plath, "Crossing the Water," *Collected Poems,* p. 190.
28. Sylvia Plath, "Pheasant," *Collected Poems,* p. 191.
29. Sylvia Plath, "Elm," *Collected Poems,* pp. 192–3.
30. Sylvia Plath, "Event," *Collected Poems,* pp. 194–5.
31. Ted Hughes, undated letter to the Merwins (last in Folder 5, 1962), Emory University Rare Books.
32. Sylvia Plath, "Event," *Collected Poems,* pp. 194–5.
33. Draft of "Event," Smith College Rare Books Room.
34. Sylvia Plath, "The Rabbit Catcher," *Collected Poems,* pp. 193–4.
35. Draft of "The Rabbit Catcher," Smith College Rare Books Room.
36. Jacqueline Rose, *The Haunting of Sylvia Plath,* p. 135.
37. Ibid., p. 143.
38. Sylvia Plath, "Apprehensions," *Collected Poems,* pp. 195–6.
39. Sylvia Plath, "The Detective," *Collected Poems,* pp. 208–9.
40. Sylvia Plath, "The Courage of Shutting-Up," *Collected Poems,* pp. 209–10.
41. See Karen Jackson Ford, *Gender and the Poetics of Excess,* 1997; Susan Van Dyne, *Revising Life,* 1993; and Jacqueline Rose, *The Haunting of Sylvia Plath,* 1992.
42. Aurelia Plath, Interview with Wagner-Martin, August 27, 1984.
43. Sylvia Plath, "Daddy," *Collected Poems,* pp. 222–4. Heather Cam makes explicit the many ties between this poem and the work of Anne Sexton (*American Literature,* 1987).
44. Eric Homberger, *The Art of the Real,* 1977, says correctly that "Daddy" is Plath's most comic poem, coming "straight out of Walt Disney or the marchen of the brothers Grimm ... comic gothic." 'Daddy' is a poem of massively felt relief at the symbolic murder of her father and husband" (pp. 164–5). Anne Ferry's *The Title to the Poem* (1996, p. 197) sees "Daddy" as performative and spoken.
45. Ted Hughes's 1993 poem "Black Coat" concludes "Set up like a decoy/ Against that freezing sea/ From which your dead father had just crawled.// I did not feel/ How, as your lenses tightened,/ He slid into me.'
46. Sylvia Plath, "Burning the Letters," *Collected Poems,* pp. 204–5.
47. Sylvia Plath, "The Jailer," *Collected Poems,* pp. 226–7.
48. "Burning the Letters," *Collected Poems,* pp. 204–5.
49. "The Jailer," *Collected Poems,* pp. 226–7.

12 Sylvia Plath, The Poet and Her Writing Life

1. Sylvia Plath, "Review of *The Stones of Troy*," *Gemini*, 1 (Summer 1957), pp. 90–103.
2. Ibid.
3. Ted Hughes to W. S. Merwin, May 24, 1962, Emory University Rare Books Room.
4. Sylvia Plath, January 10, 1963, BBC broadcast transcription for "New Comment 2," on Donald Hall's anthology, Smith College Rare Books Room; subsequent pages of discussion taken from this source.
5. Sylvia Plath, editor of *American Poetry Now*, for *Critical Quarterly*, 1961. In a folder of work which she did not include in the edition, housed at Smith College Rare Books Room, Plath had selected more poems by Anne Sexton and Adrienne Rich, poems by Sandra Hochman and May Swenson (who did not appear), Robert Lowell's "Pigeons" [for Hannah Arendt], and a number of poems by W. S. Merwin.
6. Sylvia Plath to Anne Sexton, August 21, 1962, Harry Ransom Humanities Center, University of Texas, Austin. See Wagner-Martin's *Sylvia Plath* for a more complete discussion of this key relationship.
7. See Eric Homburger (*The Art of the Real, Poetry in England and America Since 1939*, 1977) and Alicia Ostriker (*Stealing the Language: The Emergence of Women's Poetry in America*, 1986) and a more traditional view (of even Plath's work) in M. L. Rosenthal and Sally Gall's *The Modern Poetic Sequence*, 1983.
8. Sylvia Plath, Introduction to *American Poetry Now*, p. 2.
9. See Hughes-Merwin correspondence, Emory University Rare Books Room.
10. Sylvia Plath, *Journals*, p. 186.
11. See Wagner–Martin's *Sylvia Plath* for fuller accounts of these matters, and for the chronology of her last year.
12. Sylvia Plath, "A Comparison," *Johnny Panic*, pp. 62–4.
13. Ted Hughes, "Introduction," *Johnny Panic*, pp. 12–13, 16–18.
14. Sylvia Plath, *Journals*, p. 186.
15. Ted Hughes, "Sylvia Plath's *Collected Poems* and *The Bell Jar*," *Winter Pollen*, pp. 475–7; the reader should note, too, that Hughes's analysis of this period in Plath's writing, day by day, depends heavily on which phase of the moon is occurring.
16. Ibid., p. 477.
17. See Marjorie Perloff, "Sylvia Plath's *Collected Poems*," *Resources for American Literary Studies* (1981) and "The Two Ariels: The (Re)making of The Sylvia Plath Canon," *American Poetry Review* (1984) and Steven Axelrod, "The Second Destruction of Sylvia Plath," *American Poetry Review* (1984).
18. Robert Lowell, "Foreword," *Ariel*, by Sylvia Plath. New York: Harper & Row, 1965, pp. vii–ix; several disturbing elements control the effect of this seemingly praising commentary – she is "hardly a person at all, or a woman, certainly not another 'poetess,' but – regretfully, in all her accomplishment, a "heroine," never a hero. Lowell's description of her

in class, as modest and abashed, jars with his greatest praise, that she is "more powerful than man.'

19. Ted Hughes, letter to Andrew Motion about Wagner-Martin's biography.
20. A. Alvarez, *The Review*, 9, pp. 4–26.
21. Ted Hughes, the group of his essays on Plath's work in *Winter Pollen* (1995), pp. 161–211, 466–81.
22. Sylvia Plath to her mother, *Letters Home*, p. 468, October 16, 1962; a poignant corrective balance to that temporary exuberance is her earlier *Journal* comment, "I see only an accelerated work pattern until the day I drop into the grave" (p. 222).
23. Sylvia Plath, drafts of "Ariel," Smith College Rare Books Room.
24. Sylvia Plath, drafts of "The Couriers," Smith College Rare Books Room.
25. Sylvia Plath, "Elm," *Collected Poems*, p. 192.
26. St. Augustine, *Confessions*, p. 100; another of Plath's underlined maxims is "Everywhere the greater joy is ushered in by the greater pain" (p. 155).
27. Sylvia Plath, "Words," *Collected Poems*, p. 270.
28. St. Augustine, *Confessions*, p. xii.
29. Quoted in Timothy Materer, *Modernist Alchemy*, 1995, p. 68.
30. Timothy Materer, *Modernist Alchemy*, p. 126.
31. Ibid., p. 51.
32. On Sylvia Plath's gravestone.
33. Sylvia Plath, "Years," *Collected Poems*, pp. 255–6; "Paralytic," Ibid., pp. 217–18; "Mystic," Ibid., pp. 268–9. Plath's poems might well be read in the company of several of Ted Hughes's later poems, "Heptonstall Cemetery" (in which "Esther and Sylvia" are described as "living feathers') and the dedicatory poem from that volume, *Remains of Elmet* (1979) and his "Kreutzer Sonata," in which the persona stabs his "wife's sweet flesh...A sacrifice, not a murder" (*New Selected Poems*, 1982).
34. Sylvia Plath, "Letter in November," *Collected Poems*, pp. 253–4.

13 The Usurpation of Sylvia Plath's Narrative: Hughes's *Birthday Letters*

1. Katha Pollitt, "A Note of Triumph" [*The Nation* 234 (January 16, 1982)], in *Critical Essays on Sylvia Plath*, ed. Linda W. Wagner (Boston: G.K. Hall, 1984), p. 69.
2. Dave Smith, "Sylvia Plath, the Electric Horse" [*American Poetry Review* (January 1982)], in *Sylvia Plath, The Critical Heritage*, ed. Linda W. Wagner (London: Routledge, 1988), p. 273.
3. Michael Kirkham, "Sylvia Plath" [*Queen's Quarterly* (Spring 1984)], ibid., p. 277.
4. William H. Pritchard, "'An Interesting Minor Poet?'" [*New Republic* (December 30, 1981)], ibid., p. 268.

5. Sylvia Plath, *The Unabridged Journals of Sylvia Plath*, ed. Karen V. Kukil (New York: Random House, 2000), p. 422.
6. Sylvia Plath, "Whiteness I Remember," *Collected Poems*, p. 103.
7. Ted Hughes, "Sam," *Birthday Letters* (New York: Farrar, Straus and Giroux, 1998), p. 11.
8. Ted Hughes, "Night-Ride on Ariel," *Birthday Letters*, p. 174.
9. Ibid., p. 175.
10. Sylvia Plath, "The Rabbit Catcher," *Collected Poems*, p. 194.
11. Ibid.
12. Ted Hughes, "The Rabbit Catcher," *Birthday Letters*, p. 145.
13. Ibid., p. 144.
14. Ibid., p. 145.
15. Sylvia Plath, "Man in Black," *Collected Poems*, p. 120.
16. Ted Hughes, "Black Coat," *Birthday Letters*, p. 103.
17. Ted Hughes, "Perfect Light," *Birthday Letters*, p. 143.
18. Janet Burroway, "I Didn't Know Sylvia Plath," *Five Points* (Summer 2001), p. 45.
19. Katha Pollitt, "Peering Into the Bell Jar," *New York Times Book Review* (March 1, 1998), p. 4.
20. Calvin Bedient, "Minotaur Baby," *Nation* (April 20, 1998), p. 25.
21. Jack Kroll, "Answering Ariel," *Newsweek* (February 2, 1998), p. 59.
22. Michiko Kakutani, "A Portrait of Plath in Poetry for Its Own Sake," *New York Times* (February 13, 1998), p. B43.
23. Ted Hughes, "The Dogs Are Eating Your Mother," *Birthday Letters*, p. 195.
24. Frieda Hughes, "Readers," *Wooroloo* (New York: HarperCollins, 1998), p. 61.

Select Bibliography

Primary

Plath, Sylvia, *Ariel*. New York: Harper & Row, 1966.
——, *The Bell Jar*. New York: Harper & Row, 1971.
——, *The Collected Poems of Sylvia Plath*, ed. Ted Hughes. New York: Harper & Row, 1981.
——, *The Colossus and Other Poems*. New York: Alfred A. Knopf, 1962.
——, *Crossing the Water*. New York: Harper & Row, 1971.
——, Interview, *The Poet Speaks*, ed. Peter Orr. New York: Barnes & Noble, 1966, pp. 167–72.
——, *Johnny Panic and the Bible of Dreams and Other Prose Writings*. London: Faber and Faber, 1977.
——, *The Journals of Sylvia Plath*, ed. Frances McCullough. New York: Dial Press, 1982.
——, *The Unabridged Journals of Sylvia Plath, 1950–1962*, ed. Karen V. Kukil. New York: Random House, 2000.
——, *Letters Home by Sylvia Plath, Correspondence 1950–1963*, ed. Aurelia Schober Plath. New York: Harper & Row, 1975.
——, *Plath Reads Plath*. Cambridge, MA: Credo Records, 1975.
——, "Review of *The Stones of Troy*," *Gemini*, 1, No. 2 (Summer 1957), pp. 98–103.
——, *Winter Trees*. New York: Harper & Row, 1972.
——, ed. *American Poetry Now: A Selection of the Best Poems by Modern American Writers. Critical Quarterly Poetry Supplement*, 2, 1961.

Extensive manuscript material and correspondence at both the Lilly Library, Indiana University, and the Rare Books Room, Smith College (the largest Plath archives), as well as University of Texas, The Harry Ransom Humanities Research Collection; Emory University Rare Books Room; the Houghton Library at Harvard University; and the Berg Collection, New York Public Library. The author's own file of interview transcriptions, correspondence, and other materials date from 1982 to 1996.

Secondary

Ahearn, Catherine, "An Archetype of Pain: From Plath to Atwood and Musgrave," *Still the Frame Holds, Essays on Women Poets and Writers*, ed. Sheila Roberts. San Bernardino, CA: Borgo Press, 1993, pp. 137–56.
Alexander, Paul, ed. *Ariel Ascending: Writings about Sylvia Plath*. New York: Harper & Row, 1984.
——, *Rough Magic*. New York: Viking, 1991.

Alvarez, A., *The Savage God: A Study of Suicide*. New York: Random House, 1972.

Ames, Lois, "Sylvia Plath: A Biographical Note," *The Bell Jar*, pp. 203–16.

Annas, Pamela J., *A Disturbance in Mirrors: The Poetry of Sylvia Plath*. Westport, CT: Greenwood, 1988.

Axelrod, Steven Gould, *Sylvia Plath: The Wound and the Cure of Wounds*. Baltimore, MD: Johns Hopkins University Press, 1990.

Barnard, Caroline King, *Sylvia Plath*. Boston: Twayne, 1978.

Bassnet, Susan, *Sylvia Plath*. London: Macmillan Education Ltd., 1987.

Bedient, Calvin. "Minotaur Baby," *The Nation* (April 20, 1998), pp. 25–6.

Benjamin, Jessica, *The Bonds of Love: Psychoanalysis, Feminism, and the Problem of Domination*. New York: Pantheon, 1988.

Bennett, Paula, *My Life a Loaded Gun*. Boston: Beacon Press, 1986.

Barnard Hall, Caroline King. *Sylvia Plath, Revised*. New York: Twayne, 1998.

Britzolakis, Christina. *Sylvia Plath and the Theatre of Mourning*. New York: Oxford University Press, 1999.

Broe, Mary Lynn, "A Subtle Psychic Bond: The Mother Figure in Sylvia Plath's Poetry," *The Lost Tradition: Mothers and Daughters in Literature*, ed. Cathy N. Davidson and E. M. Broner. New York: Ungar, 1980, pp. 217–30.

Bundtzen, Lynda K, *Plath's Incarnations: Woman and the Creative Process*. Ann Arbor: University of Michigan Press, 1983.

——, *The Other Ariel*. Amherst: University of Massachusetts Press, 2001.

Burroway, Janet. "I Didn't Know Sylvia Plath," *Five Points* 5, no. 3 (Summer 2001), pp. 24–47.

Butscher, Edward, *Sylvia Plath: Method and Madness*. New York: Seabury Press, 1976.

——, ed. *Sylvia Plath: The Woman and the Work*. New York: Dodd, Mead, 1977.

Cam, Heather, "'Daddy': Sylvia Plath's Debt to Anne Sexton," *American Literature*, 59 (October 1987), pp. 429–32.

Davison, Peter, *Half Remembered, A Personal History*. New York: Harper & Row, 1973.

De Lauretis, Teresa, "Rebirth in *The Bell Jar*," *Women's Studies*, 3 (1975), pp. 173–83.

Diehl, Joanne Feit, *Women Poets and the American Sublime*. Bloomington: Indiana University Press, 1990.

Erkkila, Betsy, *The Wicked Sisters: Women Poets, Literary History, and Discord*. New York: Oxford University Press, 1992.

Faas, Ekbert, "Chapters of a Shared Mythology: Sylvia Plath and Ted Hughes," *The Achievement of Ted Hughes*, ed. Keith Sagar. Athens: University of Georgia Press, 1983, pp. 107–24.

Ferry, Anne, *The Title to the Poem*. Stanford, CA: Stanford University Press, 1996.

Ford, Karen Jackson, *Gender and the Poetics of Excess: Moments of Brocade*. Jackson: University Press of Mississippi, 1997.

Friedman, Susan Stanford, "Creativity and the Childbirth Metaphor: Gender Difference in Literary Discourse," *Feminist Studies*, 13 (Spring 1987), pp. 49–82.

Gaebler, Max D., "Sylvia Plath Remembered" (unpublished interview, March 14, 1983), Smith, Plath Archive.

Gilbert, Sandra M., "A Fine, White Flying Myth: The Life/Work of Sylvia Plath," *Shakespeare's Sisters: Feminist Essays on Women Poets*, ed. Sandra M. Gilbert and Susan Gubar. Bloomington: Indiana University Press, 1979, pp. 245–60.

——, "In Yeats' House: The Death and Resurrection of Sylvia Plath," *Critical Essays on Sylvia Plath*, ed. Linda W. Wagner, pp. 204–22.

——, and Susan Gubar, *No Man's Land*, I and II. New Haven, CT: Yale University Press, 1988, 1989.

Graves, Robert, *The White Goddess, A Historical Grammar of Poetic Myth*. New York: Vintage, 1948.

Hampl, Patricia, "The Smile of Accomplishment: Sylvia Plath's Ambition," *Iowa Review*, 25 (1995), pp. 1–28.

Hayman, Ronald, *The Death and Life of Sylvia Plath*. London: Heinemann, 1991.

Helle, Anita, " 'Family Matters': An Afterword on the Biography of Sylvia Plath," *Northwest Review*, 26, No. 2 (1988), pp. 148–60.

Homberger, Eric, *The Art of the Real, Poetry in England and America Since 1939*. Totowa, NJ: Rowman and Littlefield, 1977.

Hughes, Frieda. *Wooroloo*. New York: HarperCollins, 1998.

Hughes, Ted, *Birthday Letters*. N.Y.: Farrar Straus Giroux, 1998.

——, "Black Coat," *New Yorker* (January 11, 1993), pp. 62–3.

——, "The Error," *New Yorker* (June 26 & July 3, 1995), pp. 156–57.

——, Foreword to *The Journals of Sylvia Plath, 1950–62*, ed. Frances McCullough. New York: Dial Press, 1982.

——, "Heptonstall Cemetery," *Remains of Elmet*. New York: Harper & Row, 1979, p. 122. (Also, dedicatory poem in that volume.)

——, Interview with Blake Morrison, *The Sunday Review Page, The Independent* (September 5, 1993), p. 32.

——, Introduction to *The Collected Poems of Sylvia Plath*, ed. Ted Hughes. New York: Harper & Row, 1981.

——, Introduction to *Johnny Panic and the Bible of Dreams and Other Prose Writings*. London: Faber and Faber, 1977.

——, "Kreutzer Sonata," *New Selected Poems*. New York: Harper & Row, 1982, pp. 85–6.

——, "Sylvia Plath's *Crossing the Water*: Some Reflections," *Critical Quarterly*, 13 (Summer 1971), pp. 165–72.

——, *Winter Pollen, Occasional Prose*, ed. William Scammell. New York: Picador, 1995.

Juhasz, Suzanne, *Naked and Fiery Forms, Modern American Poetry by Women: A New Tradition*. New York: Harper Colophon, 1976.

Kakutani, Michiko. "A Portrait of Plath in Poetry for Its Own Sake," *New York Times* (February 13, 1998), p. B43.

Kirkham, Michael. "Sylvia Plath," *Sylvia Plath: The Critical Heritage*, ed. Linda W. Wagner (London: Routledge, 1988), pp. 276–91.

Klein, Elinor, 'A Friend Recalls Sylvia Plath,' *Glamour*, November 1966, pp. 168, 184.

Kroll, Jack. "Answering Ariel," *Newsweek* (February 2, 1998), pp. 58–9.

Kroll, Judith, *Chapters in a Mythology: The Poetry of Sylvia Plath*. New York: Harper & Row, 1976.

Kurtzman, Mary, "Plath's 'Ariel' and Tarot," *Centennial Review*, 32 (Summer 1988), pp. 286–95.

Lameyer, Gordon, "Letters from Sylvia," *Smith Alumnae Quarterly*, 67 (February 1976), pp. 3–10.

——, *Who Was Sylvia? A Memoir of Sylvia Plath* (unpublished manuscript).

Lane, Gary, ed. *Sylvia Plath: New Views on the Poetry*. Baltimore, MD: Johns Hopkins University Press, 1979.

Lant, Kathleen Margaret, " 'The big strip tease': Female Bodies and Male Power in the Poetry of Sylvia Plath," *Contemporary Literature*, 34 (Winter 1992), pp. 620–69.

Libby, Anthony, *Mythologies of Nothing, Mystical Death in American Poetry, 1940–1970*. Urbana: University of Illinois Press, 1984.

Lowell, Robert, Foreword to *Ariel* by Sylvia Plath. New York: Harper & Row, 1966, pp. vii–ix.

Macpherson, Pat, *Reflecting on The Bell Jar*. London: Routledge, 1991.

Mademoiselle, College Board issue, August 1953.

Malcolm, Janet, "Sylvia Plath, The Silent Woman," *The New Yorker*, 69 (August 23 and 30, 1993), pp. 84–97, 100–59. [*The Silent Woman*]

Markey, Janice, *A Journey into the Red Eye, The Poetry of Sylvia Plath – A Critique*. London: The Women's Press, 1993.

Martin, Elaine, "Mothers, Madness, and the Middle Class," *French American Review* 5 (Spring 1981), pp. 24–47.

Materer, Timothy, *Modernist Alchemy: Poetry and the Occult*. Ithaca: Cornell University Press, 1995.

Mazzaro, Jerome, "The Cycles of History: Sylvia Plath (1932–1963)," *Postmodern American Poetry*. Urbana: University of Illinois Press, 1980, pp. 139–66.

Meyering, Sheryl, *Sylvia Plath: A Reference Guide, 1973–1988*. Boston: G. K. Hall, 1990.

Miller, Alice, *For Your Own Good: Hidden Cruelty in Childrearing and the Roots of Violence*. New York: Farrar, Straus & Giroux, 1983.

Mossberg, Barbara, "A Rose in Context: The Daughter Construct," *Historical Studies and Literary Criticism*, ed. Jerome J. McGann. Madison: University of Wisconsin Press, 1985, pp. 199–225.

Newman, Charles, ed. *The Art of Sylvia Plath: A Symposium*, reprint *TriQuarterly*. Bloomington: Indiana University Press, 1970.

Oberg, Arthur, *Modern American Lyric: Lowell, Berryman, Creeley, and Plath*. New Brunswick, NJ: Rutgers University Press, 1981.

Ostriker, Alicia, *Stealing the Language: The Emergence of Women's Poetry in America*. Boston: Beacon, 1986.

Perloff, Marjorie, "Sylvia Plath's *Collected Poems*: A Review Essay," *Resources for American Literary Studies*, 11 (1981), pp. 304–11.

——, "The Two Ariels: The (Re)making of The Sylvia Plath Canon," *American Poetry Review*, 13 (1984), pp. 10–18.

Plath, Aurelia Schober, "Authors' Series Talk," March 16, 1976, Wellesley College Club (in Smith Plath Archive).

——, ed. *Letters Home by Sylvia Plath, Correspondnce 1950–1963*. New York: Harper & Row, 1975.

——, and Robert Robinson, "Sylvia Plath's *Letters Home*: Some Reflections by Her Mother," *The Listener*, 95 (April 22, 1976), pp. 515–16.

Plath, Otto Emil, *Bumblebees and Their Ways*. New York: Macmillan, 1934.

Pollitt, Katha. *"Birthday Letters," New York Times Book Review* (March 1, 1998), pp. 4, 6.

——, "A Note of Triumph," *Critical Essays on Sylvia Plath*, ed. Linda W. Wagner (Boston: G.K. Hall, 1984), pp. 67–72.

Pratt, Annis, *Archetypal Patterns in Women's Fiction*. Bloomington: Indiana University Press, 1981.

Pritchard, William H. "An Interesting Minor Poet?" *Critical Essays on Sylvia Plath*, ed. Linda W. Wagner (Boston: G.K. Hall, 1984), pp. 72–7.

Ramazani, Jahan, " 'Daddy, I have had to kill you': Plath, Rage and the Modern Elegy," *PMLA*, 108 (1993), pp. 1142–56.

Reilly, Erline, "Sylvia Plath: Talented Poet, Tortured Woman," *Perspectives in Psychiatric Care*, 16 (May–June 1978), pp. 129–36.

Rose, Jacqueline, *The Haunting of Sylvia Plath*. Cambridge: Harvard University Press, 1992.

Rosenstein, Harriet, "Reconsidering Sylvia Plath," *Ms.*, September 1972, pp. 45–51, 96–9.

Rosenthal, M. L. and Sally Gall, *The Modern Poetic Sequence: The Genius of Modern Poetry*. New York: Oxford University Press, 1983.

Sagar, Keith, *The Art of Ted Hughes*, 2nd edition. London: Cambridge University Press, 1978.

Sanazaro, Leonard. 'The Transfiguring Self: Sylvia Plath, A Reconsideration," *Centennial Review*, 27 (Winter 1983), pp. 62–73.

Sarot, Ellin. "To Be 'God's Lioness' and Live: On Sylvia Plath," *Centennial Review*, 23 (Spring 1979), pp. 105–28.

Shook, Margaret. "Sylvia Plath: The Poet and the College," *Smith Alumnae Quarterly*, 63 (April 1972), pp. 4–9.

Silverman, M.A. and Norman Will. "Sylvia Plath and the Failure of Emotional Self-Repair Through Poetry," *Psychoanalytic Quarterly*, 55 (1986), pp. 99–130.

Simpson, Louis, *A Revolution in Taste*. New York: Macmillan, 1978.

Smith, Dave. "Sylvia Plath, the Electric Horse," *Sylvia Plath: The Critical Heritage*, ed. Linda W. Wagner (London: Routledge, 1988), pp. 268–76.

Smith, Stan, *Inviolable Voice, History and Twentieth-Century Poetry*. Dublin: Gill and Macmillan, Ltd., 1982 ('Waist-Deep in History: Sylvia Plath,' pp. 200–25).

Spivack, Kathleen, *Robert Lowell and the Teaching of Poetry, Boston/Cambridge, 1959–77* (unpublished manuscript).

Steiner, Nancy Hunter, *A Closer Look at Ariel: A Memory of Sylvia Plath*. New York: Popular Library, 1973.

Stevenson, Anne, *Bitter Fame: A Life of Sylvia Plath*. Boston: Houghton Mifflin, 1989.

Strangeways, Al, *Sylvia Plath: Poetry and Influence*. Selinsgrove, PA: Susquehanna University Press, 1998.

Tabor, Stephen, *Sylvia Plath: An Analytical Bibliography*. London: Mansell, 1987.

Tennant, Emma. *Sylvia and Ted*. New York: Henry Holt, 2001.

Thomas, Trevor, *A Memoir of Sylvia Plath* (typescript).

Uroff, Margaret Dickie, *Sylvia Plath and Ted Hughes*. Urbana: University of Illinois Press, 1979.

Van Dyne, Susan R., "Fueling the Phoenix Fire: The Manuscripts of Sylvia Plath's 'Lady Lazarus,'" *Massachusetts Review*, 24 (Winter 1982), pp. 395–410.

——, "Rekindling the Past in Sylvia Plath's 'Burning the Letters,'" *Centennial Review*, 32 (Summer 1988), 250–65.

——, *Revising Life: Sylvia Plath's Ariel Poems*. Chapel Hill: University of North Carolina Press, 1993.

Voices and Visions: Sylvia Plath, videotape dir. and prod. by Lawrence Pitkethly. Washington, DC: Annenberg CPB Project, 1988.

Wagner, Linda W., ed. *Critical Essays on Sylvia Plath*. Boston: G. K. Hall, 1984.

——, "*45 Mercy Street* and Other Vacant Houses," *American Literature: The New England Heritage*, ed. James Nagel and Richard Astro. New York: Garland, 1981, pp. 145–65.

——, "Modern American Literature: The Poetics of the Individual Voice," *Centennial Review*, 21 (Fall 1977), pp. 333–54.

——, "Plath's *The Bell Jar* as Female *Bildungsroman*," *Women's Studies*, 12 (February 1986), pp. 55–68.

——, "Plath's *Ladies' Home Journal* Syndrome," *Journal of American Culture*, 7 (Spring-Summer 1984), pp. 32–8.

Wagner-Martin, Linda, *The Bell Jar: A Novel of the Fifties*. New York: Twayne/Macmillan, 1992.

——, "Reflections on Writing the Plath Biography," *The Literary Biography: Problems and Solutions*, ed. Dale Salwak. London: Macmillan, 1996.

——, *Sylvia Plath: A Biography*. New York: Simon & Schuster, 1987.

——, ed. *Sylvia Plath: The Critical Heritage*. London: Routledge & Kegan Paul, 1988.

——, *Telling Women's Lives: The New Biography*. New Brunswick, NJ: Rutgers University Press, 1994.

Whittier, Gayle, "The Divided Woman and Generic Doubleness in *The Bell Jar*," *Women's Studies*, 3 (1976), pp. 127–46.

Yalom, Marilyn. *Maternity, Mortality, and the Literature of Madness*. University Park: Pennsylvania State University Press, 1985.

Yeats, William Butler, *A Vision, A Reissue with the Author's Final Revisions*. New York: Macmillan, 1961.

Young, James E., "'I may be a bit of a Jew': The Holocaust Confessions of Sylvia Plath," *Philological Quarterly*, 6 (1987), pp. 127–47.

Yorke, Liz, *Impertinent Voices, Subversive Strategies in Contemporary Women's Poetry*. New York: Routledge, 1991.

Zajdel, Melody, "Apprenticed in a Bible of Dreams: Sylvia Plath's Short Stories," *Critical Essays on Sylvia Plath*, ed. Linda W. Wagner (1984), pp. 182–93.

Index

CPSIA information can be obtained at www.ICGtesting.com
Printed in the USA
LVOW07s0900011013

354897LV00002B/217/P